Becoming an Ally

Becoming an Ally

Breaking the Cycle
of Oppression
in People

Third Edition

Anne Bishop

Fernwood Publishing
Halifax & Winnipeg

Cartoons on pages 7 and 127 are copyright © Bob Haverluck, *Confessions of a Jailbird: The anti-racism comic book*. Winnipeg: Family Life Centre of Winnipeg North. Reprinted with permission. The song on pages 23–24 is copyright © Leon Rosselson, *The World Turned Upside Down (The Diggers' Song)*. England: Fuse Records (1975). Reprinted with permission. The flower of power on page 150 is copyright © Rick Arnold et al., *Educating for a Change*. Toronto: Between the Lines (1991). Reprinted with permission.

Editing: Brenda Conroy
Cover photos: Eric Ourique
Cover design: John van der Woude
Printed and bound in Canada

Published by Fernwood Publishing
32 Oceanvista Lane, Black Point, Nova Scotia, B0J 1B0
and 748 Broadway Avenue, Winnipeg, Manitoba, R3G 0X3
www.fernwoodpublishing.ca

Fernwood Publishing Company Limited gratefully acknowledges the financial support of the Government of Canada through the Canada Book Fund and the Canada Council for the Arts, the Nova Scotia Department of Communities, Culture and Heritage, the Manitoba Department of Culture, Heritage and Tourism under the Manitoba Publishers Marketing Assistance Program and the Province of Manitoba, through the Book Publishing Tax Credit, for our publishing program.

Canadian Heritage   Patrimoine canadien   The Canada Council for the Arts / Le Conseil des Arts du Canada   NOVA SCOTIA   Manitoba

Library and Archives Canada Cataloguing in Publication

Bishop, Anne, 1950-, author
Becoming an ally : breaking the cycle of oppression in people
/ Anne Bishop. -- Third edition.

Includes index.
ISBN 978-1-55266-723-1 (pbk.)

1. Oppression (Psychology). 2. Social psychology. 3. Social control. I. Title.

HM1033.B58 2015   303.3'3   C2015-900668-6

Contents

About the Author ix
Acknowledgements x
Big Words xii
Preface to the Third Edition 1
Preface to the First Edition 4

Images: Competitive Oppressions 6

1. **Why Write a Book About Becoming an Ally?** 8

2. **Step 1: Understanding Oppression — How did it come about?** 14
   The Conquest of "Old Europe" 19
   The Conquest of North America 21
   The Enclosure Movement 23
   Forms of Power 30

   Journal Entry:
   "They Wouldn't Be Able to Pick Us Off One by One" 34

3. **Step 1: Understanding Oppression — How is it held in place?** 35

   Morality, Duty and Being True to Yourself 44

4. **Step 1: Understanding Oppression — The personal is political** 45

   A Story: Racism and Sexism 60

5. **Step 2: Understanding Different Oppressions** 62
   Differences 63
      Visible and Invisible 63
      Specific Histories of Peoples 63
      Aboriginal/Non-Aboriginal Groups 64

Class and Other Forms of Oppression 64
Similarities Among All Forms of Oppression 67
    Power and Hierarchy... 67
    Stereotyping.. 67
    The Structure of Violence... 69
    Assumptions/Slurs Concerning Sexuality............................ 69
    Assumptions Concerning Treatment of and Access
    to Children and Efforts to Separate the Oppressed
    from Children, Even Their Own 70
    Desire to Separate and Distinguish..................................... 72
    Specific Similarities.. 72
Distinctions within the Major Oppressions 72

Two Quotes: Breaking Silence, Healing....................................... 76

6. Step 3: Consciousness and Healing..**77**

7. Step 4: Becoming a Worker in Your Own Liberation **81**

Journal Entry: Racism and Sexism 86

8. Step 5: Becoming an Ally..**87**
Learning about Yourself as an Oppressor................................. 92
How to Become an Ally.. 94
How to Work with Allies When You
Are a Member of the Oppressed Group 100
Working for Liberation and Becoming an Ally:
Using the Lessons Back and Forth 101
Balance and Clarity..101
Criticism of the Ally Approach to Privilege............................ 102

Journal Entry: How Not to Be an Ally —
An Open Letter to the Young Man Who Spoke
at our Memorial Rally on December 6th................................. 106

9. Notes on Educating Allies **108**
What Is the Process of "Unlearning" Oppression?..................109
The Organizational Context of Ally Education.........................113
Computerized Equity Education 115
The Basic Structure of Popular Education................................116
    Naming Ourselves...116
    Reflecting on Experience..117
    Analysis.. 118

Strategy and Action *119*
Reflection, Evaluation, Closure *119*
A Note on Emotional Responses... 120
Knowing What to Say 122
A Note on Homogenous and Mixed Groups 124
Homogenous or Mixed Leadership Teams?........................... 125
Reflections on Educating Allies... 126

10. Step 6: Maintaining Hope...**128**

The Dream 128
Idealism 129
Hope... 129

Glossary...**133**
Appendix... 149

Toolkit 149

References **166**
Index 179

For Hélène Moussa, who started me on this path.

About the Author

Anne Bishop discovered sexism when she noticed that professors didn't hear what she said in class. If a male student repeated the point, it suddenly became worthy of attention. Later she went public as a lesbian and discovered what it feels like to be spit at, threatened over the telephone and told by complete strangers that she was going to hell. She also experienced the reassurance and effective voice that allies can provide.

At the same time as she was reflecting on her own oppression, Anne was becoming increasingly involved in anti-poverty and anti-racism work. This forced her to see herself in another way, as a member of an oppressor group. These contrasting experiences planted the seeds for this book.

Anne completed a BA in philosophy and religious studies in her early twenties. After twenty-five years of life education, she completed a master's degree in adult education two days before her fiftieth birthday. The road between included travel and work across Canada, in the United States, the United Kingdom, France, Iceland, Malta, Ghana, Togo, Nigeria, Guatemala, El Salvador and Nicaragua.

In her mid-twenties, she spent a year at the Centre for Christian Studies in Toronto intending to become a deaconess in the United Church of Canada. The Centre's radical and collective approach to education at the time changed her. She became a social activist and left the church. However, it was at the Centre that she learned the social analysis and facilitation skills that have formed the basis of her life's work.

Anne has had two "real jobs" — three years as coordinator of development education for Canadian University Services Overseas (cuso) and eleven years of teaching adult continuing education. This included a skill-development program for leaders of low-income and marginalized communities, based on a similar course at the Centre for Christian Studies (Bishop with Jeanne Fay 2004).

She now makes her living with freelance contracts in group facilitation, writing, editing, teaching, research and community development. She has also worked at various times as a camp counsellor and director, fishplant worker, grape picker, union organizer, dog walker, farm worker, industrial sewing machine operator, used clothing store manager, cooperative development officer and restaurant host.

She lives on a small farm with her partner and an ever-changing menagerie of sheep, chickens, cats and a workaholic Border Collie.

Acknowledgements

Any work like this reflects many interactions, conversations, joint tasks and ideas bounced back and forth so many times that no one can remember where they began. Some of these exchanges happen face to face, others through written work. It is impossible to thank everyone who took part. However, I would like to thank a few of my special teachers:

Susan George, who suggested I start keeping a journal;

Karen Saum, who pointed out how much can be written in fifteen minutes a day;

Julie Vandervoort, who went over the manuscript of the first edition in great detail, several times;

Fyre Jean Graveline, who helped write the story that introduces Chapter 5.

Wanda Thomas Bernard, Marguerite Cassin, Debbie Castle, Jeanne Fay, Isabelle Knockwood, Toni Laidlaw and Diane Maxsym, who read the first edition manuscript and gave me many valuable comments;

my family, particularly my parents, Jean and Rodger Bishop, and my sister Ruth Bishop, who gave me the confidence that is the foundation for my life and work;

my co-counsellors and the Re-evaluation Counselling communities in Toronto, Ottawa, Nova Scotia and all over the world for their love, support, healing and excellent analysis of different forms of oppression;

all the many friends who have taught me about their oppression or their particular struggle as allies, including Valerie Farmer Carvery, Arturo and Florrie Chacon, Frances Lappé, Susanne Pharr, Barbara Kannapel and Eileen Paul, Jean and Bernie Knockwood, Faith Boswell, Lucien Royer, Victoria Biyele, Luce-Andrée Gautier, Lily Mah-sen, Toni Gorée, Donna Marshall, Pam Reid, Shirley Glass, Gabriel Epstein, Barbara Harris, Darcelle Upshaw, Elizabeth Doull, Jim McDermott, Alan Williams, Rosamaría Ruiz, Ingrid Mendonça, Shireen Samarasuriya, Ela Bhatt, Rhada Bhatt, Renana Jhabvala, Evangeline Cain-Grant, Olga Flandez, Philippa Pictou, Candy Yip, Joyce Robart, Terry Sabattis, Teresa and Frances Palliser, Charla Williams, Viki Samuels-Stewart, Holly Bartlett, Susan Buchanan, Candy Palmater, Tom Henderson, Darren Ruck, Wanda Thomas-Bernard, Liz Cumberbatch, my community leadership and community development students, the Henson College Anti-Racism

Response and Development Committee, my students in the Nova Scotia Public Service Commission's Diversity and Employment Equity course and so many others, some already named above;

the friends and colleagues with whom I developed my analysis of Canada and the world, particularly those who participated in the Centre for Christian Studies, the Ten Days for World Development, the Canadian News Synthesis Project, Oxfam-Canada, CUSO and the People's Food Commission;

the Coalition for a Non-Racist Society ("the white group"), for their pioneering thought and action as allies;

the Nova Scotia Diversity Roundtable, especially Sylvia Paris, Sharon Davis-Murdoch and Charlie Macdonald;

many people who helped me find references: Michael Bradfield, Beverly Johnson, Blye Frank, Gary Kinsman, Wendy Lill, Murray MacAdam, Lily Mah-Sen, Veronica Marsman, Dorothy Moore, Hélène Moussa, Brian O'Neill, Percy Paris, Verna Thomas and Colin Stuart;

the supportive people at Fernwood Publishing: Errol Sharpe, Bev Rach, Brenda Conroy and Anne Webb;

Bob Haverluck, for his cartoons;

Eric Ourique, for the cover photographs;

my friends who contributed their beautiful faces to the cover—Jean, Bernie and Catherine Knockwood, Donna, Brandy and Anthony Marshall, Jim Schlay, Alan Williams, Betty Peterson and Muriel Duckworth;

and Jan, researcher, supporter, critic, source of ideas, friend, life-partner.

Big Words

In the beginning, I had hoped this book could be written using only words that are part of everyday conversation. Above all, I wanted to make it accessible to everyone interested in the topic, no matter what their formal education. However, this did not prove possible. Too many of the concepts do not have precise everyday words. I also had to make some political choices when deciding what words to use. At the back of the book there is a glossary containing brief comments on some of the words and concepts used in this book.

A Note on Internet Resources

Since the first edition of *Becoming an Ally* in 1994, the Internet has become an important research tool. You will find many URL addresses in the endnotes and bibliography. Whenever possible, I have given a standard publication reference as well. All of the Internet references given were active in February 2015.

Preface to the Third Edition

The first edition of *Becoming an Ally* was published in 1994, the second in 2004. In twenty years, some things have changed; some have stayed just the same. Neoliberalism has visibly spread, making progress on free trade, privatization and the cutting of social programs. As a result, there is a greater gap between rich and poor, all over the world, than there was two decades ago. In response, and because of our unprecedented global electronic connections, there is now an anti-globalization movement that is larger, better coordinated and more international than ever before. For me, this is a great source of hope.

Unfortunately, twenty years on, oppression based on gender, race, ability, sexual orientation and many other differences among people is still alive and well. It is nourished by the growing inequalities in our class structure and continues to play a role in causing them. Competition is still there as well, between and among those who suffer different forms of oppression.

Since *Becoming an Ally* first appeared, I have received many responses — from people I know and complete strangers, from people who are working only on their own liberation and see *Ally* as something they want their oppressors to read, and from people who are on their own journey of becoming allies. I have taken part in many interesting discussions. Three topics stand out: the distinction between being an ally and taking abuse for your good intentions; the evolving field of equity education; and, above all, internal conflict in social justice groups. The section of the book on the latter topic stimulated more response than any other.

For this third edition, I have made many small changes and some larger ones. I have tried my best to update the resources named in the endnotes and bibliography, including many discovered because people who read *Becoming an Ally* pointed me in the right direction.

The principal addition to this third edition is a greatly expanded Chapter 9: Educating Allies. In the first edition, Chapter 9 was an afterthought. At the last minute before publication, the question came up of why I had not included anything about educating allies, since my work was in the field of adult education. I quickly assembled some of the exercises and resources I and my colleagues were using in workshops and included them.

Between the first and second edition, I was taken aback by how my quickly offered exercises were sometimes misused. As a result, in the second edition, I expanded the chapter, adding discussion of the principles behind ally education, the skills and context required for it to be effective and when it should not be attempted at all.

Between the second edition and this one, I have done a great deal of growing as an adult educator. For thirty-five years I taught almost exclusively people who chose to take part. This gave me an open, vulnerable facilitation style, sharing leadership as much as possible with participants, and a relatively positive picture of my fellow citizens' willingness to become allies. From 2006 to 2011, I took on a contract teaching mandatory equity courses to provincial civil servants. I soon met fierce resistance, both open and subtle. My relatively privileged position in life and as a teacher of adults who want to learn had lulled me into complacency. Abruptly I had to re-learn an old lesson in just how widespread and determined bigotry can be under the veneer of the "nice" Canadian. I also realized the teaching methods that had served me so well up to that point were just about useless. Battered by one particularly vicious session, I considered quitting, but my pride in my facilitation skills and belief in the possibility of a more just world, along with the loving challenge and support of my partner, would not let me walk away. I began to experiment with surprise and humour, honesty and clarity, deeper and more extensive knowledge of my subject, thoughtful listening, more skilled timing and a better balance between firmness and openness. I received support and insight from colleagues, concerned managers, human resource professionals, union leaders and members of the Public Service Commission's Diversity Roundtable. Before long, I began to get much better responses from participants.

As I learned and changed through this experience, I thought about writing a book solely about educating allies, but then discovered that someone else has already written it. Tema Okun has published her analysis and methods in a book called *The Emperor Has No Clothes: Teaching About Race and Racism to People Who Don't Want to Know* (2010). She divides the concepts up and names them a little differently than I do, but she has basically said much of what I wanted to say. As a result, I shelved the idea of a separate book. Instead, I added a summary of her analysis to Chapter 9 along with what I have learned from the experience of teaching mandatory equity education. I also expanded my analysis of Canadians' responses to learning about their privilege at the beginning of Chapter 8.

I began writing *Ally* because I was concerned about how many people, deeply engaged in the liberation of their own group, seemed not to be able to see their role in oppressing others and how that comes full circle and perpetuates their own oppression. Like Margaret Green (1987), I don't believe anyone would choose to be an oppressor, but we do so unconsciously out of our emotional scars. I was intrigued by how we reproduce oppression in spite of our best intentions. I was also anxious to communicate my own experience of becoming aware first of my oppression, then my role as an oppressor of others. I wanted more people to know how complementary the two processes are. Above all I wanted to create a guidebook for would-be allies.

For a few months after the publication of *Ally*, I felt a great sense of accomplishment. I had summed up about fifteen years of learning and given it to the world. I had said all that I wanted to say and wondered if I would ever feel that pressing a need to say something again.

Within a few months, however, I found myself acting as an ally in a situation where everything I knew about that role was not enough. I had an analysis of the individual journey to becoming an ally, but I was caught in a situation of institutional oppression. I learned quickly that institutions are more than the sum of their parts; their patterns go beyond those of the individuals who participate in them. Understanding something about how oppression becomes encoded into our individual psychological makeup was not enough. I began a new piece of the journey, trying to understand how oppression becomes encoded into our institutions.

As a result, *Becoming an Ally* is now the first half of a larger work. Its original subtitle was *Breaking the Cycle of Oppression*. Now it is *Breaking the Cycle of Oppression in People*. The sequel, published in 2005, is *Beyond Token Change: Breaking the Cycle of Oppression in Institutions*. They are intended as a pair.

I hope this new edition of *Becoming an Ally* goes out around the world as the first and second editions did, bringing back new contacts, colleagues, ideas and learning. As a first time reader or an old friend, may this book stimulate your thinking, move you to action and give you pleasure.

Preface to the First Edition

For several years, I co-led a workshop called "Unlearning Racism" with African-Nova Scotian community leader Valerie Carvery (Bishop and Carvery 1994). Early on in the process, we drew a line down the middle of the floor and participants moved back and forth between the "privileged" side and the "exploited" side. First men went to one side, women to the other. Then white people went to one side, racialized people to the other, and so on. Each time, participants were asked to remember an experience which reflected that particular part of their identity. The purpose of the exercise was to help people understand that some groups in society are oppressed and others benefit from that oppression; but, as individuals, we have all experienced both at some point.

As a woman and a lesbian, I am oppressed by the structures and attitudes of the dominant culture in Nova Scotia, where I live. I am also white, anglophone, employed, able-bodied, hearing and sighted, born a Canadian citizen, "normal" looking and not over-weight. These attributes place me on the privileged side of the line. Being just past middle-aged and "middle class" puts me sometimes on one side of the power line, sometimes on the other.

I consider myself amazingly blessed. First, I grew up in a family that was able to give me encouragement, support, safety and enough to eat. Throughout my life, I have had the loving and challenging friendship of many who were not as protected as I was, who grew up with poverty, racism, deprivation, abuse and war. They saved me from the *näiveté* and privilege-blindness which otherwise might have remained my outlook. I was also saved by being a lesbian and a woman who came of age in the 1960s.

This book is my attempt to answer some of the big questions of my life: Where does oppression come from? Has it always been with us, just "human nature"? What can we do to change it? What does individual healing have to do with struggles for social justice? What does social justice have to do with individual healing? Why do members of the same oppressed group fight each other, sometimes more viciously than they fight their oppressor? Why do some who experience oppression develop a lifelong commitment to fighting it, while others become oppressors?

This work is a reflection on my experience. It comes out of my social identity in this place and time. It also grows out of my world-view as a feminist. I am a community development worker and popular educator.[1] For a time I also worked in the field of international development. Over more than forty years I have been part of, and worked with, many groups struggling to achieve social justice. My observations on these experiences are the main source of material for this book. Along the way, my thoughts have intermingled with those of many other people, through reading, conversation or joint work. It would be impossible to trace the origin of every idea contained in these pages. When I have taken material directly from others' work and ideas, recently enough to be able to follow the trail back to the source, I have put a reference in the notes. I have also used the notes to give some starting points for those who would like to explore an idea further through reading, experiential education or group reflection. I have not made any attempt to back up everything I say with anything beyond my own experience.

This book is intended to be part of a conversation. I look forward to readers' responses. I have so much to learn.

note

1.   "Popular Education" is defined in the glossary near the end of this book.

Competitive Oppressions

I am watching a video of the Gay Pride March in New York. On the sidewalk a young Black woman chants loudly: "The wages of sin is death!" (PBS 1990).

A feminist friend sighs about her gay boss: "We can't get him to listen to the problems facing women in this organization. All he says is we're not as oppressed as he is."

During a march commemorating victims of the holocaust, a group of gay men come in memory of those who died for their sexual orientation. They are forced to leave the march (Emecheta 1989).

During the summer of 1990, we hold a series of rallies in support of the Mohawks who are facing the Canadian army at Oka. They are trying to protect their ancient sacred place from becoming a golf course. During his speech, a local First Nation leader attacks all Québécois, calling them "those Frenchmen."

We have an international visitor. A group of low-income single mothers is telling her about some of their organizing work. "Poverty?" she says. "What do you know about poverty? This is nothing."

For five years I led an employment equity workshop and watched some predictable arguments arise among participants over and over again; for example: Is it harder to experience a visible oppression or an invisible one? Which are more oppressed, racialized people or women? A great deal of energy and emotion is wasted in such debates. It is as if the only way we know to advance is to step on each other. How far could we go if we tossed out these divide-and-conquer scripts we've learned and figured out how to work together?

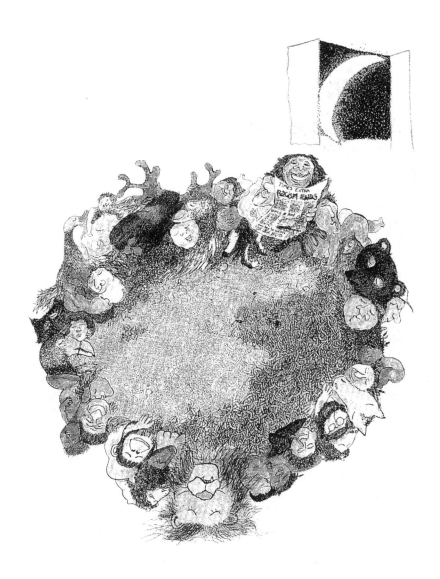

Chapter One

Why Write a Book About Becoming an Ally?

My first reason for writing this book is a dream. This dream is a deep, driving force in me, and I know many others share it. The dream is a vision of the world I would like to live in, a world based on cooperation, negotiation and universal respect for the innate value of every creature on earth and the Earth herself, a world where no one doubts that to hurt anyone or anything is to hurt yourself and those you love most, a world where everyone works to understand how everything we do will affect future generations.

I am what is called an "activist." I like to live my commitment to my dream. I distrust language, because I am tired of hearing the same words I use — "respect," "cooperation," "justice," "equality," "the people" — with their meaning co-opted by exploiters. However, it is time for me to converse with a wider network than those I can know face to face. I have something I want to say.

I have a vision of how my dream can come about. It is not detailed, because it is not for one person to predict the path of consensus. In general, though, I long to see all of us who are giving our work, ideas, energy and lives to a society that benefits the rich and powerful rise up together and say: "No more. We can develop social, political and economic structures that benefit everyone, and we will. We want to take on the challenge of moving towards equity, and we will. We are by far the majority; we can change things."

Between me and my dream stands a high wall. Its name is "Divide and Conquer." We have learned all too well to despise and distrust those who are different from us. Ironically, we have also been taught to despise and distrust people like us, because we have been divided even from ourselves. We distrust ourselves. Rather than looking within, to our own thoughts and experience, we accept the word of the media, the advertisers and the "experts."

The second reason for writing this book is anger. Again and again I see examples of division among oppressed people, as in the images before this chapter. Incidents like these rob me of hope. How can we take back our world and reorganize it to benefit everyone if we cannot even talk about our different forms of oppression without getting tangled up in the net of competition?

When I see people competing, claiming their own oppression as the "worst" or attacking the gains made by other oppressed groups, I see us all running on a treadmill. As long as we try to end our oppression by rising above others, we are reinforcing each other's oppression and, eventually, our own. We are fighting over who has more value, who has less, instead of asking why we must be valued as more or less. We are investing energy in the source of all our oppressions, which is competition itself.[1]

The truth is that each form of oppression is part of a single, complex, inter-related, self-perpetuating system. The whole thing rests on a worldview that says we must constantly strive to be better than someone else. Competition assumes that we are separate beings — separate from each other, from other species, from the earth. If we believe we are separate, then we are able to believe we can hurt another being and not suffer ourselves.

Competition also assumes that there is a hierarchy of beings. Those who "win" can take a "higher" position, one with more power and value than those who "lose." It is a short step from accepting hierarchy as natural to assuming that exploitation is just. It becomes right, even admirable, for those who have more power and value to help themselves to the labour, land, resources, culture, possessions, even the bodies, of those who have less power and value. The result is a class system, where power and privilege increase as you go up the ladder, and those standing on each rung take for granted their right to benefit from the labour and resources of those below them.

As long as we who are fighting oppression continue to play the game of com-petition with one another, all forms of oppression will continue to exist. No one oppression can be ended without all ending, and this can only happen when we succeed in replacing the assumptions of competition, hierarchy and separation with cooperation, an understanding that each being has value beyond measure and the knowledge that we are all part of one vast network of life. We cannot harm anyone or anything without harming ourselves.

The connection between different forms of oppression is often understood in the liberal[2] sense, which denies differences, ignores the continuing presence of history and blames individuals — "We're all the same, everyone has problems." I have found it difficult, when speaking in public, to say that all oppressions have one root, without my audience hearing me say that all oppressions are the same, or equal. People often feel that their oppression has been belittled. But I am not saying that all oppressions are the same or equal; equality means nothing in this context, for how would you measure? I certainly am not saying that we all have problems and should just learn to get along; this denies a long, complicated history and all the terrible scars that need healing, individually and collectively, before we can live together in peace. What I *am* saying is that all oppressions are interdependent, all come from the same worldview, and none can be solved in isolation. We can either perpetuate a society based on competition, where some win and some lose, or we can work toward a society based on cooperation, where winning and losing become irrelevant. In the first scenario, oppression will continue to exist for almost everyone. In the second, it will fade away, because it serves no purpose.

The idea that one form of oppression, or even one person's oppression, can be solved independently is of great benefit to the rich and powerful. This belief is enough to keep oppressed people fighting and jostling in competition with one another, never reaching a point of unity where we can successfully challenge those with more than their share.

Reverend Martin Niemöller, a Nazi prison survivor, recognized this:

> First they arrested the Communists — but I was not a Communist, so I did nothing. Then they came for the Social Democrats — but I was not a Social Democrat, so I did nothing. Then they arrested the Trade Unionists — and I did nothing, because I was not one. And then they came for the Jews, and then the Catholics, but I was neither a Jew nor a Catholic, and I did nothing. At last they came and arrested me — and there was no one left to do anything about it. (Bartlett 1980: 824)

I regain hope every time I see someone reach out past the boundaries of their own oppression to understand and support someone else's struggle. Hope is my third reason for writing this book.

I have a fourth reason for writing about becoming an ally. As a university-educated, Western person, when I want to know about something, one of the first places I look is in others' writing — books, articles and, more recently, websites and blogs.

I first met the concept of "ally," as I am using it here, in the mid-1980s. Up to that point, "ally" meant to me what it means to any other English speaker — "to join with another person, group, etc. to get or give support, a person or group that gives help to another" (Merriam-Webster) or an ally in the military sense. My first encounter with "ally" as a member of an oppressor group who takes action to end the form of oppression that gives them privilege came at a community meeting about an issue of race. As always, I was all wrapped up in worry about doing and saying the right things and, more importantly, not doing or saying the wrong things. I was feeling defensive about every suggestion that white people might be racist, because I certainly wasn't. How did I know this? Racists are bad people with nasty attitudes toward those who are different. I was good. I had good intensions, and that's what counts, right? I had never done anything to hurt anyone. I didn't think less of people because of their colour. Why, some of my best friends …

I don't remember whether the man who spoke — interestingly, I do remember that it was a man — was a designated speaker or contributing from the floor, and I don't remember what he said, unfortunately, but he talked about "allies" and somehow I "got it": it's not about me. It couldn't matter less if I am good or bad or what my intentions are. I am one piece in a massive, complex system, part of a people and a history. I have some advantages that I can offer to this struggle — some people will hear me who might not hear a racialized person say the same thing; I can take risks with fewer or less serious repercussions — but the shape and direction of the struggle does not belong to me. With a huge sense of relief I saw that of course I am racist — how could I not be? — and the energy I was wasting on defensiveness could be used instead to participate in change. It was like "seeing the light," a conversion experience; I left a pile of debilitating guilt right there in a heap on the floor of that meeting room, although certainly not all of it, and took up my responsibility instead — my responsibility to listen, learn and contribute when invited, my responsibility to drop my focus on "their" problem and work toward changing my own obliviously powerful and privileged people.

This dramatic moment sent me searching for fellow travellers who were writing about their experience of becoming an ally. There was a huge body of literature about the process of liberation from the perspective of the oppressed.[3] I found a few personal accounts by individuals coming to grips with their role as oppressor[4] and literature about unlearning racism, sexism and heterosexism.[5] I found a small number of writers working to understand the interrelationship of racism, sexism, heterosexism and class,[6] but what I needed to understand was the complex interweaving of all forms of oppression and how, as a member of various oppressor groups, I could become an effective ally to those seeking liberation from me and my people. In the mid 1980s, I couldn't find anything. What, exactly, I asked myself, *is* the process of becoming an ally? At least I found someone else who was asking the same question:

In *Yearning: Race, Gender and Cultural Politics* (1990), bell hooks wrote:

> One change in direction that would be real cool would be the production of a discourse on race that interrogates whiteness. It would just be so interesting for all those white folks who are giving blacks their take on blackness to let them know what's going on with whiteness. In far too much contemporary writing — though there are some outstanding exceptions — race is always an issue of Otherness that is not white; it is black, brown, yellow, red, purple even. Yet only a persistent, rigorous, and informed critique of whiteness could really determine what forces of denial, fear, and competition are responsible for creating fundamental gaps between professed political commitment to eradicating racism and the participation in the construction of a discourse on race that perpetuates racial domination. Many scholars, critics and writers preface their work by stating that they are white, as though mere acknowledgment of this fact were sufficient, as though it conveyed all we need to know of standpoint, motivation, direction. I think back to my graduate years when many of the feminist professors fiercely resisted the insistence that it was

important to examine race and racism. Now many of these very same women are producing scholarship focusing on race and gender. What process enabled their perspectives to shift? Understanding that process is important for the development of solidarity; it can enhance awareness of the epistemological shifts that enable all of us to move in new and oppositional directions. Yet none of these women write articles reflecting on their critical process, showing how their attitudes have changed.

Knowledge of this process, I felt, is crucial to overcoming all types of oppression. If we can understand how and why some people choose to give up privilege and become allies, we will have an important insight into social change.

I began keeping a journal of my observations and thoughts as I worked on anti-poverty issues, took on a public role in the campaign to include sexual orientation in the Nova Scotia Human Rights Act and co-led workshops on racism and heterosexism. After ten years, I printed the whole document. A three-inch thick stack of old-fashioned accordion computer paper formed on the floor in front of my printer. I began highlighting and connecting the key ideas. Eventually, my journal evolved into the first edition of *Becoming an Ally*, published in April 1994.

Shortly after it came out, I found a small booklet on a sale table. *With All of Who We Are* (1991) was an address given by Barbara Findlay as part of a plenary panel for the National Association of Women and the Law. I was delighted to discover that in fourteen pages she had captured the heart of what I wrote in all 137 pages of the first edition of *Becoming an Ally*.

Now, as I work on this third edition, there is an exciting collection of literature about anti-oppression allies. I am delighted to be part of the conversation, and I believe now, as I did three decades ago, that understanding the journey from resisting one's own oppression to becoming an effective ally is central in our continuing struggle to overcome racism, sexism and all other forms of inequity, including the ultimate one, class.

In my experience so far, I can define the following seven steps in becoming an ally:

1. understanding oppression, how it came about, how it is held in place and how it stamps its pattern on the individuals and institutions that perpetuate it;
2. understanding different oppressions, how they are similar, how they differ and how they reinforce one another;
3. consciousness and healing;
4. becoming a worker for your own liberation;
5. becoming an ally;
6. educating other allies; and
7. maintaining hope.

The remaining chapters expand on these steps.

notes

1. For an interesting discussion of competition, see Kohn (1986). Also see the glossary at the back of this book for further comments on the terms "competition" and "separation."

2. See the glossary at the back of the book for a discussion of liberalism and how I use the term.

3. There are too many to list here; however, key to my own understanding of the process was the work of Paulo Freire (1970, 1972, 1973).

4. In the world of books, some of my favourite examples of white people coming to terms with racial privilege are Boyd (2004), Carniol (2010), Green (1987), Helms (1990), Jensen (1998, 1999, 2005), Katz (1978), Lopes and Thomas (2006), McCaskell (1988), McIntosh (1990), Okun (2010), Pogrebin (1991), Thompson (2003) and Wise (2009, 2011).

    Examples of men writing about gender privilege are Connell (2005), Frank (1987), Johnson (2005a, 2005b), Kaufman (1987), Kimmel (2012, 2014), Lyttelton (1983/4), Robinson et al. (2003), Schacht (2001), Schacht and Ewing (1998) Schwalbe (1996), Snodgrass (1977), Stoltenburg (1999, 2000) and Tolson (1977).

    There are a huge number of writers on the Internet working at coming to terms with their privilege as members of oppressor groups. Type "white privilege," "male privilege," "heterosexual privilege," "able-bodied privilege," "age privilege," "thin privilege" or any other form of privilege into your search engine. Be cautious, though. Along with honest exploration of our oppressive histories, searches using these key words produce reactionary material, including hate.

5. Resources for unlearning racism include the white privilege references listed above along with Brown (1982), CUSO (1988), James (1989), Lee (1985), Obedkoff (1989), Thomas and Novogrodsky (1983a, 1983b) and Thomas (1984).

    Resources for unlearning heterosexism include Obear (1990) and Thompson (1990). Also see Blumenfeld (1992), Pharr (1988) and the many publications of PFLAG <community.pflag.org>.

6. Writers who were particularly helpful to me in learning the connections among racism, sexism, heterosexism and class are bell hooks (1990), Audre Lorde 1980) and Suzanne Pharr (1988); also helpful was and the "structuralist" school of social work, including writers Maurice Moreau, Gisèle Legault, Pierre Racine and Peter Leonard.

Chapter Two

Step 1:
Understanding Oppression
— How did it come about?

Sometimes when I teach about the dynamics of power and oppression, I have participants do an exercise. First we discuss different value systems and how they shape societies. We define separation and connection, hierarchy and equal value, competition and cooperation. The participants are then divided into small groups and given this task:

> You are a society with a social structure based on separation, hierarchy and competition. In keeping with your beliefs, you have conquered another nation and taken possession of their land and resources. In general, they have darker skin than yours.
>
> The conquered nation has a society based on connection, equal value and cooperation. Before you came along, they lived in peace, and each person, regardless of gender, age and ability, had the right to self-determination and everything they needed to live. Since all species and all elements of nature were included in their understanding of connection, equal value and cooperation, nothing could be owned or exploited the way you do it in your society.
>
> For the time being, you are forcing your system on them, which is not difficult, since they were not prepared to defend themselves; war is incomprehensible in their belief system. However, you do not want to invest in armed occupation forever. You want their next generation to think and behave the way you do and therefore be able to assimilate into your society.

I give participants flipchart paper and markers. On the first sheet, they list, in two columns, the characteristics they would expect to find in the conquered

Web Chart: Conquest of a Peaceful Culture

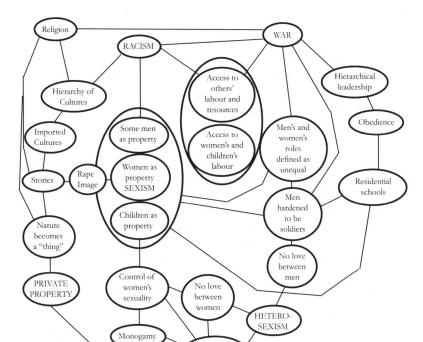

society and the contrasting characteristics of their own imaginary competitive society. Next, they decide on a first step to begin the task of assimilation. We use a technique called a "web chart." They write their first tactic near the centre of the paper and circle it. Then they work backward from this first step, that is: "In order to do this, first we must do this." Each idea is written in a new circle and connected to the last one by a short line. They continue for as many steps as they can imagine. Then they go back to all of their circles and work forward, that is: "If we do this, then this will happen." They continue this process as far as they can. Finally, they look at all the steps, forward and backward, and use lines to connect any that are related.

It is fascinating to watch groups work on this task. They start with different tactics. Some, especially if there are Aboriginal people present, start with residential schools. Groups with feminist women in them sometimes start with taking away women's property rights or introducing the men in the conquered society to the idea of violence against women. Other groups begin with introducing private property or racism or control of sexual and emotional expression.

Wherever the group begins, by the time they have worked their way through all the requirements for and results of their first tactic, many other possible tactics are present on the page. In a very short time, most groups complete a large portion of the whole jigsaw puzzle of oppression. They discover for themselves that no one form of oppression can stand alone without the others and that, as long as the basic assumptions of competition, separation and hierarchy are present, everything else follows.

Here is an example. Let us follow a group that began by introducing the idea of private property. Their final drawing is reproduced at the start of this chapter. Working backwards, they came up with this list of steps:

In order to introduce the concept of private property, it will be essential to introduce a belief system that portrays the earth, animals, plants and resources as "things," separate from large ecological systems, with no value except what they can be used for by their owners. This might require some cultural action, perhaps some stories that glorify the killing, conquest and domination of nature and the benefits of these activities. What about portraying nature as female and her conquest as rape? A religion that believes humans are superior to nature would be useful, too.

Writers, playwrights, performers and media people who can write and disseminate these stories may have to come from our culture at first. We must set up systems to import culture.

In order to have rape work as a positive image for oppressors, we must set up its reflection in the society. We must make women into "things," "possessions" to be conquered and dominated, and make sure men get benefits from doing this. The most effective benefit would be to make women the property of men once they are "conquered" by rape and give the man the right to use the woman's labour to make his life easier and wealthier.

Why stop at making women into things to be conquered and used? What about children? The elderly? All those too weak to be conquerors themselves? This idea of defining people as "things" connects back to defining the natural world as "things."

Even men could be property in some cases, but we must be sure that there are clear distinctions between those who can own and those who are designated as property. Easily identifiable differences would be best — like skin colour, height, eye shape, accent when speaking. The owning of other men must give the owners the same benefits as the owning of women — access to their labour. The owners could also take possession of the conquered men's land and resources. This could eventually be developed into full-blown racism.

Even if the property owners don't "own" other human beings outright, they can control others' labour, because anyone who doesn't have property must work for them. This is the basis of an economic class system — some (usually a minority) own the productive resources, like land, raw materials and machines. Others (the majority) have no choice but to work for the owners to survive.

At this point, the group returned to the circles already on the page and began to work forward from each one: If we import culture, the result will be a better grasp of a hierarchy of cultures — ours is superior to theirs. Others must also be judged and placed in the hierarchy. It would be good to label some as inferior to theirs so they can take out their frustration at being inferior to us on someone else. This connects back to racism and makes sure various conquered peoples won't combine forces against us (divide and conquer.)

Once the idea of getting possession of the labour, land and resources of "inferior" cultures is firmly established, the next thing we need our conquered people to do is go to war and conquer someone else. If they go to war, they will have to stop valuing all their people equally and begin to put more value on physical strength, aggression and mobility, less on nurturing, home-making and gentleness. This will tend to give greater value to men for their physical strength and devalue women's roles of bearing and breast-feeding children. Men and women will become more role-defined and unequal.

If women become defined by "hearth and home" and men by war, women and those they nurture — children, the weak and the elderly — will become thought of increasingly as in need of men's protection. This helps reinforce the idea that women and other weaker people are men's property and men can rightfully benefit from their labour. In return, men offer weaker folk protection.

When men go to war they must be hardened. Masculinity must be defined as toughness and violence.[1] Men must be able to kill and withstand seeing their companions maimed and killed. They must be able to step over a comrade's body and go on. This will require the bond between men to change from the friendships they experienced as part of a peaceful culture. They must bond with each other as "brothers" or "comrades" in an abstract sense only. Their loyalty must also be to ideas rather than people — ideas such as country or race. They must not love each other as individuals. This means that love between men must be strongly discouraged. A method of doing this would be to make men who love men one of those male groups that is owned by other men and defined as female, like all other possessed people, and therefore subject to rape and conquest. Now we have part of heterosexism added to the picture.

Another way to make men fight and kill is to establish an absolute hierarchy of leadership and to reward only obedience. This will also give the mobility and speed of response required by war. Hierarchical leadership connects back to a number of other circles. The process of teaching people to value obedience must apply to all the possessed people — women, children, slaves. Also, hierarchy and obedience among individuals reinforces the notion of a hierarchy among peoples inherent in racism.

Some other elements of heterosexism come from the concept of women and children as property. If women and children are the property of men, then each man must be able to control his woman's (or women's) sexuality. This gives him control over her/them and an assurance that her/their children are his. The best way to do this would be to stress male-dominated monogamous or polygynous marriage and make adultery a crime, especially for women, who can be punished for it by execution, to be sure she is not carrying an "illegitimate" child. These types of marriage would be useful in establishing a patrilineal system of inheritance, necessary to allow all of the family property to be passed down from father to son. Men's property rights will be reinforced generally.

Another important step in allowing men to control women's sexuality would be to limit sex to procreation. This is where we connect to the heterosexism circle again. Same-sex love, even friendship, must be suppressed among women as well as men; sexuality-for-procreation-only gives a justification for destroying gay and lesbian people.

Going back to the circle that defines children as possessions, childrearing and education must be done in such a way that this whole network of values is deeply internalized. Children must be taught obedience. They must experience violence so that they will be angry enough to practice violence on others when they can. When they take this step, they must experience the rewards of controlling others through violence. Boys and girls must learn their roles, and children from the dominant culture and other cultures must learn their relative values by reproducing the whole society in the home and school settings. The best way to do this, particularly at first, would be to establish residential schools and remove the children completely from any nurturing elements in their families. Even after the conquering culture is firmly established, residential schools will continue to be a good way to ensure that the ruling elite of men is thoroughly taught the values and practices of competition, separation and hierarchy.

This example shows how a group starting with private property discovered the necessity of introducing sexism, racism, ageism, adultism, heterosexism and ableism.[2] I am sure the reader can see how a group starting with something else — residential schools, for example, or the elimination of women's property rights — would also eventually uncover the whole system.[3]

In my experience, this exercise leaves everyone completely depressed. Participants discover how much they know about oppressing others. It is very important to have a full debriefing process when the exercise is finished. People need to be reminded that just knowing the dynamics of oppression well does not mean we are somehow evil. We are children of this network of values. We have learned how it works from our first days, largely unconsciously. It is also important not to leave participants before they have had an opportunity to use what they have learned to build strategies for change.

However, before going on to strategy building, I risk deepening the depression for a short time by having the group reflect on the likelihood of the conquered society resisting these tactics. They usually conclude that at first it would be very difficult, because their social structures, technology, values and behaviour are all organized around cooperation. They would be most likely to welcome the conquerors as friends and discover the exploitative intentions too late. Later they would likely develop organized resistance, but in order to do that successfully, they would have to reorganize their culture to include the conqueror's competitive values, war technology and social structures. The resistance might go on for years or even centuries, but the essential nature of the cooperative society would be severely damaged or lost altogether.

The purpose of this exercise is to learn about the complex and necessary interrelationships among different forms of oppression. The scenario is extremely simple and would be unlikely to occur in such a "pure" form. However, there are signs in history, mythology and archeology that versions of the dynamics described by this educational exercise have happened, in different times and places, all over the world.

No one knows where competitive, conquering societies began, but the earliest archeological evidence of such societies dates from roughly 3500 BCE (Eisler 1990: 49; Starhawk 1982: 38). This is not very long ago for a species that was living in groups, creating art and using tools by at least 35,000 BCE.

Wherever and however the notion of competition and conquest began, there are numerous stories of contacts between conquering peoples and peaceful, cooperative ones where the cooperative society was eventually transformed by processes resembling the ones my classes drew on sheets of newsprint. These dynamics also occur within a society when a class or group with competitive social values becomes strong enough to extend its control to other parts of its own society.

I must leave thorough study of these dynamics to scholars of history, mythology and archeology, but I want to give three brief examples, based on others' work. The first two illustrate contact between conquering and cooperative peoples, one in Europe from 4300 to 2800 BCE, and the other in North America in the sixteenth century. The third example involves a wealthy class expanding their power over others in their own society. It took place during the sixteenth and seventeenth centuries in England.

The Conquest of "Old Europe"

My first example, that of Europe between 4300 and 2800 BCE, comes from Riane Eisler, *The Chalice and the Blade* (1990: 42–54), and Marija Gimbutas, *Goddesses and Gods of Old Europe* (1982: 9–10, 17–18) and *The Language of the Goddess* (1989: xix–xxi).

Marija Gimbutas was an archeologist whose life work was unearthing the remains of the Neolithic Period (7000 to 3500 BCE) in what she called "Old Europe," an area stretching north from the Adriatic and Aegean seas to former Czechoslovakia, southern Poland and western Ukraine.[4] She organized the thousands of objects, particularly art objects, found in this area to reveal the basic worldview of Old Europe. Using the archeological work of others, she extended her analysis of the artifacts to include western and northern Europe (where the

Neolithic Period was later, 4500 to 2500 BCE) and the Mediterranean and the Middle East (where the Neolithic Period was earlier, 10,000 to 8000 BCE). In *The Language of the Goddess*, she made the links between her work with artifacts and studies of mythology, folklore, language and ethnography.

What emerges is a picture of a complex and advanced civilization farming in rich river valleys. The social organization was complicated, with sophisticated religious and governmental organizations and extensive specialization of crafts and roles. These people used metal and had written communication.

Above all, she found that the Old Europeans lived in peace and equality. Their cities were located close to good water and soils, with a view over agricultural land. No attention was paid to defensible locations, nor were there walls and fortifications. There is no sign of damage from warfare nor any portrayal of warfare in art. Metal was used for art objects, decoration and tools, not for weapons. According to the artwork, women played leading roles in every area of life along with men, and a study of grave-goods and housing reveals no difference in wealth to be found between men and women or between classes of people.

There are many indications that the society was matrilineal. Eisler developed the term "gylanic" (by combining gy from *gyne*, for woman, and an from *andros*, for man) to describe these gender-equal societies. The greatest deity for the Old European peoples was a mother-goddess, the Earth Mother, whose gifts included birth, sustenance and natural death. Her worship is much older than the Neolithic Period. She and her symbols, as catalogued by Gimbutas, can be traced back to Paleolithic art, beginning around 35,000 BCE.

However, the peaceful, egalitarian civilizations of Europe were not able to survive. Another people, with a very different worldview, were growing in strength just to the north-east of them, in the area between the Caspian and Black Seas. Gimbutas calls these the "Kurgan" people, after the round burial barrows (*kurgan* in Russian) that cover the funerary houses of their important males. She identifies them as part of what is called "Proto-Indo-European" culture. The Indo-Europeans are also called the "Aryans."

Kurgan culture was also agricultural but was centred on animal breeding and grazing. The Kurgan people had domesticated the horse and were semi-nomadic. They had also developed weapons and war. The horse and weapons featured prominently in their religion, where the central deity was a fierce, angry male warrior who lived in the sky. Images of the warrior-god always show him holding a sword or an axe, his belt hung with daggers. The society was male-dominated, hierarchical, authoritarian and patrilineal.

The Kurgan people began to move across Europe, conquering the peaceful sedentary population there. Gimbutas identified three "waves" of invasion — 4300 to 4200 BCE, 3400 to 3200 BCE, and 3000 to 2800 BCE. The archeological records show how the life of Old Europe was transformed. In some Kurgan camps in Europe, the bulk of the female population was not Kurgan, but rather women captured from conquered towns in Old Europe. Men were buried with not only immense wealth arrayed around them, including weapons, but the bodies of their sacrificed wives, children, slaves and animals as well.

The highly developed culture of Old Europe disappeared. The large towns, paintings, written scripts, temples, sculptures and thousands of female figurines found in earlier levels are absent in later levels. Settlements became much smaller and were built in defensible positions, with fortifications.

What Gimbutas describes as "hybrid cultures" begin to appear, showing aspects of both the Old European and the Kurgan cultures, although the Kurgan culture dominates. She speculates that this reflects the assimilation of the conquered culture into the conquering one.

A great transformation accompanied the Kurgan invasions into Europe. The indigenous culture, centred on the power to give and nurture life, was gradually changed into a culture dominated by the power to take life. A gender-equal, relatively classless society gradually became a highly stratified, male-dominant one. Although the real, historical process was long and complicated, it seems to reflect some of the same dynamics identified by my students as the origin and interrelationship of different forms of oppression.

The Conquest of North America

My second example took place in North America, during the colonization of North America's Aboriginal peoples by European invaders. The whole story, again, is long and complicated, and the documentation required to make a complete account would fill rooms and take years to study. I want to give only one quote, albeit a long one. It comes from *The Sacred Hoop: Recovering the Feminine in American Indian Traditions* by Paula Gunn Allen (1986). She, in turn, quotes extensively from the journal of Father Paul LeJeune, a mid-sixteenth-century Jesuit missionary among the Innu of the St. Lawrence Valley, the people the Europeans called Montagnais-Naskapi. LeJeune seemed to see clearly the necessity of undermining the power of women, introducing interpersonal violence, changing the treatment of children and establishing authoritarian male leadership in order to "civilize" (that is, dominate) the "savages." He even foresaw the residential school system, which did not appear until three centuries later:

> The Jesuits, under the leadership of Fr. Paul LeJeune … determined to convert the Montagnais to Christianity, resocialize them, and transform them into peasant-serfs as were the Indians' counterparts in France centuries earlier.
>
> To accomplish this task, the good fathers had to loosen the hold of Montagnais women on tribal policies and to convince both men and women that a woman's proper place was under the authority of her husband and that a man's proper place was under the authority of the priests.

The system of vassalage with which the Frenchmen were most familiar required this arrangement.

In pursuit of this end, the priests had to undermine the status of the women, who according to one of LeJeune's reports, had "great power." A man may promise you something and if he does not keep his promise, he thinks he is sufficiently excused when he tells you that his wife did not wish him to do it." Further, the Jesuit noted the equable relations between husbands and wives among the Montagnais. He commented that "men leave the arrangement of the household to the women, without interfering with them; they cut and decide to give away as they please without making the husband angry. I have never seen my host ask a giddy young woman that he had with him what became of the provisions, although they were disappearing very fast."

Undaunted, Paul LeJeune composed a plan whereby this state of affairs could be put aright. His plan had four parts, which he was certain, would turn the Montagnais into proper, civilized people. He figured that the first requirement was the establishment of permanent settlements and the placement of officially constituted authority in the hands of one person. "Alas!" he mourned. "If someone could stop the wanderings of the Savages, and give authority to one of them to rule the others, we would see them converted and civilized in a short time." More ominously, he believed that the institution of punishment was essential in Montagnais social relations. How could they understand tyranny and respect it unless they wielded it upon each other and experienced it at each other's hands? He was most distressed that the "Savages," as he termed them, thought physical abuse a terrible crime.

He commented on the "savage" aberration in a number of his reports, emphasizing his position that its cure rested only in the abduction or seduction of the children into attendance at Jesuit-run schools located a good distance from their homes. "The Savages prevent their [children's] instruction; they will not tolerate the chastisement of their children, whatever they may do, they permit only a simple reprimand," he complains.

What he had in mind was more along the lines of torture, imprisonment, battering, neglect, and psychological torment — the educational methods to which Indian children in government and mission schools would be subjected for some time after Conquest was accomplished. Doubtless these methods were required or few would have traded the Montagnais way for the European one. Thus his third goal was subsumed under the "education" of the young.

Last, LeJeune wished to implement a new social system whereby the Montagnais would live within the European family structure with its twin patriarchal institutions of male authority and female fidelity. These would be enforced by the simple expediency of forbidding divorce. He informed the men that in France women do not rule their husbands, information that had been conveyed by various means, including Jesuit education, to other tribes such as the Iroquois and the Cherokee. (Allen 1986: 38–40, with quotations from Thwaites 1906: 2: 77)[5]

This single example of Father LeJeune's observations contains several steps in the transformation of a cooperative, connected, egalitarian social system into a competitive, hierarchical society based on separation. These themes appear over and over again in accounts of the European colonization of North America, particularly those written from a First Nations point of view.[6]

The Enclosure Movement

At the same time that Father LeJeune and his colleagues, both religious and secular, were "bringing civilization" to "savages" who lived in a relatively egalitarian way, inseparably connected with an earth that they believed to be alive and female, a similar process was happening in England. The sixteenth and seventeenth centuries were a time of rapid transformation there as the propertied class established its dominance over the rest of the population. Major changes occurred in the economic base, class and gender relations, and social and religious values.

My first contact with the story of this period was a song, "The World Turned Upside Down (The Diggers' Song)," by Leon Rosselson:

> In 1649 to St. George's Hill,
> A ragged band they called the Diggers
> came to show the people's will.
> They defied the landlords; they defied the laws.
> They were the dispossessed reclaiming what was theirs.
>
> "We come in peace" they said, "to dig and sow.
> We come to work the lands in common
> and to make the waste ground grow.
> This earth divided we will make whole,
> So it will be a common treasury for all.
>
> The sin of property we do disdain.
> No man has any right to buy and sell the earth for private gain.
> By theft and murder they took the land.
> Now everywhere the walls spring up at their command.
>
> They make the laws to chain us well.
> The clergy dazzle us with heaven

or they damn us into hell.
We will not worship the god they serve,
The god of greed who feeds the rich while the poor folk starve.

We work, we eat together, we need no swords.
We will not bow to the masters or pay rent unto the lords.
Still we are free, tho' we are poor.
You Diggers all stand up for glory, stand up now."

From the men of property, the orders came.
They sent the hired men and troopers
to wipe out the Diggers' claim.
Tear down their cottages, destroy their corn.
They were dispersed, but still the vision lingers on.

You poor take courage, you rich take care.
This earth was made a common treasury
for everyone to share
All things in common, all people one.
"We come in peace" the order came to cut them down.[7]

Curious about the Diggers, I began to search for information. For about twenty years in the mid-seventeenth century, there was "a great overturning, questioning, revaluing, of everything in England" (Hill 1972: 12). During what is now called the English Civil War, or the English Revolution, Parliament and its army defeated the forces of King Charles I, executed him and established a republic. Feudal society and its structures of loyalty and dependence came to an end. Eventually a new order was established that suited the gentry and wealthy merchants, "a world safe for businessmen to make profits in" (Hill 1972: 12), but not before a period of "glorious flux and intellectual excitement" (12). Various groups of common people came forward trying to establish their own vision of political, religious and economic equality (11). Some of these were the Levellers, Fifth Monarchists, Baptists, Quakers, Muggletonians, Seekers, Ranters, Anabaptists, Familists and also the Diggers. Apart from the Baptists and Quakers, these names are little known today because their political and economic solutions to the problems of poor people in their time were swept away when the gentry, king and bishops, along with the newer class of merchants, were re-established in 1660 (11–12, 21–23). As Christopher Hill says:

> There were, we may oversimplify, two revolutions in the mid-seventeenth century England. The one which succeeded established the sacred rights of property ... gave political power to the propertied ... and removed

all impediments to the triumph of the ideology of the men of property — the protestant ethic. There was, however, another revolution which never happened, though from time to time it threatened. This might have established communal property, a far wider democracy in political and legal institutions, might have disestablished the state church and rejected the protestant ethic. (1972: 12)

In 1648, the disruptions caused by economic change and war were intensified by a disastrous harvest. People were starving. A writer of the time tells us that "the poor did gather in troops of ten, twenty, thirty, in the roads and seized upon corn as it was carrying to market, and divided it among themselves before the owners' faces, telling them they could not starve" (quoted in Hill 1972: 86). A contemporary Leveller pamphlet declared that "necessity dissolves all laws and government, and hunger will break through stone walls" (86). Soldiers were being disbanded without payment of wages owed them, causing mutiny in some Parliamentarian regiments, and many felt betrayed when the king was executed in January 1649 and the republic set up without the social reforms they were fighting for (87).

Against this backdrop, on Sunday, April 1, 1649, a band of about twenty poor labourers began farming common land on St. George's Hill, at the edge of Windsor Great Forest. They called themselves the Diggers, or True Levellers. They identified sin with private property and tried to re-establish the right of poor people to make a living from the land. They invited all to join them, promising them food and clothing, a significant offer in a place accessible to the starving millions of London (87, 89). Their spokesperson, Gerard Winstanley, claimed to have had a vision in a trance telling him to make a public statement that "the earth should be made a common treasury of livelihood to whole mankind" (90). Over the next year, other Digger communities were established in at least nine locations in south and central England, with three more in the planning stages (99, 101). In 1650, when food and money ran short in the original Digger colony they sent out two emissaries to visit other colonies and groups of sympathizers. Their journey visited thirty-four locations in eight counties (101–02). By the time the first colony was destroyed, there were at least seventy-three men living there with their families (91).

Throughout the year of their existence, the St. George's Hill community was harassed by local landlords. They organized raids and an economic boycott and kept them tied up with a series of expensive legal actions, a tactic still common today (Landry 2014). In April 1650, in a final series of raids, they chased the Diggers out of the area, destroyed their crops and burned their cottages (90–91).

The Diggers were part of a much longer resistance of the English peasant class to what is now called the "enclosure movement." Enclosure was a long and complex process, starting in the fifteenth century and continuing into the nineteenth, reaching the peak of its impact on peasants from the mid-sixteenth to the mid-eighteenth centuries (Allen 1992: 13–15; Mingay, introduction to Gonner

1966: xli; Starhawk 1982: 185). At the heart of the enclosure movement were wealthy landlords claiming as their own private property land that had previously been seen as a community resource. "The tradition of looking to the ruling classes for protection [was] broken," and instead, "the eagerness to enclose ... together with the primacy given to legal rights to property, over-rode any scruples that the major interests might have had over the consequences for the poorer elements of the village community" (Mingay 1997: 153–54).

English society was already stratified into classes at the beginning of the sixteenth century and subject to almost continuous warfare but there were many remnants of the ancient, cooperative societies that had existed in much earlier times. For example, although the land belonged in name to the lords and tenant farmers paid rent, there was a complex system of "rights of common" that gave peasants access to the food, fuel, medicinal herbs and building materials available in the fields, marshes, pastures and forests. Many peasants worked their land communally, making decisions and owning equipment in common, and dividing the harvest. Even the poorest family had at least a cow, a pig and some poultry, along with access to marsh and forest, to provide food and fuel (Gonner 1966: 3, 31, 34; Mingay 1990: 14–15; Mingay 1997: 34, 126; Starhawk 1982: 190–91).

The majority of the population were Christian, but communal festivals still reflected an earlier time. Celebrations of seasonal cycles dated back to the Neolithic Period and some even to Paleolithic times. The beliefs of the common people also came from a much older time. "Common sense" still said that the earth was a sacred living being, the mother of life. Her skin was the soil; her bloodstream the rivers and her breath the wind. Her soul lived in stone and the bones of the ancestors under the ground. Human beings lived on the skin of Mother Earth like micro-organisms live on human skin (Mander 1991: 211, summarizing Merchant 1980). Wise women and men, or witches, who practised ancient methods of healing, preventive public health and midwifery were not only the peasant population's "doctors" but also held important leadership positions in the community. Many kept up the rituals of the ancient traditional religions of Europe. Their knowledge was learned orally and was often extensive. The witches discovered many medicines that are still in use today (Starhawk 1982: 202).

However, Western culture was undergoing a profound ideological revolution. The idea was taking hold that the earth is a dead piece of rock, or a machine, valuable only as a raw material for human use. From this basic notion, new understandings emerged. Land was beginning to be thought of as a commodity, to be bought and sold. Mining was permissible if the earth was not a living being (Mander 1991: 211–12). Knowledge, too, was being transformed into a commodity to be owned by professionals trained in a university and licensed to practise. Since women and poor people were excluded from formal education, they were also excluded from the newly emerging professions, such as religious leadership and medicine (Starhawk 1982: 200–201).

Also in the sixteenth century, several things happened to cause the landlords to want the people removed from the land. European markets were flooded with gold and silver from the Americas, causing extreme inflation and making the peasants' low rental payments almost worthless. New demand for agricultural products were emerging from the growing populations of the first industrial areas and the armies fighting in England, continental Europe and America. These products could also be transported over greater distances because of new canals and roads. At the same time, demand was growing for wool in the newly mechanized English textile industry and in other European countries. There were profits to be made from raising sheep. Mining had also become a profitable pursuit, with markets opening up for coal, iron, lead, copper, stone and slate. Landowners began to pressure for enclosure and fencing, so that they could use the land for mining or raising sheep, cattle and crops for sale. They worked to transform the land from a resource with multiple uses for the whole community to private property for private profit (Mingay, introduction to Gonner 1966: xli, xlvi; Mingay 1997: 32, 34, 44, 48, 149; Starhawk 1982: 192–93).

A central piece of this transition was the "extinction of common." There were several legal mechanisms for accomplishing this, and they changed over the long period of time during which enclosure took place (Mingay, introduction to Gonner 1966: xlii; Gonner 1966: 43, 71). The end result, however, was the destruction of a system of rights that allowed peasants to take the necessities of life from, or even live on, land that they did not legally own. In the new system, landlords could punish as poachers those who tried to take fish and game, as trespassers those who tried to collect herbs and berries, and as squatters those who lived on the land (Starhawk 1982: 193–94; Yelling 1977: 227–28).

The destruction of forests, marshes and wild areas changed the landscape forever and dispossessed whole communities of peasants and craftspeople who had been living self-sufficiently in these areas, far from the laws of the lords and bishops (Hill 1972: 35–38). Some were "outlaws" who,

> opposed to the king and his laws ... specialized in robbing those who ground the faces of the poor, enclosers of commons, usurers foreclosing on land, builders of iron mills that grub up forests ... cheating shopkeepers and vintners, but not rent-racked farmers, needy market folks, labourers, carriers or women. (Hill 1972: 35–36)

These "outlaws" have been immortalized for centuries by the Robin Hood ballads. Other denizens of the forests were those who still followed the ancient pre-Christian traditions of England. Large networks of pagans met there to celebrate their annual cycle of festivals and to study magic and healing. The pagan understanding of the earth and all its life forms as sacred was being violated by new ideas of nature as dead raw material, valuable only when exploited for profit (Hill 1972: 38; Starhawk 1982: 194, 197).

Oliver Goldsmith, a poet living in the late eighteenth century, wrote of the enclosure movement:

> But times are alter'd; trade's unfeeling train
> Usurp the land and dispossess the swain;
> Along the lawn, where scatter'd hamlets rose,
> Unwieldy wealth, and cumbrous pomp repose.
> Ill fares the land, to hastening ills a prey,
> When wealth accumulates, and men decay:
> Princes and lords may flourish or may fade;
> A breath can make them, as a breath has made;
> But a bold peasantry, the country's pride,
> When once destroy'd, can never be supplied.
> (quoted in Mingay 1997: 124)

Then, as now, the dispossession of the poor was justified by labelling the victims as lazy and immoral. As G.E. Mingay says:

> The hastening of profitable reform was fuelled also by contemporary morality. Property-owners were likely to agree with those who saw the commons as a cause of idleness and fecklessness, a means of enabling the poor to live without the discipline of regular full-time work. Some went beyond this and thought that the commons encouraged not merely idleness but also dissipation and crime. (1997: 154)

Mingay quotes Matthew Boulton, partner of James Watt in their steam engine works, referring to those living on common land as "idle beggarly wretches, addicted to laziness and crime" (1997: 44). Mingay also quotes a "well-known agricultural expert," writing in 1798: "In sauntering after his cattle, the cottager acquired a habit of indolence.... Day labour becomes disgusting to him ... and at length the sale of a half-fed calf, or hog, furnishes the means of adding intemperance to idleness" (Billingsley, quoted in Mingay 1997: 135). Hill records an Elizabethan surveyor's opinion: "So long as [the cottagers] may be permitted to live in such idleness upon their stock of cattle, they will bend themselves to no kind of labour. Common pasture ... is a ... maintaining of idlers and beggary" (1972: 40–41). In a quote reminiscent of modern "poor-bashing"[8] aimed at women on social assistance, an early nineteenth-century commentator on enclosure said that peasant women were "very lazy; they do nothing but bring children and eat cake" (Mingay 1997: 155).

Women and children were particularly affected by enclosure. In the old system, while the man of the house worked as a labourer on larger farms, the women and children took care of the cows, pigs, sheep, vegetables and poultry the family kept on common land, producing the family's food and clothing from them. Once the family was separated from the common land and therefore their livestock, the role of women and children disappeared. Some found work in industry, but a woman could only expect to earn half a man's wages, and children even less (Mingay 1997: 135; Starhawk 1982: 195).

In many areas the dispossessed peasantry resisted enclosure. There were protests, marches and public meetings. Resisters pulled down fences and pulled up surveyors' stakes. There were riots in Somerset, Cornwall, Wiltshire, Gloucester, North Devon and many other areas of the country. Marsh dwellers destroyed drainage systems (Mingay 1997: 51–52; Starhawk 1982: 196). The Diggers were part of this resistance. Women lost disproportionately more of their livelihood than men did and were also very active in the leadership of resistance actions. In one example the workmen enclosing the moors were "held up by mobs of hostile poor who might number as many as a hundred and fifty, and included women armed with dripping pans" (Mingay 1997: 132).

Women who were dispossessed by these economic changes and those who took part in resistance were particularly at risk. Witch hunting reached England in the sixteenth century. Although not as vicious or widespread as the witch hunts on the European continent, the English witch hunt had the effect of spreading fear in peasant communities. It helped destroy the unity that made resistance to enclosure possible by making people afraid of each other, for anyone could accuse someone of being a witch. It also encouraged people to channel the despair and anger accompanying their growing poverty towards women. For this reason, although almost half of the witches were men, the witch hunts were directed almost entirely at women (Starhawk 1982: 196–97).

The sixteenth and seventeenth centuries gave us a legacy of property, gender, race and class relations that persist into the present.[9] All over the world, women struggle toward equity, taking many steps backward as well as forward.[9] Resource exploitation companies continue to use centuries-old methods to dispossess Indigenous peoples (Bowles and Veltmeyer 2014; CBC 2013), and the commons are forever under attack (Haiven 2014; McMurtry 2013; Mies and Shiva 1993: 98-107; Shiva 2005).

Since the mid-1970s, the pace of our current version of the "enclosure movement" has picked up. The governments of Ronald Reagan in the United States and Margaret Thatcher in the United Kingdom launched the age of neoliberalism, marked by lower taxes for the rich, cuts to social welfare and public services and the public employees who delivered both, erosion of democracy and environmental protection, privatization of formerly public debt, lands, spaces, institutions, research and services, deregulation of industry, attacks on labour organization and standards, open borders for trade and investment, and currencies floating free of the gold standard. The collapse of the U.S.S.R. in 1989 removed a threat and an alternative to private property, and the modern "enclosure movement" gained more speed.

John McMurtry, in his book *The Cancer Stage of Capitalism* (2013), compares the out-of-control privatization of the decades since the 1970s with the growth and metastasization of cancer, not just as a metaphor but as a parallel process on a collective scale. Among other things, he examines the ability of capitalism to use its ownership of the media to disguise its takeover of life processes in the same way that cancer avoids immune system detection by mimicking normal growth. His parallel for the immune system on the cellular level is the civil commons on the social level. It is in the civil commons, he says, that we preserve the ground of life in opposition to the pathology of "the market paradigm in its recent carcinogenic eruption" (Preface). Our struggle to survive this collective cancer, according to McMurtry, takes the form of our battles to preserve and expand the civil commons, just as English peasants tried to do in the sixteenth and seventeenth centuries.

Forms of Power

Each of these stories — the conquests of Old Europe and North America and the enclosure movement (although far more complex than the brief summary I have provided here) — demonstrates some of the same processes that appear whenever people with competitive, hierarchical, separation-based values come into contact with people who practise a more connected, cooperative way of life. The end result is that the more cooperative group eventually is forced to absorb and live by competitive values. The essence of this transition is a transformation in the forms of power used in a society.

Like most other women of my class I have been afraid of power most of my life. I thought power was automatically evil and that cooperation depended on the refusal to use it. More often, I denied the power I had in many situations. This, I finally realized, is because, like most people formed by a competitive society, I thought power could only mean power over others.

I encountered a much deeper understanding of power in the work of Starhawk (1987: 8–20). She defines four kinds of power. "Power-over" is domination or force, the power I had been afraid of. "Power-over" also includes its flip side — rebellion. Rebellion is the reaction of people trying to protect themselves or get some control of a situation where they are being hurt by a person or system with power over them. Rebellion can be a dramatic fighting back or can take the form of quiet manipulation, the "power of the powerless," used, for example, by children to control adults even though adults are stronger and, in this culture, are the "owners" of children. If rebellion succeeds, the roles simply reverse and the situation of "power-over" continues.

There are, however, forms of power which have nothing to do with the domination of others. The first is "power-within." This refers to one's own centredness, one's grounding in one's own beliefs, wisdom, knowledge, skills, culture and community. The second is "power-with," or power exercised cooperatively among equals. The third is "authority," that is, the wisdom, creativity or expression of a group's energy by an individual that is recognized and agreed to by others as right at a certain time.

The history of conquest by patriarchal cultures is a lesson in the relationship between "power-over" and "power-with." Cooperative cultures practise "power-with," along with "power-within" and "authority." Decisions are made by consensus, among equals. If one person's views have more weight, it is because of wisdom, experience or an insight that sums up the group spirit at that time. These forms of power vary in strength, shift from person to person, and can be earned and lost, although they tend to accumulate with age.

When a culture practising "power-with" meets a culture that practises "power-over," the former group does not stand much of a chance. People from a cooperative culture tend to trust others, make themselves vulnerable and give with the knowledge that something of value will come back in due time. They assume a connection with others that makes injuring or killing another person very rare. They do not accumulate goods. They do not think in terms of self-defence or distrust. The two cultures are not evenly matched.

On a smaller scale, within an organization, even one person who wants control and uses the methods of "power-over" can destroy an experiment in consensus methods. In my experience, when the controlling manipulations begin, the other members of the group have to choose among three options. The first choice is to band together in complete unity to resist the person's attempt to take over. In the second case, one or more members lead the resistance, entering into a power struggle, which in turn demands the use of "power-over" tactics and ends the cooperative nature of the group. The third option is to break up the group.

The first choice is a good one, but the total agreement required is very difficult to achieve, especially if there is discontent in the group or the person initiating the take-over has done some groundwork and convinced others to support the effort, or, as is often the case, people are simply not able to figure out what is happening. Often the person seeking control is doing it unconsciously, making it even more difficult for others to see the dynamics. Even if the group is successful in forming a united opposition to the one member who is using power-over methods, consensus decision-making must be abandoned, at least for a time, in favour of majority rule. Otherwise the single member can block consensus forever. Unless this change to majority rule is conscious and limited, the group may not go back to consensus after the problem is solved.

The second choice is similar to the usual result of a cooperative culture facing conquest. The resistance may be successful, but the egalitarian, consensus-based nature of the group is sacrificed. The third option is by far the most common. Many organizations, successful in establishing internal cooperation for a time, have faced this painful choice. The interaction of "power-over" and "power-with" in groups is discussed further in Chapter 4.

Oppression is an inevitable result of "power-over." In order to end it, our challenge is to discover how we can restore the skills, methods and culture of "power-with."

notes

1. The term "violence," as I am using it here, is defined in the glossary near the back of this book.
2. These terms are defined in the glossary.
3. An account similar to this one, unravelling the net of social values woven around war-making, can be found in Starhawk (1987) Chapter 2, "The Dismembering of the World" (47–67). Starhawk also explored these connections in a fictional work, *The Fifth Sacred Thing* (1993).

   There is other interesting material on some of the other connections made in this account: on also relationship between women and the environment, see Merchant (1980); on the relationship between heterosexism and sexism, see Grahn (1984), Pharr (1988) and *New Internationalist* (1989); on the relationships among heterosexism, sexism, conquest and war, see Altman (1989), Barry (1979, 1985), Brock-Utne (1973, 1981), Easlea (1987) and Enloe (1983). In *Sexual Suicide* (1973), Brock-Utne quotes George Gilder, writing of training in a Marine boot camp:

   > From the moment one arrives, the drill instructors begin a torrent of misogynistic and anti-individualist abuse. The good things are manly and collective; the despicable are feminine and individual. Virtually every sentence, every description, every lesson embodies this sexual duality, and the female anatomy provides a rich metaphor for every degradation. (from unpaginated transcript)

   Brock-Utne adds the comment: "When you want to create a soldierly group of male killers, that is what you do, you kill the woman in them."

   Another reflection of the relationship between heterosexism and war is the inscription on the tombstone of Leonard Matlovitch, a gay man who died of AIDS in 1988. The stone stands in the military cemetery in Arlington, Virginia: "They gave me a medal for killing five men, and a dishonourable discharge for loving one."

   In February 1992, the Halifax *Daily News* reported that scientists working on non-lethal weapons were running into resistance from the Pentagon because it was felt that non-lethal weapons were not manly enough; masculine means killing. A similar connection appeared in another Halifax paper, the *Mail Star,* in September 1992 in a report on the rape and harassment of female officers and civilian female passers-by at a party held to thank troops for their work in the Gulf War. Some of the high-ranking Navy personnel quoted felt that to curb such behaviour would demoralize the male officers.

   References on men conquering other men by rape can be found in Barnett (1979), Cole (1989), Hanmer and Maynard (1987), Kleinberg (1987: 131), MacKinnon (1987), Troiden (1988) and Mies and Shiva (1993: 122–23, 129–130).
4. Marija Gimbutas's life and legacy is portrayed in a film by Donna Read and Starhawk, *Signs Out of Time: The Story of Archeologist Marija Gimbutas* (Belili Productions, 2003).
5. There is a similar but more scientific account contrasting the high status of women and the gentle rearing of children in a "primitive" society with the subservience of women and punishment of children in Western "civilization" in Bronislaw Malinowski's classic anthropological study of Triobrand society (Papua New Guinea), *Sex and Repression in Savage Society* (2001 [1927]: 25–39).
6. Ronald Wright has collected and studied post-colonial accounts by North American Aboriginal people. In *Stolen Continents: The "New World" Through Indian Eyes* (1992),

he told the story of the European conquest from the point of view of five First Nations: Aztec, Maya, Inca, Cherokee and Iroquois.

7. Leon Rosselson (Wembley Park, Middlesex, U.K.: Fuse Records, 1975). The song can be heard on Rosselson's recordings *For the Good of the Nation* and *That's Not the Way It's Got to Be*. It is also on Dick Gaughan's *A Handful of Earth*, Billy Bragg's *Between the Wars* and *Aya! A Benefit Tape for* AIDS *Vancouver*, by the Vancouver trio Aya (Slim Evans Records and Tapes, 2149 Parker St., Vancouver, BC, V5L 2L6).

8. For an analysis of modern "poor-bashing" in Canada see Swanson (2001a).

9. For current information on the state of the world's women, look at the websites of Human Rights Watch <www.hrw.org/topic/womens-rights>, the United Nations Population Fund <www.unfpa.org/rights/women.htm> and the Association for Women's Rights in Development <www.awid.org/eng>. Current information on Canadian women can also be found at Human Rights Watch. As well, see Elghawaby (2012) and the bibliography on women's rights assembled by Childcare Canada <www.childcarecanada.org/resourcesation-and-child-care---still-central-women's-equality/back>.

"They Wouldn't Be Able to Pick Us Off One by One"

January 21, 1992

Pearline Oliver, a leader in Nova Scotia's Black community, was interviewed on CBC this afternoon. She is a founder of the Black United Front of Nova Scotia, but said she would like to see BUF change its name and become a people's movement against poverty and social problems. The interviewer argued, more than once, that every "special interest group" has its own advocacy organization; Black people would risk having no one to speak for them. Oliver responded that if people were united, "they wouldn't be able to pick us off one by one."

Step 1: Understanding Oppression — How is it held in place?

This book is about the relationships between people experiencing different forms of oppression. My aim is to uncover what is required so that we may achieve understanding based on our mutual dispossession. I believe we need unity in order to create a power base strong enough to change the system we live in. I spend very little time in this book speaking of those who are benefitting from and actively promoting our oppressions and the divisions between us. It may seem as if I am forgetting about them and suggesting that we, the exploited, are to blame for our situation because we keep ourselves and each other down. We certainly help keep ourselves and each other down. We reproduce the social, economic and political system that formed us by playing out our internalized oppression against ourselves and each other. However, I do not mean to suggest that our mutual oppression is the whole story.

The backdrop for any discussion of oppression is an understanding of class. In all three of the case studies in Chapter 2, a small but powerful group expropriated for themselves resources that were formerly used to maintain life, community and culture for all or most of the population. This is how class functions. Class is both the foundation and the result of all other forms of oppression.

In the twenty-first century, the elite classes are still grabbing even more control of the world's natural resources, along with human life and labour, to benefit only themselves. Our "rights of common" are still being "extinguished" as what is left in the public realm is turned into private property. Our transportation infrastructure — including even the sea bed under our harbours — our formerly public parks, public meeting places, prisons, power utilities, postal systems, water supplies, schools, public services, the seeds we grow, even our human genetic code are gradually being declared private property and sold to the highest bidder (McMurtry 2013; Mies and Shiva 1993: 98–107; Shiva 2005, 2010). In Canada, our public health care system, something we have fought for and treasured for forty years, is under intense attack. Our federal and provincial governments are carrying out the destruction, but the benefits of the process go to the private health and insurance companies.[1] We can no longer even keep track of the impact of service cuts and privatization because our public science and statistics agencies are among the hardest hit (Nelson 2013; Polster 2014).

In our time, the driving force of this process, the structure of the elite classes, takes the form of transnational corporations and financial institutions. They have woven a web of control around the world. In *Global Reach* (1974), an early analysis of globalization, Richard Barnet and Ronald Muller described the top executives of multinational corporations as "world managers because they are "the first men in history to make a credible attempt at managing the world as an integrated unit" (quoted in Morgan 1979: 275). They are using their overwhelming influence with powerful international organizations like the International Monetary Fund, the World Bank, the World Trade Organization, the European Union and the G8 to make themselves the most powerful actors on earth. Through bilateral and multilateral trade agreements such as the North American Free Trade Agreement and Canada's draft agreements with Europe and China, the multinational corporations have succeeded in entrenching their right to profit over the power of any government to protect the health and safety of its citizens or the environment. For example, the Ethyl Corporation sued Canada for banning the use of lead in gasoline. Canada was forced to lift the ban and pay Ethyl Corporation U.S. $13 million in damages. Sun Belt Water Inc. of California claimed U.S. $10.5 billion in compensation because the British Columbia government banned bulk water exports. S.D. Meyers Inc. sued Canada for U.S. $20 million in damages for banning PCBs (Swenarchuk 1999).[2]

Am I evoking a "conspiracy theory"? Unfortunately, the multinationals do not need a conspiracy to coordinate their activities. In the introduction to *A Fate Worse Than Debt*, Susan George explains:

> I DON'T BELIEVE IN THE CONSPIRACY THEORY OF HISTORY. I take special pains to state this, because I've been accused of just such beliefs the moment I pointed out that a great many forces were converging in a single direction. They don't have to conspire if they have the same worldview, aspire to similar goals, and take concerted steps to attain them. (1988: 5)

On the other hand, these "world managers cannot have a grip on everything. As Malvina Reynolds wrote in one of her songs: "They've got the world in their pocket, but the pocket's got a hole" (1975). Hundreds of people protested at the World Trade Organization meeting in Seattle, Washington, in November/ December 1999, initiating an era of large international protests at meetings of the G8, International Monetary Fund/World Bank, European Economic Summit, World Petroleum Congress, Organization of American States and North Atlantic

Treaty Organization (*Telegraph* 2012). The secretive World Economic Forum, a coordinating body for international neoliberal economic and policy development, which meets annually in Davos, Switzerland, is countered by the World Social Forum (wsf), an annual international gathering to coordinate action for justice, human rights and the environment. The wsf has popularized the anti-globalization slogan: "Another world is possible" (Chossudovsky 2013; George 2004; Porto Alegre 2013). The Organization for Economic Cooperation and Development abandoned its Multinational Agreement on Investment, called "the constitution of a single global economy" by the director general of the World Trade Organization, in October 1998, because of strong resistance in several key countries, including Canada and France (Barlow and Clarke 1998; Richardson 1997).

All over the world, there are thousands of resistance actions at the local level. Farmers in India prevented Cargill and other huge grain companies from privatizing public seed resources (Singh 1993). Bolivians successfully resisted the privatization of their water (Clarke 2002; Spronk 2006). The Mi'kmaw people and their allies are resisting hydraulic fracturing (fracking) for natural gas in Northern New Brunswick (Ward 2014), and people all over the world camped in public squares and parks to draw attention to the growing wealth of a tiny proportion of the population during the Occupy Movement in 2011. Thanks to Occupy, millions of people now know the meaning of "We are the ninety-nine percent" (Wikipedia 2014b).

Whenever reporters give the leaders of anti-globalization protests a few seconds of air-time or print-space, they make the point that they are not opposed to economic development or trade, but to the growing control exercised by the transnational corporations over all aspects of life. Ever since the draft Multilateral Agreement on Investment was leaked to the public in February 1997, the transnational corporations have not been able to organize the world to their liking in complete secrecy and with no opposition (Barlow and Clarke 1998). If we are vigilant, they will not be able to do it at all.

In addition to the more confrontational forms of protest, thousands of people are involved in quieter forms of resistance to globalization by creating alternative networks and communities; experimenting with sustainable food and fibre production; developing socially and environmentally aware methods of energy generation, production and trade; teaching, writing, making theatre, film and art; publishing books and magazines; preserving wilderness and species at risk; and the list goes on.

The Internet, created for military purposes and quickly picked up by university-based researchers, has become overwhelmingly a tool of multinational corporations (Brignall 2002), but here too "the pocket's got a hole." Resistance organizations and networks are using it to accumulate and distribute information, coordinate action and gather thousands of names on crucial petitions in just a few days. Online activists are coordinating strategies for election, environmental, social justice and LGBT activism, all online (Carty 2009; Gerbaudo 2012).[3] In 2011, during what is now called the "Arab Spring," the world watched in amazement as protest movements in twenty Middle Eastern, African and Central Asian countries without open media and communication used social media to host political debates, spread ideas, coordinate actions and attract international attention. They overturned the governing regimes of four countries and made important changes in others (Howard et al. 2011; Eltantawy and Weist 2011; Stepanova 2011).

For centuries, the structures and institutions representing the international elite class have had a huge investment in hierarchy, competition and divide-and-conquer tactics. They put vast resources into keeping the world the way they want it. They prefer to do it quietly, invisibly if possible, but, if necessary, they will use the influence they have over our governments. Governments, in turn, use their armies, intelligence services, media, police, schools and weapons to maintain control of the population.

A world of systems designed to preserve injustice and inequality is held in place by several interrelated expressions of "power-over": political, economic, ideological and physical force.

Political power works by putting only members of a certain group in positions where they can make decisions affecting everyone. In North America, decisions with an impact on vast numbers of people are, for the most part, made by white, straight (or perceived as straight), upper-class and upper-middle-class males. Political power tends to concentrate in fewer and fewer hands, because those who make the decisions favour their own group, giving themselves increasing power.

Economic power — where one group has access to more economic resources than others — tends to concentrate in the same way. The favoured class uses its resources to further increase its wealth and, with that, its economic power. In Canada in 2005, the most recent year for which this information is available, the richest 10 percent of people held 58.2 percent of the wealth. The bottom 90 percent held 41.8 percent of the wealth. The bottom 50 percent held 3.2 percent of the wealth. The income figures reflect this huge inequality as well. In 2007, the richest 0.01 percent of Canadians had an average income of $3.83 million. The richest 0.1 percent had an average income of $1.49 million. For the richest 1 percent, the average income was $387,400. For the richest 10 percent, $119,600 The average Canadian income that year was $38,200 (Canadian Centre for Policy Alternatives 2012).

The gap is getting larger. Between 1997 and 2007, the richest 1 percent got 32 percent of income growth. Between 1980 and 2009, the richest 20 percent of households had an income increase of 38.4 percent while the middle 20 percent lost 0.3 percent of their income and the poorest 20 percent lost 11.4 percent of their income (Macdonald 2014). Between the late 1970s and 2007, the richest 1 percent doubled their share of the national income; the richest 0.01 percent quintupled their share (Hennessey 2014).

The international picture is similar. Worldwide, the richest 1% own 46% of global wealth, the richest 10% own 68%. The poorest two-thirds of the world's population each owns less than $10,000 in assets, a total of 3% of the world's wealth (Piketty 2014; Freeland 2012).

This appalling gap is widening, nationally and internationally, because of public-policy decisions heavily influenced by the wealthiest citizens. The way they use their spending power, along with their political power, affects millions of other people's lives.[4]

Political and economic forms of power are backed up by the power of physical force. Large corporations, drug cartels and governments back up their control over others through action or threat of action by security forces, paramilitaries, thugs and armies.

There is another form of power that makes the previous three possible. This is ideological power, the power of belief. Ideological power allows an individual or group to influence others' concepts of reality and their idea of what is possible and valuable. If people believe that injustice and inequality are right, or at least inevitable, they will not try to change their society. This silence and inaction becomes the ballast that steadies the whole system. It creates an appearance of peace and order; people's discouragement about the possibility of changing the *status quo* keeps the current power relationships in place without obvious force having to be used.[5]

Specific beliefs that prop up injustice include the following:

- the myth of scarcity — the belief that there is not enough to go around, frequently used to disguise the fact that a large proportion of the world's resources benefit very few people. The world's resources are adequate to give everyone a good quality of life. The problem is domination of resources by a few powerful people. In other words, the problem is the inequalities of class;
- the myth of objective information — the belief that it is possible for one group, particularly straight white males in this part of the world, to stand back and observe humanity without their own biases influencing what they see;
- stereotyping — the belief that all members of a group are the same;
- blaming the victim — the belief that people are responsible for their own oppression. An example is the strong tendency in North American culture to blame a woman for being raped, beaten, or harassed. The first questions asked are what was she wearing, what did she do and what kind of a woman is she, as if she brought the violence down on her own head. Another example is the assumption that poor people are "lazy." When many people believe that the poor are to blame for their own misfortune, attention is directed away from the real causes of poverty.[6] This attitude is internalized by the poor themselves, who then tend to live in shame and hostility towards other members of their own group;
- might is right, or "majority rule," in situations where only a small minority are really calling the shots. The majority can be threatened, manipulated, bought or given only the appearance of choice;

- separation, competition and hierarchy — the belief that human beings are isolated individuals in competition with one another for positions on a ladder of status.

These beliefs are maintained by:

- tokenism — a few members of an oppressed group are given high-status positions and then used as examples, with the claim that any member of that group can "make it." It is not unusual for organizations to put the tokens in competition with one another, labelling some as "good," others as "bad." This reinforces the behaviour that is expected of those who would share the benefits offered by the institution or system (Bishop 2005; Kanter 1977, 1993);
- assimilation — absorbing marginalized cultures into the dominant one;
- private ownership of information;
- private ownership of the means to communicate information. Those who hold political and economic power also own most of the media that brings us our news. In Canada the short list of media corporations includes Bell, Shaw, Rogers, Newcap and Quebecor (Faguy 2013). In 1970, a Special Senate Committee on Mass Media was concerned that the three biggest newspaper chains controlled 45 percent of circulation when they had controlled only 25 percent in 1958. By the time the Kent Royal Commission on Newspapers reported in 1980, these three chains controlled 57 percent. In 2011 they controlled 65 percent. The largest five controlled 84 percent (Wikipedia 2013). The same process of media concentration in the hands of a few large corporations is repeated all over the world (Wikipedia 2014a). Ordinary people are constantly exposed to the version of the truth carried by these information media, a version of the truth acceptable, in the long run, to the owners of the media. David Radler of Hollinger Inc., owner of 151 newspapers during the 1990s, said: "I don't audit each newspaper's editorial each day, but if it should come to a matter of principle, I am ultimately the publisher of all these papers, and if editors disagree with us, they should disagree when they're no longer in our employ. The buck stops with the ownership. I am responsible for meeting the payroll; therefore, I will ultimately determine what the papers say and how they're going to be run" (Winter 2007);
- violence or the threat of violence. Oppression is held in place ultimately by violence in its many forms — visible, such as injury and death, or less visible, like exclusion, denial of access and denial of needs. Violence prefers not to show its face. Whenever possible, oppression is held in place by the fear of violence.

Anyone involved in social justice activism sees this fear all the time. People often do not fight for what they need or believe is right because of this pervasive fear of reprisal. When you ask people to sign a petition on the sidewalk, many look at you with fear in their eyes and back away. When the possibility of a march or demonstration arises in a group, people tend to immediately think of reasons why they should not do it.

There is political repression in Canada, although most of it is hidden from sight and excluded from history texts. Miners and other unionists have been shot on picket lines (Abella 1974; Allen 1973; Calhoun 1983; Kuyek 1990: 17–25; Mellor 1983). People's leaders and organizers have been imprisoned (Salutin 1980). Tear gas, pepper spray and police horses disperse demonstrations. Guns have been hidden in leaders' houses to be found again when the police come to search.[7] Telephones are tapped and files kept. Opponents of uranium mining have been harassed by helicopters flying repeatedly over their houses.[8] Groups have been infiltrated. Activists have been intimidated, bribed and threatened with release of private information until they agree to become informants (Fidler 1978; Mann, Lee and Penner 1979; Sawatski 1980). Many, many social change activists, even those who simply begin to speak up a little for themselves, experience a backlash from members of the oppressor group. Gay and lesbian activists receive anonymous threats of death or rape. Such terrifying calls and notes also plague feminist, Aboriginal and Black activists who gain the public's attention.[9] Those who try to change oppressive relationships on an individual level can experience violence as well. For example, women who try to change unequal relationships with their male partners sometimes receive verbal, psychological or physical violence in response.

In Canada, those who speak up against injustice or immoral uses of power are more likely to experience indirect reprisals than outright physical violence. They may lose their livelihood, become painfully isolated, have their reputation smeared or be branded as "troublemakers." For example, four scientists working for Health Canada experienced "persistent harassment by management, including conspiracy, threats, intimidation, and defamation" after pointing out gaps in the study used to prove the safety of bovine growth hormone, a genetically altered hormone injected into dairy cattle to increase their milk production (Mills 2002). Two journalists in the United States were fired for producing a documentary including some of the same questions about bovine growth hormone raised by the Canadian scientists.[10] Labels like "socially maladjusted" carry with them the threat of institutionalization for psychiatric "care" (Blackbridge and Gilhooly 1985).

Canada is not Guatemala or Azerbaijan. We do not face the extreme repression carried on in many other parts of the world. However, a little violence goes a long way here. An occasional, unpredictable display of repression can make an average, law-abiding citizen refuse to sign a petition. This is the principle of terrorism. For every person hurt, a thousand more are persuaded not to rock the boat. Direct, violent repression is always a possibility, in the background, but for us in Canada, it is more important to understand fear and the other quiet, invisible, self-perpetuating methods of control the elite classes have established.

One could argue that Canada is an advanced example of invisible oppression.

Our government is quietly handing our country to our current colonial masters, the United States and the transnational corporations, wrapped and tied up with a bow (McQuaig 2010). Our international reputation continues to be surprisingly positive despite our abandonment of public-interest science, peacekeeping, multilateral action against poverty, disease and climate change, and our former role as a trusted mediator in world affairs (Heinbecker 2010; McLeod Group 2013; Nutt 2011). Our national reputation continues to glow with innocent good will in spite of the increasing inequality within our borders and our deteriorating record on gender and human rights (Clark 2013; Farber 2013). We continue to write off the violence we practise systematically against each other as aberrant individual cases.[11] Groups working towards alternatives are so dependent on government funding that they feel they have to compete with one another whenever a bit of funding is dangled in front of them. We seem to have a national case of wearing rose-coloured glasses.

We must overcome these methods of control if we are to take the first steps toward unity, equality, justice and a humane culture — a culture with a future.

notes

1. Organizations monitoring public health care in Canada include the Canadian Health Coalition <healthcoalition.ca>, Canadian Doctors for Medicare <www.canadiandoctorsformedicare.ca> and the Council of Canadians <www.canadians.org>.

2. Analysis of transnational corporations and their strategies can be found in the work of Sarah Anderson (2000), Mark Ackbar et al. 2003, Susan George (1976, 2004, 2010, 2013), Naomi Klein (2007), Jerry Mander (1991, 2012), John McMurtry (2013), Linda McQuaig (2001), Linda McQuaig and Neil Brooks (2012), and Vandana Shiva (2005, 2010; and Maria Mies and Vandana Shiva 1993), to name a few. There are also websites monitoring the activities of transnational corporations, including CorpWatch <www.corpwatch.org>, The Council of Canadians <www.canadians.org>, Focus on the Global South <www.focusweb.org>, Susan George's Home Page <www.tni.org/george/index.htm>, *The Multinational Monitor* <multinationalmonitor.org>, *New Internationalist Magazine* <newint.org>, and many others.

3. Some of the organizations pioneering the use of online activism are Amnesty International Canada<www.amnesty.ca>, Avaaz <www.avaaz.org>, Sum of Us <sumofus.org> and All Out <www.allout.org>. There are many more.

4. A detailed account of how this process works can be found in McQuaig (1987).

5. Ideological power was first defined and explored by Antonio Gramsci (1988). For a chilling example of the use of ideological power in apartheid South Africa, see Lambley (1980: 12–36, 159–223). Maria Mies gives a detailed example of the use of ideological power to keep oppressed people in place in "The Myth of Catching-up Development," in Mies and Shiva (1993: 55–69, 124–27).

6. An excellent analysis of "poor-bashing" can be found in Swanson (2001a).

7. This is from a speech by Georges Erasmus, telling the story of resistance to the first natural gas pipeline proposed for the Mackenzie Valley, at a workshop called "North and South: What's the Connection?" sponsored by Project North, held at the Centre

for Christian Studies, Toronto, March 1975.

8. Experience of friends involved in lobbying for the ban on uranium mining in Nova Scotia, 1981–82.

9. Personal experience and firsthand accounts from friends, colleagues and community leadership students.

10. The two journalists were Jane Akre and Steve Wilson. There is information on their case at <www.foxBGHsuit.com>.

11. For an excellent example of attributing systematic violence to aberrant individuals, look for Canadian press coverage of the murder of fourteen women in Montréal, December 6, 1989, and the subsequent anniversaries of that occurrence. Examples are McGillivray (1990), Lalonde (1991), and Conlogue (1991).

Morality, Duty and Being True to Yourself

We admire people who oppose the regime in a totalitarian country and think they have courage or a "strong moral sense" or have remained "true to their principles" or the like. We may also smile at their *naïveté*, thinking, "Don't they realize that their words are of no use at all against this oppressive power? That they will have to pay dearly for their protest?"

Yet it is possible that both those who admire and those who scorn these protesters are missing the real point: individuals who refuse to adapt to a totalitarian regime are not doing so out of a sense of duty or because of *naïveté* but because they cannot help but be true to themselves. ...

Morality and performance of duty are artificial measures that become necessary when something essential is lacking. The more successfully a person was denied access to his or her feelings in childhood, the larger the arsenal of intellectual weapons and the supply of moral prostheses has to be, because morality and a sense of duty are not sources of strength or fruitful soil for genuine affection. Blood does not flow in artificial limbs; they are for sale and can serve many masters. What was considered good yesterday can — depending on the decree of government or party — be considered evil and corrupt today, and vice versa. But those who have spontaneous feelings can only be themselves. They have no other choice if they want to remain true to themselves. Rejection, ostracism, loss of love and name calling will not fail to affect them; they will suffer as a result and will dread them, but once they have found their authentic self they will not want to lose it. And when they sense that something is being demanded of them to which their whole being says no, they cannot do it. They simply cannot. — Alice Miller (1983: 84–85)

Chapter Four

Step 1: Understanding Oppression — The personal is political

> The problem, unstated 'til now, is how to live in a damaged body in a world where pain is meant to be gagged uncured ungrieved-over. The problem is to connect, without hysteria, the pain of any one's body with the pain of the body's world.
>
> — Adrienne Rich (1986)

Twice in my life I have been part of experiments in cooperative group functioning that I would call completely successful. One was a workplace, the other a voluntary group. Both practised collegiality, consensus decision-making, cooperative planning, shared work, a negotiated division of tasks, personal support and opportunities for learning — for a time. Neither lasted more than two years. Both broke up quickly, completely, dramatically and, for me, painfully.

My work sometimes involves mediating conflicts in voluntary organizations. I see the patterns of my own painful experiences repeated over and over again. Sometimes I feel I am watching the same play performed by different theatre companies.

The pattern is this: after months of muttering outside of the decision-making forum, a person or small group suddenly tries to establish control, sometimes directly, but more often through hidden, manipulative means. While attempting to take control, they express feelings of being persecuted or unsafe. They often believe that someone is trying to overpower them, and sometimes they seem even to be unconscious of the steps they are taking to gain control. They challenge whomever they perceive to be in a position of leadership. If the challenge is accepted by the person or people challenged, or by someone else, a power struggle follows. Once a power struggle begins, anything goes — backroom organizing, running to get support from someone who is perceived to have more power over the situation, dramatic performances, lies.

In the end, it seems, the only option is to destroy the whole experiment, or at least its spirit, since the cooperative spirit cannot be controlled and survive. As with a consensus-based culture trying to resist conquest by a competitive one, once the battle for control begins, "power-over" tactics must be resisted by using "power-over" tactics. The prerequisites for "power-with" — openness, trust, vulnerability, creativity, risk, emotional expression, honesty, giving before receiving — become impractical. Anyone who tries to maintain these ways of interacting is bound to lose what is now structured as a win-lose battle and perhaps be injured in the process.

During these incidents, everyone involved experiences extreme confusion, pain and a sense that the real problem is underlying and unspoken. The surface expression of the disagreement seems shallow or completely irrational or shifts quickly among several different points of disagreement. Consensus becomes impossible. People are forced to take sides. The tension is personalized — people cease to like, trust or cooperate with one another. Above all, the depth of emotion, distrust and the sense of danger go far beyond any actual threat present in the group. The power of the feelings in such a situation is amazing; people are passionate about the stands they take, even while unclear exactly what their stands are.

Where do these dramatic, emotional group disintegrations come from? Why do people who have so much in common do this to one another? Why do the best of our cooperative experiments seem to explode with the greatest intensity? How does the practice of "power-over" become so deeply ingrained that even those of us who have committed our lives to finding different ways of being together fall back into it so completely?[1]

The first time I was part of a story like this from beginning to end, I was in the midst of the experience when I received a clue. A friend took part in a workshop on counselling adult survivors of childhood abuse. When she told me about it, she listed symptoms that may indicate childhood abuse, including sharp intelligence, watchfulness, competitiveness, well-developed skills in manipulating people and a strong need to control every situation. I began to wonder about the person who was trying to control our situation. Later, after all was said and done, it turned out that she was indeed a survivor of incest. Her awareness of her past had been emerging during our conflict.

This led me to ponder a possible connection between child sexual abuse and some adults' need to exert control over others. Such a connection would have huge implications for our efforts to change power relationships. Childhood sexual abuse is not uncommon. About a third of the hundreds of women I know as friends, associates and acquaintances, all over the world and across many races and cultures, have at some time told me about their memories of childhood sexual abuse.

Now thirty years old, the only national study of child sexual abuse in Canada was the 1984 Committee on Sexual Offences Against Children and Youths (Badgley Committee). In 1988 the data collected was analyzed again by the author, who concluded the following:

- one out of two females (53 percent) and one out of three males (31 percent) in Canada have been victims of at least one unwanted sexual act;
- four out of five of these are committed when the victim is a child or youth;
- four out of one hundred young females have been raped;
- two in one hundred young people have experienced unwanted anal penetration;
- three out of five sexually abused children were threatened or physically coerced;
- one out of four assailants is a family member; one out of five is the child's father; one out of two is a friend or acquaintance (Badgley 1988).

The Canadian Centre for Justice Statistics produces reports on childhood sexual abuse. Their statistics include the following:

- while children and youth under eighteen account for 21 percent of the population, they are the victims in 60 percent of sexual assaults reported to police, five times more often than adults;
- for every 100,000 young females, 320 are victims of a reported sexual assault; for the same number of young males, there are 86;
- in 98 percent of reported sexual assaults against young people, the perpetrator is known to the victim; in 30–40 percent of cases, the perpetrator is a family member (2001, 2002, 2003, 2007).

These figures do not begin to tell us the extent of child abuse in Canada, as the power to commit sexual abuse also includes the power to silence the victims with threats, shame and a strong sense of family privacy. According to David Finkelhor, in *Sexually Victimized Children* (1979), 63 percent of abused girls and 73 percent of abused boys who reported their abuse as adults did not tell anyone while they were children. Researchers estimate that only 3 percent of child abuse cases and 12 percent of child rapes are reported (Finkelhor 1994; Hanson et al. 1999). Many children bury the memory in their subconscious. The memory may resurface in later years, sometimes not until old age. Even when children do disclose abuse, it is more common for the adults in their lives to accuse them of making it up than to challenge the perpetrator (Salter 2003).[2]

I began to watch similar situations and to look for literature on the connection between childhood abuse and a need to control others. I found very little. Most writing on child sexual abuse is concerned with how adult survivors function emotionally and sexually and in intimate relationships. Few articles look at survivors' use of power.[3]

My personal observations told me that there is some connection between child sexual abuse and a need to control situations later in life, but there is not a consistent pattern. Of the dozens of women I know who experienced sexual abuse as children, I have seen only a few abuse power in groups. On the other hand, I have seen some abuse power who, as far as I know, did not experience sexual abuse as children.

Then I clicked. I had been swept away by the drama of sexual abuse. The key is not the sexual nature of the abuse but rather the child's experience of powerlessness. Children's experience of powerlessness at the hands of adults is so common worldwide, that it passes for "normal."

Adult power over children is unavoidable. It should be used to protect children, set healthy boundaries and maintain their well-being. It can be accompanied with explanations, negotiation and fair demands made on everyone in the household, young and old. It can be limited to protecting the child's health and well-being, while the child's own decisions are supported in situations where the consequences are not as serious. Adult power must be used to fill the needs of children. All too often, though, it is used to fill the needs of the adults, and childrearing becomes centred on obedience instead of child development. Obedience-centred childrearing undermines children's self-esteem and discourages them from thinking for themselves.

When programs are introduced in schools to help children value themselves and think independently, a significant number of parents actively resist. For example, in 1987, Timberline Press in Eugene, Oregon, developed a dragon puppet called Pumsy, with accompanying lessons to be used by teachers and guidance counsellors. The objective of the program was to help children think clearly, increase their confidence and respect others. The exercises involved children in such activities as visualizing saying "no" to a drug dealer or discussing what they would do if they found twenty dollars. Pumsy was used in 16,000 schools in the United States and was challenged by parents in eight states in 1992 alone. According to the Halifax *Daily News*, most of the objections criticized the lessons that help children learn decision-making. The parents were upset because the dragon "undermines parental authority" and "contradicts Christian beliefs that only parents, or a higher power, have the right to tell children how to act" (Halifax *Daily News* 1993).[4]

Fortunately, Pumsy won many of these battles, but the parental objections demonstrate the commonly held understanding that children should think of themselves as lesser beings and as under their parents' authority in all things. This belief, along with the experience of being raised this way, encourages adults to keep children in a state of anxiety, to undermine their self-esteem and to stress unquestioning obedience. This collection of conditions is often referred to as emotional abuse. Sometimes children are intentionally treated this way; more often it is a reflection of the adults' own state of anxiety, low self-esteem and training in obedience.

Almost all North American children grow up experiencing some form of emotional abuse. Alice Miller's series of three books, *For Your Own Good* (1983), *Prisoners of Childhood* (1981) and *Thou Shalt Not Be Aware* (1986), explores the cruelty and humiliation hidden in some of the most commonly held beliefs about childrearing in Western culture.[5] She also examines how abusive methods of controlling children — methods designed to break a child's will rather than develop a child's awareness and skills— are perpetuated, generation after generation. The isolation, shame and secrecy of the patriarchal nuclear family help ensure that abusive childraising methods are passed down through families without examination.

Even when children generally do not experience abuse from their parents or family, they may experience pain and powerlessness in other settings. Anyone who spends time in Aboriginal communities or communities made up of people from Africa, Latin America, the Caribbean, Asia or the Pacific Islands, sees children everywhere. They often have a voice in family and community decision-making and participate in every community event, playing on the floor when they get bored, falling asleep in a corner when they get tired. No one is bothered by their noise and activity. A babysitter is rare.

Western culture, on the other hand, does not place much value on children's opinions or welcome them as part of adult activities. When a child cries in at supermarket, concert, movie or public presentation, even on public transit, the parent tries urgently to shush them while other adults cast annoyed glances in their direction. Margaret Green, a white South African Jewish psychotherapist, says: "Try as a parent to let your child carry on crying on a bus or pee in a public place or even try breastfeeding beyond the first year or two. You will be criticized, ridiculed, and made to feel extremely isolated. Our culture has institutionalized the oppression of children" (1987: 207).[6]

On the structural level too, Western culture demonstrates the low value it assigns to children. In 2003, Joel Bakan, a law professor at the University of British Columbia, made a film called *The Corporation*, where he explored the parallels between the symptoms that are used to diagnose psychosis and the defining qualities of a successful corporate chief executive officer. The film includes an interview with Lucy Hughes of Initiative Media, the largest purchaser of advertising time and space in the world. She is the co-creator of a research project called "The Nag Factor," a major study of why and how children nag their parents. The purpose of the research was not to help parents deal with nagging children, but to help corporate advertisers teach children how to nag more effectively. "You can manipulate consumers into wanting and therefore buying your products," says Ms Hughes. "It's a game.... Children are your future consumers. If you build a relationship with them when they're younger, you've got them as adults" (Ackbar et al. 2003).

In 2011, Bakan followed up on this segment of the movie with a full-length book that explores the evolution of "kid marketing" since the neoliberal governments of the mid-1970s began the process of deregulating products and media aimed at children. The book is truly frightening, documenting how the multinational corporations are using video games, violence, addiction, sexualization, unhealthy foods, tobacco, caffeine and prescription medications — supporting the development the whole field of child psychiatry along the way — to make money from children. "From [the corporations'] self-interested perspectives," he says, "Childhood vulnerabilities that should demand protection — tender and turbulent emotions, forming intellects, inexperience and lack of guile — instead are targeted for easy exploitation" (Bakan 2011: 47).

The Nag Factor research was part of the corporate advertisers' goal of driving a wedge between children and the adults in their families. "Rebelliousness, stoked by marketers is ... aimed at severing ties to parents and family in order to create bonds to brands, products, endorsed celebrities and athletes, websites, TV shows and networks, mascots, characters, bands and musicians, and anything else that will help marketers and corporations generate profit" (196).

The harm done is beyond calculation. Bakan quotes Gordon Neufeld and Gabor Maté, authors of *Hold On to Your Kids*: "[Children] need bonds with parents and others to develop self-esteem, independence and identity.... When these bonds are breached, children become more difficult to parent, students are harder to teach, aggression and violence among children are escalating, adolescents are failing to mature, bullying is on the rise, children are becoming desensitized and insolence and defiance are increasing" (370).

If child abuse is defined as the exploitation of children for the benefit of adults, deregulation of marketing to children, along with privatizing schools, failing to ban child labour and disposal into the environment of toxic chemicals, to which children are especially vulnerable, constitute child abuse on a huge scale, as a structural feature of Western culture.

Children also experience pain and powerlessness when they encounter the oppressions that are the subject of this book — racism, poverty and discrimination based on disability, learning style, language, geographic location, religion and gender. Some children have families who help them understand and deal with the pain and injustice of oppression; others are not so lucky. Some children's families can help them learn survival tactics; some cannot because the family does not share the oppression. This is often the case when the child's oppression results from a disability, a bisexual, gay or lesbian sexual orientation or a transgendered identity. Sometimes when other family members do not share the oppression, they contribute to the child's experience of powerlessness by rejecting, patronizing, overprotecting or trying to change the child.

The severity of adult power abuse varies greatly. It can range from comments that make a child feel self-conscious to treatment that could be called torture. Also, different people carry childhood abuse into adulthood in different ways and to different degrees. There seems to be little correspondence between the adult reaction and the severity of the abuse, if, indeed, severity can be judged. What most North American children carry with them into adult life, however, are the fear and low self-esteem that come from experiences of powerlessness and the strategies they learn for self-protection.

What are the strategies children learn to protect themselves from powerlessness? They learn to be afraid, to distrust, to be watchful and to make clear distinctions between "us" and "them," safe and dangerous. They learn that they are part of a hierarchy based on deception and force. They learn to judge the situation and make the choice that faces all people who lack power — whether to go along with the situation, fight or run away.

When they decide to go along with the situation, they obey, conform and stay silent. Children learn to cozy up to those who can hurt them, say what the adults want them to say, please and protect adults, act on their behalf, disguise their own intelligence and power, and pretend to take pleasure in their own abuse. They learn to be afraid of what power they do have; they learn to deny it and see themselves as even more powerless than they really are. They also blame themselves for the situation, thereby reducing their self-esteem.

When children decide to fight back, they learn to take every opportunity to grab a little power for themselves and use it to the limit. They can develop a large repertoire of methods for manipulating, controlling and disempowering others, even for destroying them. Abuse survival, whatever form it takes, requires great intelligence and skill.

Survival also requires the suppression of feelings — emotion can make a person with too little power even more vulnerable. Even in situations where abuse is not involved, emotional expression is heavily discouraged in North American anglophone culture. A society structured around competition for control of others requires the control of self, for both the controller and the controlled. Alice Miller writes that denial of emotions separates people from their deep moral sense and therefore makes people obedient and "adaptable," that is, capable of being used for anything. Part of Miller's explanation of this phenomenon is included as a quote at the beginning of this chapter (Miller 1983: 83–85). This relates closely to the process of making men into soldiers, discussed in Chapter 2. Emotion, like sexuality, must be crushed to make a man able to fight and kill.

An African friend once arrived at a meeting feeling shaken. She had been walking along a Toronto sidewalk and passed through a group of people. Afterwards, she realized that they had just emerged from a funeral parlour. She was shocked by the disrespect she had shown the mourners and also because she could not tell they were mourners. There was no crying, no wailing, no expression of grief at all. Her comment was: "No wonder North Americans can be controlled so easily!" At the time I did not understand what she meant; now I do.

Expressing emotions is healing and liberating. When a person is physically wounded, bleeding prevents infection, or, if infection has already taken place, the wound gathers pus that must be released for healing to take place. Likewise, tears release pain, shouting and physical movement release anger, shaking releases fear, talking and laughing release tensions, conversation and physical touch communicate loving support between human beings. All these are necessary for emotional healing to take place.[7] When emotions are released, they can be seen and shared, and others who have experienced the same feelings can offer support. This can begin the process of collective healing as well, for the first step is to discover that we are not alone, not imagining it and not to blame and that there is no reason for shame. Every time someone breaks through the bounds of shame — the "privacy" taught by our dominant culture — others are drawn to them saying, "Yes, that happened to me too." By repressing physical and emotional expression, the culture we live in blocks individual healing and the possibility of people uniting around shared pain.

Because emotional healing is often denied by the adults in a family or the general culture or both, a child experiencing powerlessness must deal with the pain in some other way. It is sometimes buried in the unconscious mind. Many adults who were abused as children have no memory of the experience. Memories may emerge later in life, usually as flashbacks, sometimes when the person is middle-aged or older. Until then, healing or even conscious reflection cannot be initiated, but the pain is still there, affecting the person's reactions to new situations. George Santayana (2006) said: "Those who do not remember the past are condemned to repeat it." Canadian actor, playwright, novelist, television host and open lesbian Ann-Marie MacDonald, in a speech about remembering and healing her parents' viciously negative initial reaction to her sexual orientation (2014), quotes her eleven-year-old daughter: "If you forget the past, it grows inside you." Both sentiments are deeply true in relation to children's experiences of pain and powerlessness.

Unhealed childhood pain seems to be a key mechanism for learning how to behave as oppressors and oppressed. Childhood scars leave a deep distrust of the possibility of safety and equality, and many of us as adults react by using and accepting "power-over," creating hierarchies wherever we go.

Margaret Green has made a very direct connection, not just between unhealed childhood pain and unconscious oppressive attitudes in general, but between the experience of a particular oppressive attitude and its later expression. The context of her experience is her leadership of "unlearning racism" classes for white women. She says: "The most interesting feature of emotional work on being racist is that hardly anyone ever sticks to the topic ... if one attempts to work with any one of [the participants] they will invariably revert to the hurts related to their own oppression" (1987: 193). "From the emotional work done in these [workshops], it becomes evident that experiences of oppression in early childhood provide the fertile ground in which the unconscious roots of racism develop and are allowed to flourish. The common factor linking the many and varied experiences of oppression is the conscious and unconscious abuse of power in relation to children" (179).

For example, she describes women searching for the source of their fear of asking questions about other cultures. They find it in childhood memories of what seemed to them adults' bizarre behaviour in the presence of racialized people. A woman remembered her grandmother telling her that people were Black because they were covered in chocolate. Another was told out of the blue that a Black man standing nearby was no different than she was and she should remember that. As children, these women knew the information was untrue, and when they questioned further, the adult became upset and dragged them away. The memories were painful because it was clear that they were lied to by someone they loved and then silenced when they tried to figure it out. They experienced powerlessness in the face of something that didn't make sense.

Another participant lived in a mixed-race neighbourhood and enjoyed it until she had a baby of her own. She then became frightened of her Black neighbours and worried about her baby's safety. She wanted to move away and yet felt guilty because she knew that her attitudes were racist. Work on her memories and feelings brought back a childhood incident where her grandmother had read her a story about Black people in Africa being cannibals and eating white babies. This information had frightened her at the time but was later repressed along with the memory of its source.

Another example involved a woman who was short-tempered with Black women who attended a clinic where she worked. As she explored her feelings, it emerged that she was upset at the number of children they had while she had been trying to conceive for over a year. This experience connected with early messages about Black women's fertility.

A woman found it difficult to be warm and welcoming with the male immigrants who came to the advice centre where she worked. As she explored the roots of this reaction, she uncovered her experience of being unwelcome in her own family.

Green says:

> It is the internalization of our personal experiences of oppression which perhaps cause us to feel inadequate, ugly, ridiculous, invalidated, objectified, fearful or terrified. If these experiences remain unresolved, we then project on to the external world. Who or what we perceive as embodying a threat to our existence, be it personal, social or economic, is very much determined by institutionalized prejudice and prevailing myths and stereotypes which serve to manipulate and fuel our fears. (196–97)

How exactly does it work? How does the pain of childhood powerlessness become adult abuse of power or acceptance of abuse, adult oppression or acceptance of oppression? This is a question that has intrigued many researchers, scholars, philosophers and writers, particularly those who have survived times and places of obvious cruelty, such as Germany under Hitler or Latin America under U.S. domination. From among many explanations, I have found five that make sense to me.

The first I found in re-evaluation counselling, a program I participated in, on and off, for ten years. Although it originated with Harvey Jackins, re-evaluation counselling theory has been built by the collective thinking of hundreds of re-evaluation counsellors who communicate through the various journals that serve as their network.[8] According to this theory, unhealed pain is like a gully carved in our thinking. Each time we see a situation that looks anything like the one that hurt us, we do not stop to think creatively, we simply react with whatever behaviour protected us in the past. In this way, childhood survival tactics are used automatically and irrationally by adults who have more power in their current circumstances and could react more creatively. The situation itself may be similar to the original hurtful situation in only one respect. Suddenly, however, it is as if the person is back in the situation of abuse — hurt, frightened and powerless in the face of someone with much more power. The old survival skills click into action, judge the situation, distrust everyone, go along with what is happening, denying what power you do have, or fight back by manipulating and controlling.

Sometimes survivors whose childhood pain has never been allowed to heal will abuse a less powerful person if their survival reaction has been triggered by the belief that their victim has power over them. For example, men who batter their partners often see their action as controlling a person who will hurt them if they do not strike first.[9]

Margaret Green points out that some roles in society institutionalize this cycle.

> Teachers will say how they never intended to treat children "that way." But they find themselves shouting, for example, or about to use violence. They may begin to see themselves pitted against the children rather than as the allies and collaborators they had always intended to be. Of course, there is hardly anyone alive today who has not experienced some form of mistreatment at school. Being in the position of teacher sanctions the re-enactment of childhood hurts. There are for instance schools where corporal punishment is still allowed. If that is the case, then lesser everyday crimes like invalidation, ridicule and humiliation, and the suppression of creativity will surely go unnoticed. (1987: 207)[10]

A second theory on how childhood pain becomes adult abuse of power can be found in the work of Alice Miller. She uses a Freudian theory, "splitting and projection," to explain the mechanism (Miller 1983: 79–91). According to her analysis, abused children split off the parts of themselves they have learned to hate, particularly their weak, powerless child-state. Later, as adults, they project these hated parts of themselves onto children, or others less powerful than themselves, and then punish the children, or others, for their own feelings of helplessness. This theory could explain why we so often direct our power against members of our own oppressed group. If we have suffered because we are women, Aboriginal, gay/lesbian, Black or because we have a disability, we may split off that feared and hated characteristic of ourselves. Later we may direct our fear and hatred at whoever exhibits that part of our identity, particularly if they are proud of it.

A third explanation can be found in the writings of several therapists who work with adult survivors of child abuse. They document a tendency of adult survivors of abuse to distrust and severely test, even abuse, any person or group that expresses love towards them. This reaction comes from low self-esteem — the feeling that one could never be worthy of kindness, love, and support.[11]

A fourth explanation comes from the work of Arno Gruen. He believes that when children experience pain from their parents, they adapt by dissociation; that is, they split their interior and exterior worlds apart. They see their parents as the parents see themselves — loving, kind, good — and suppress their own perceptions of their parents as a source of pain. They lose consciousness of their own inner life, particularly their feelings of helplessness, and can only play the roles expected of them by those more powerful than themselves. They create the illusion that they share adults' power by obeying and pleasing them. When they grow up they can become destructive, abusive people because they have lost empathy with others, along with all their other feelings, are terrified of powerlessness and suffer from self-hatred — a result of betraying themselves and submitting their will to others. (Gruen seems to feel that children choose to submit. To my mind, children are too dependent on their parents to choose; however, it seems very common for adults to believe that they chose to submit to abusive treatment as children.) In this dissociated state, people can be manipulated by those willing to take power over them, and they can feel alive and safe only when they take power over others. They believe, however, that their destructive "power-over" is love, just as they were taught to believe that their parents' power over them was love. With no feelings and no inner life, they cannot tell the difference (Gruen 1987).

A fifth explanation is that the pain of extreme loss of control, unhealed, becomes the source of extreme fear of loss of control. Adults who carry this fear with them seek control in every situation in order to feel safe (Laidlaw, Malmo and Associates 1990: 46).

The five psychological mechanisms described here — adult use of childhood survival skills; splitting and projection; distrust of good treatment; dissociation; and extreme fear of loss of control — help me understand why members of groups who seem to have everything in common and have operated cooperatively for some time can be triggered by something that brings controlling behaviour into play, destroying the group. The unhealed pain from past experience of powerlessness, buried in individuals, builds the intensity of these battles.

There have been many experiments in creating communities based on similarities — all-lesbian communities for example. The point is to leave behind the conflicts arising from diversity. The problem is that participants in such communities still take their scars along with them. Within a short time unhealed injuries from past experiences have the group tearing each other apart. The community, based on similarity, experiences all the same struggles as the most diverse of coalitions.

Because we all carry the roles of both oppressor and oppressed deeply rooted in us, it becomes difficult for alternative ways of functioning to gain a foothold. Cooperation, equality, consensus, negotiation and power sharing are constantly sabotaged by fear and the beliefs about reality sealed into our old scars. I am not suggesting that we should blame individuals who break down experiments in cooperation because of their childhood scars. Rather, I am looking for the mechanisms that cause us all to reproduce oppression generation after generation in Western society. These mechanisms are obviously complex and may vary from culture to culture. My analysis is, of course, limited by such factors as my class, gender, colour, ideology and location in the world.

The phenomenon I have observed of an oppressed individual becoming an oppressor may also work on the collective level. I remember my surprise when I was involved in anti-apartheid work and first learned that during the Anglo-Boer War, the Afrikaners were the ones who were oppressed. They faced the well-equipped professional army of the British with rag-tag guerrilla bands, while much of their population died of hunger in concentration camps and their farmland was laid waste.[12] I had thought of them only as the people whose government developed the oppressive system of apartheid in South Africa. I wondered why their humiliation and defeat seemed to give them, or rather their leaders, a determination to oppress others, instead of sympathy for those trying to resist oppression and scrape a livelihood from the land. How could a safe, prosperous, independent homeland be achieved by the methods they used? Their logic was that of an unhealed survivor.

Abuse is sometimes used deliberately to teach children to fit into the system of oppression when they become adults. Two examples of this are boarding schools for upper-class young men and the Indian residential schools. In the case of boarding schools for upper-class young men, the boys are separated from their families, particularly their mothers, at a very young age. The lessons of repressed emotion, hierarchy, competition and obedience are reinforced constantly. Above all, in many of these schools there is a tradition of "hazing," or the "fag" system as it is called in the U.K. Older students are encouraged to torment and abuse younger students. In school, then, young boys first experience oppression, then later are in a position to oppress others.[13] This is excellent training for young men who will someday wield power in industry, government, the civil service and the justice system, the very institutions that maintain the oppressive *status quo*. Margaret Green calls this system

> the perfect training ground for the colonial administrator who would be expected to treat his Third World underling with similar contempt. The role provides the opportunity, and the person filling it experiences enhanced social status, a sense of self-worth which contradicts his early experience, and at the same time a release of tension which accompanies the re-enactment of a hurt in a position of greater power. (1987: 207)

The second example, Indian residential schools, is one of child abuse being used to force a people to internalize what their conquerors thought to be their rightful place in a racist, sexist, class-stratified society. The Truth and Reconciliation Commission has been holding events across Canada since 2008. Hundreds of residential school survivors have taken this opportunity to document the physical, emotional and sexual abuse they suffered as children (Truth and Reconciliation Commission 2014).[14] In Chapter 2, I included a long quote discussing the ideas of

Father Paul LeJeune, a missionary to the Innu people in the sixteenth century. Even that early, LeJeune saw clearly that in order to teach Aboriginal people the hierarchy, competitiveness and violence of Europe's dominant cultures, they would have to take their children away from their communities' protection and abuse them.

The same methods have been used on Indigenous people all over the world. Malidoma Patrice Somé, a scholar and author in the West but an initiated shaman in his own Dagara culture in West Africa, was kidnapped by a Jesuit missionary at the age of four to be trained as a priest. His powerful autobiography, *Of Water and the Spirit* (1995), is more about his journey of healing and finding his calling than the damage inflicted by his schooling, but he does not spare us the details of the brutal and humiliating physical, psychic, spiritual and sexual abuse that accompanied the seminary's efforts to strip him of his language and culture.

At first glance it may seem strange that the same methods have been used to train both upper class men and Aboriginal people, both oppressor and oppressed. This illustrates that oppression is a single system, in which most of us play both roles. Learning to reproduce that system is a single process. Margaret Green says: "If one imagines a person on a see-saw alternating between the two possibilities, oppressor and victim, then emotional work on either role undermines the fulcrum and eventually the whole structure will collapse" (1987: 195).

Many children who have experienced the pain of powerlessness with inadequate opportunity to heal survive by learning to use a variety of tactics. If they feel they can control the situation, they do so; if control is impossible, they learn to protect themselves by obeying and pleasing, or they undermine others. In other words, they learn that they have a place, with some people more powerful than they are, some less. They learn hierarchy and its forms of power well, not consciously, but as a pattern in their deepest survival instincts.

Upper-class men are supposed to learn not only to oppress others but also to respect and obey those above them in the hierarchy. The intention with Aboriginal people, as well, was for them to learn both subservience to whites and oppression of their own people. Both groups learned to maintain the structures of oppression, no matter where they fit into them at any given time. Paula Gunn Allen observes this logic in Father LeJeune's journal: "How could they understand tyranny and respect it unless they wielded it upon each other and experienced it at each other's hands? He was most distressed that the 'Savages,' as he termed them, thought physical abuse a terrible crime" (Allen 1986: 39).

Unfortunately, many of us raised in our abusive society can understand no other forms of power besides power over another or another's power over us. We carry within us a blueprint of the culture's oppressive patterns to be reproduced wherever we have influence. The name for this is "internalized oppression." Thus, the ways of "power-over" follow their cycle from macrocosm to microcosm and back again. We, as individuals, are the DNA of our cultural patterns of misused power. "Power-over" is self-perpetuating. The personal is indeed political.[15]

notes

1. A very interesting book has been inspired by infighting among lesbians, which examines the ethics and values that prevent us from working together. See Hoagland (1988).

2. Up-to-date information on child abuse for Canada can be found on the website of the National Clearinghouse on Family Violence <www.phac-aspc.gc.ca/ncfv-cnivf/index-eng.php>, and other relevant information can be found on the Department of Justice information page on child abuse <www.justice.gc.ca/eng/rp-pr/cj-jp/fv-vf/caw-mei/pdf/caw_2012.pdf>. For U.S. statistics, information and research, see the National Clearinghouse on Child Abuse and Neglect Information <www.childwelfare.gov>. Other sources of information include: Region of Waterloo Research and Planning (RAP) Sheet on Childhood Sexual Abuse <www.preventingcrime.ca/userContent/documents/RapSheet_ChildhoodSexualAbuse-v6.pdf>, Calgary Communities Against Sexual Abuse: Child Sexual Abuse Myths <www.calgarycasa.com/resources>, Little Warriors <littlewarriors.ca/info/statistics-research> and Canadian Centre for Child Protection: "Child Sexual Abuse: It Is Your Business" <www.cybertip.ca/pdfs/C3P_ChildSexualAbuse_ItIsYourBusiness_en.pdf>. For more information on incest, see Butler (1978).

3. I have found the following research articles that make some connection between childhood abuse and a need to control others: Brickman (1984: 49–67, 1992: 128–39), Courtois and Sprei (1988: 270–308), Johnson (1988: 405–28) and Laidlaw, Malmo and Associates (1990: 46). A strong connection is made between authoritarian, male-dominant homes and incest, and the implications for the perpetuation of these power structures in families and society are discussed in Asher (1988).

4. Gloria Steinem tells a similar story of right-wing reaction against self-esteem programming. The programs were carried out by the California Task Force to Promote Self Esteem. Measurable positive results were achieved in a very short time in schools, prisons and women and youth centres. However, the final report was greeted by anger and an attempt to reproduce the Task Force on a national level was defeated by right-wing forces that saw an increase in self-esteem as dangerous for obedience to God and "legitimate" authority. See Steinem (1992: 26–33).

5. Also see Chapter 2, Rose (1991) and Starhawk (1987: 206–7).

6. Vandana Shiva discusses the exclusion of children from the Western development model in "The Impoverishment of the Environment: Women and Children Last," in Mies and Shiva (1993: 70–88).

7. My comments on the healing power of emotional expression and the patterns that result from unhealed pain come from my ten years of involvement with the re-evaluation counselling community. Much of my understanding of oppression generally also comes from this experience, although it is impossible to disentangle my experience with co-counselling from the many other experiences I have had with oppression. One of the strengths of re-evaluation counselling is its understanding of the collective nature of oppression and its effects on the individual. The community and its caucus groups (Black, Jewish Women, etc.) publish excellent newsletters full of insights into the nature of oppression. For further information on this system of counselling, go to their website <www.rc.org> or read its basic principles in Jackins 1973 and Personal Counsellors 1962. A more theoretical discussion of healing through emotional expression can be found in Scheff (1979).

8. See note #7.
9. For further explanation of batterers' perception that their female partners have more power than they do, see Canadian Advisory Council on the Status of Women (1987).
10. Nova Scotia playwright Wendy Lill portrays exactly this phenomenon in her play *Sisters* (1991), the story of a young nun teaching in the Shubenacadie Indian Residential School. Her play *The Occupation of Heather Rose* (1987), explores a similar response in an idealistic young nurse who goes north to work in an Aboriginal community.
11. Low self-esteem is mentioned in virtually every book and article about childhood abuse survivors. The specific problem of being unable to accept good treatment is discussed in Brickman (1992: 128–39), Cahill, Llewelyn and Pearson (1991: 117–30), Courtois (1988: 98–99), Courtois and Sprei (1988: 270–308) and Laidlaw, Malmo and Associates (1990: 178).
12. I discovered this aspect of the history of the Afrikaner people in Harrison (1981), Michener (1980) and Sparks (1990), particularly Chapter 6, "The Great Trek Inward" (119–46), and Chapter 7, "The Rise of Apartheid" (147–82). Information on the concentration camps can be found online at the website of the Anglo-Boer War Museum in Blomfontein, South Africa <www.anglo-boer.co.za>.
13. I learned what I know of life in upper-class boy's boarding schools from conversations with friends who had the experience and from occasional news reports of hazing incidents that have gone too far. The only discussions I have seen in writing are Leemon (1972) and Huysamer and Lemner (2013).
14. There is a rapidly growing body of literature on the Indian residential schools. See Brooks (1991: 12), Campbell (1991: 28), Fontaine (2010), Haig-Brown (1988), Knockwood (2001), Lill (1991), Milloy (1999), Niezen (2013), Regan (2011), Royal Commission on Aboriginal Peoples (1996) and Sellars (2013).
15. "The personal is political" was one of the key insights of feminism. Our foremothers saw the division of life into "home" and "world," "private" and "public," with women assigned to one, men to the other, as one of the foundation stones of women's oppression.

A Story

Racism and Sexism

This interaction of racism and sexism took place at a weekend workshop designed to introduce a group of white Canadians to some aspects of First Nations culture. The event arranged for the first evening was a sweat ceremony, led by a respected Elder. We travelled to the First Nation community and spent the day visiting sites of ceremonies and gatherings, asking questions and listening to stories told by the Elder who was our host. We watched a group of young men prepare the sweat lodge for our ceremony later in the day.

Evening came. We were divided into gender groups and told that the women would go first. We had a briefing from the young men assisting the Elder. One member of our group had not yet decided to go through the experience with us. She confessed to occasional experiences of claustrophobia and wanted to know if she would be allowed to leave if she began to feel panic. The young men assured her that she would, so she decided to go ahead with it.

Once inside the sweat lodge, she did begin to feel claustrophobic. We were seated in a circle around a pit filled with scalding rocks. The air was close and filled with the incense of burning cedar. The moment arrived when the tarpaulin was to be pulled down over the door. Our friend decided that she could not stand to be closed in after all. She asked if she could leave before the tarpaulin was closed. The Elder, who was seated between her and the door, said no. She panicked, rose to her feet and tried to scramble past him through the still open doorway. The Elder rose too and pushed her back into her place. She tried to escape again and again was forced back to her seat. The rest of us asked him to let her go and continue with the rest of us. He refused, instead offering us lessons, telling us that white people are weak and soft, undisciplined and divorced from the earth.

I agreed with much of what he said. By then, however, all of us felt trapped and afraid. Our fears of male violence had been aroused, instilled in us by our own culture and experiences. It was a relief when the Elder said he wanted nothing more to do with us and told us to get out of his sweat lodge. The men's sweat ceremony followed. They had a good experience.

The next morning we rejoined the First Nations members of our workshop to discuss our experience in the sweat lodge the night before. It was an angry, tense session. We tried to explain how we, as women, felt trapped by male violence. Even many of the white men did not understand what we were trying to say about our disempowerment as women. The First Nations people explained to us the absolute respect they have for their Elders and their long, painful experience of white people despising their culture. To them, once again, a group of white people had shown disrespect to a leader of their community, a wise man held in great esteem.

The interaction between racism and sexism is always very complex, and many of us barely learn to grasp one of these realities. It has taken me years to even begin to understand what they may have been saying. One piece fell into place when a friend told me of another unsuccessful introduction of a group of white people to a sweat ceremony. The Elder in her situation had explained that the sweat ceremony, like many other spiritual rituals in the Aboriginal tradition, is meant to be an initiation or trial. The purpose is to persist through the discomfort and pain and, by doing so, move to a new spiritual level. When white people (or anyone else) go through the experience for recreation, fun or because it is "interesting," we are not taking the spirit of the ceremony seriously. A friend who is a First Nation Elder is constantly annoyed when white people remark that the sweat lodge must be "just like a sauna." We bring with us our assumption that pain and discomfort are abnormal and something to be "gotten rid of," something to be ended quickly by leaving the situation or even popping a pill. We are missing the point, staying in the role of uninvolved observers and taking an important part of Aboriginal culture very lightly. This is indeed the spirit in which we had entered upon our experience of the sweat ceremony.

Another possible clue was a statement by another Elder about his discomfort with white women. He confessed that his first memory was of being beaten by a white woman, a nun at the residential school. If the Elder who had led our sweat ceremony had similar memories, no wonder our actions were disrespectful and threatening to him.

At the workshop where this sweat ceremony took place, we did not succeed in reaching a common understanding where we could all feel heard and respected. Everyone had come to the weekend intending to work at overcoming our long history of oppression, but the remainder of the workshop was marked by distrust and anger. Unfortunately, we did not part as friends. Even if the experience had been positive, perhaps it was unrealistic to expect we could have any impact on hundreds of years of oppression and lifetimes of conditioning in a weekend.

Chapter Five

Step 2: Understanding Different Oppressions

If only it were possible to draw a line through humanity with the Oppressor on one side and the Oppressed on the other — for example, Capitalists on one side, Workers on the other — liberation would be so much simpler. But it does not work like that. There are probably a few people in the world, members of the international elite, who fall almost completely on the oppressor side. There are also some who are almost entirely oppressed; for example, street children in cities of the South.[1] The vast majority of us, however, belong somewhere in between; oppressors in some parts of our identity and oppressed in others.

As long as separation, hierarchy and competition are the underlying assumptions, this interweaving of power roles helps keep the whole system in place. For example, imagine an anglophone, heterosexual, white woman with a disability who sits on the board of her family's multinational corporation and an able-bodied professional Black man who is gay and has a first language understood by only a few thousand people. If both of these individuals wish to maintain their own sense of superiority, each has several reasons to look down on the other. If they become aware of their oppression and desire to move towards liberation, they can each claim that the other is their oppressor. In the process, they reinforce their own oppression by maintaining the cycle of hierarchy and competition. It would take a long time and a great deal of work for them to ever become allies. Only a complete and complex understanding of their own contradictory roles as oppressors and oppressed would allow them to recognize their shared interests.

To begin an analysis of ourselves as oppressor and oppressed, it is important to give some thought to the differences and similarities among the forms of oppression we experience.

Differences

Visible and Invisible

There seems to be a cycle of envy between visible and invisible oppressed groups. The visible resent the ability of the invisible to blend in with the mainstream for purposes of getting jobs, housing, education and all the other advantages normally reserved for the more privileged. The invisible envy the greater progress that is made on visible oppression issues because the presence and size of a visible oppressed group cannot be ignored. Also, the invisible envy visible minority people because they can find each other in order to organize and see each other in order not to feel alone in a room. These points of envy create an unfortunate and damaging division between oppressed people.

This division appears within the ranks of those who are struggling with issues of disability because some physical differences are visible and others are not. The visible suffer the immediate discrimination of people who become uncomfortable in their presence, treat them as children or ignore them altogether; the invisible must continually make decisions about whom to tell, when and why. They do not get the sympathy for their cause that those with the more visible disabilities receive.

Another example is the tension between gay and lesbian people and racialized communities. When I travel or eat in a restaurant with racialized friends, I am grateful that I am not visible. Some racist incident, small or large, happens at least every half-hour. It is harder for them to see some of the things faced by those subject to an invisible form of oppression like heterosexism; for example, the insulting comments people sometimes make because they assume everyone present is heterosexual, the damage done to our self-worth when we hide or lie to cover up our sexual orientation, or the fear that we will be separated from our partners in the event of injury or illness.

The issue of visibility/invisibility invites us to play "my oppression is worse than yours." It is an issue that deserves attention for the sake of everyone's liberation.

Specific Histories of Peoples

The form that oppression takes is affected greatly by the particular history of the group in question. Compare the oppression of Jewish people to that of Deaf people. The identity of Jewish people has taken shape through a history of being forced to leave one country after another. Jewish members of the re-evaluation counseling community have written about the imprint this history has left on them, collectively and individually. They say it is difficult for them to feel welcome anywhere.[2]

According to the Deaf individuals I know or whose work I have read, their oppression revolves around the accessibility of communication and the legacy of poor literacy and education from lack of communication, mistreatment of deaf children and the misdiagnosis of deaf children as intellectually challenged.[3] Such different specific sources of oppression are bound to shape the struggles of these two peoples in completely different ways. They will be hurt by different things, aim their efforts at different problems and fight different institutions, to the point where they may not recognize each other as potential allies at all.

Sometimes these histories cause hostility between people experiencing different forms of oppression. For example, many African-Nova Scotians attest to the acceptance they find in their church communities and the importance of the Christian tradition to their survival.[4] Part of the teaching of that tradition, however, is that gay and lesbian people are sinful and an "abomination." Ironically, the word "abomination" has racist roots. It refers to the practices of another culture and religion that are despised and considered inferior by one's own culture and religion.[5] Most gay and lesbian people have had a negative history with Christianity. Various churches have strongly supported our oppression — sometimes our destruction — since the Inquisition.[6] Sometimes these different historical relations to Christianity lead to tension between the Black community and gay and lesbian people and a painful rift in the lives of some LGBT people who are Black.

Aboriginal/Non-Aboriginal Groups

The particular nature of Aboriginal rights can sometimes create tensions between First Nations people and others involved in various human rights struggles. Aboriginal people in Canada, like Indigenous people everywhere, have a special connection with and certain rights to their land, in this case the North American continent, that other groups do not have. The Aboriginal struggle is not only for the resources, protection and respect they deserve as human beings and as peoples, that is, basic human rights, individual and collective. It is also a struggle to recover their nationhood and their right to their homelands, that is, their Aboriginal rights.[7] Aboriginal people still need human rights; the people of a First Nation can suffer under their own leadership as well as under foreign domination. However, the tendency of many people to throw the struggle of Aboriginal people in with all other human rights struggles disregards the unique nature of Aboriginal rights and leads some Aboriginal activists to separate themselves from other human rights issues. For example, I have seen exchanges on more than one occasion between African-Nova Scotians who want to take a unified stand with Mi'kmaw people against racism while the Mi'kmaq resist because they do not want the common cause of racism to disguise the differences between the two groups over the issue of Aboriginal rights.

Class and Other Forms of Oppression

Class is the layering of our society into different levels according to how much access people have to wealth and power. When we speak of the "high," "upper" or "elite" classes, we mean people who control a great deal of wealth and power. When we speak of the "lower" classes, we mean people who are poor and vulnerable to decisions made by others. In some ways class is similar to other forms of oppression, but in another very important way it is unique. The similarity or difference depends on whether you are looking at the cultural aspects of class or its political and economic aspects. Class has both, and we must use different strategies to deal with both in our social justice work.

Class as a cultural phenomenon affects relationships among individual people in the same way that other oppressions do: there are degrees of privilege, for the most part invisible to those who have more. It is very difficult, but not impossible, for good-willed and conscious people in the more privileged levels of the class hierarchy to become allies of those with less. In a cultural sense, class is an idea or perception, just like the other oppressions. In other words, there are strengths and weaknesses, advantages and disadvantages to membership in different classes. A working-class person can appreciate not being as naïve as some professional people are, or someone who grew up in a "middle-class" family can be happy that they were not separated from their parents like many "upper-class" children who grew up in nurseries, summer camps and boarding schools. In a purely cultural sense, it is only because society says that "upper" class is better than "lower" class that one is often experienced as better than the other.

In the same way, white is not better than Black, male better than female, nor heterosexual better than gay or lesbian. The unequal values assigned to these differences are also ideas and perceptions. When we work to change these cultural oppressions, many of our tactics are ideological or cultural. They are aimed at ending shame and developing pride in those who have internalized the understanding that they have a lower value than another group. When the issue is class, it is also

Diagonal Oppressions: Racism, Sexism, Heterosexism, Discrimination based on Disability, National Origin, Religion, etc.

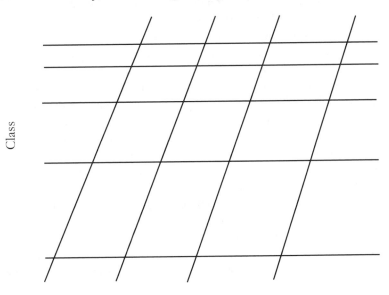

Class

important to deal with the cultural aspect and fight peoples' sense of shame over being rich or poor.

However, on a structural level, class is different from other forms of oppression such as racism, ageism and sexism. Class is not just a factor in inequalities of wealth, privilege and power; it *is* that inequality. Other forms of oppression help keep the hierarchy of power in place; class *is* that hierarchy. Class is the beginning point and end product of all other forms of oppression. It is the essential structure of society, the sum total of all the other inequalities.

I sometimes explain the relationship between class and other forms of oppression by drawing a series of horizontal lines on a piece of paper, then a series of diagonal lines cutting across the horizontal lines. The horizontal lines represent class; the diagonal ones represent other forms of oppression. The diagonal oppressions, such as racism, for example, cut across all classes, but the lower you go in class levels, the more racialized people you will find. Racism affects all racialized people, no matter what their class, but it will affect those in the higher classes less than those in the lower classes, because those with wealth and power can use their resources to ease the impact of racism on their lives.

Another example is disability. You will find more people with disabilities the lower you go in the class strata, because discrimination based on disability affects the education and employment opportunities of people with disabilities and poverty increases a person's likelihood of acquiring a disability. Like racism, disability limits the options of a person in a lower class more than it does someone who can use wealth and power to overcome the barriers they face. A person with resources can buy a van equipped with a wheelchair lift, for example, or hire a sign-language interpreter for a lecture they want to attend.

Racism, discrimination based on disability and the other "diagonal oppressions" are causes and effects of the class system and help hold it in place. For example, when people's time is taken up by the struggle to survive or make ends meet, it is difficult to take part in the kind of reflection that makes one aware of inequalities and the structures that cause and perpetuate them.

A second example is the process of scapegoating. When low-income tenants complain that the landlord collects their rent and doesn't keep up their buildings, they will often focus on the fact that the landlord is white or Jewish, for example, rather than the fact that the landlord-tenant relationship is one of class. "Middle-class" people will blame low-income people for their poverty because of their colour or because they are women, instead of seeing the class structure that causes their poverty by exploiting them. It is so much less risky to blame the vulnerable rather than the powerful. These reactions reinforce class inequality by taking attention away from it and blaming the suffering it causes on some other difference instead.

When we are fighting the diagonal forms of oppression, sooner or later we come up against class, because sooner or later we must address the real lack of power and resources faced by people forced to bear the stigma of other oppressions.

This is usually the point where we hit real resistance as well. Those who already have wealth and power in our society are often ready to accept token changes, for example, a change of attitude, but not real structural change, like redistribution of wealth or power.

When we fight class inequalities, we are not just trying to change attitudes. We are trying to change people's access to resources and their real voice in political decision-making. As one of my friends says, "When we fight racism, the purpose is not to make people white; when we fight sexism the point is not to turn women into men; but when we fight poverty, the purpose is to get people out of poverty."[8]

Likewise, we can conduct many fights against other forms of oppression with few resources, because ideological strategies depend more on creativity, sharp analysis and people's readiness to take risks and express themselves. When we reach the point of challenging class, the struggle itself requires resources — either funding or some other alternative — because the people involved do not have the resources to carry on the fight. Even basic things like getting to meetings or finding someone to care for children while adults talk are out of reach when poverty is the issue or a significant part of the issue.

These differences illustrate the unique aspect of class as a form of oppression. Class is a political and economic structure as well as an ideological one. The other oppressions are building tools; class is the wall. The other oppressions are cause and effect; class is the resulting structure. The other oppressions make it possible for some people to justify having access to the resources of others; class is the fact that they have that access. We must deal with the cultural aspects of class, but class is not just another form of oppression.[9]

Similarities Among All Forms of Oppression
Power and Hierarchy
The basic common denominator among different forms of oppression is power and hierarchy, that is, class. One group of people believes they are superior over another and can back it up with "power-over." The "power-over" can come from physical strength, weapons, wealth, resources, information or greater control of the decision-making and communication mechanisms of the society. These allow the oppressor group to control the oppressed group and help take the less powerful group's resources. They can also effectively spread the idea that the less powerful group is inferior. Both groups internalize this hierarchical thinking and begin to act it out through the mechanisms described in Chapter 4. "Power-over" and hierarchy are fundamental components of all oppressions. They constitute the basic class structure in which all other forms of oppression operate.

Stereotyping
Stereotyping is tricky because it does not come out of the blue. Stereotypes are usually built on a real observation of a culture, just as prejudices often evolve from

a kernel of truth. A comment that is a damaging stereotype in one situation, from one person, can be a compliment somewhere else, from someone else.

For example, in North America Jewish mothers have been at the centre of some cruel humour that combines sexism and anti-Semitism to portray a large group as simple-minded, overbearing and possessive. This group includes scientists, carpenters, artists, deep spirits, great minds, loving women, women with a sense of humour, women struggling with addictions, peacemakers — name it, you will probably find it among Jewish mothers, along with every conceivable variety of childrearing beliefs and skills. All of these women, however, are pushed into one limited, insulting picture. That is the damage of stereotypes.

On the other hand, some of the humour about Jewish mothers can be taken as appreciation for the love, care and concern that many women give to their children in the highly valued family structure of the Jewish community. What makes the difference is the relationship between the person making the comment and the Jewish mother who is the object of the humour, along with the exact audience, content, tone, implications, words and connotations.[10]

Absolute judgements are difficult to make on whether a given remark, story, joke or portrayal is a damaging stereotype or an affectionate, supportive one. The person speaking may have the best intentions but catch the recipients at a point in their struggle where the remark is hurtful. If twenty people hear the comments, there will probably be twenty different reactions on a scale between damage and compliment. Even in a small group where people are well known to one another, you cannot count on a stereotype being received exactly as you intend.

It is very difficult to avoid stereotypes. They seem to be present all the time, almost a form of conversational shorthand. However, even though stereotypes are almost unavoidable and can be positive, they are most often used in a damaging way against marginalized groups. Many have suffered and died because negative images of their people were established in the institutions with the power to imprison, kill, forcibly hospitalize, take jobs and homes away, and separate people who love one another.

Stereotyping is part of the concept of separation. It divides people into "us" and "them." A dominant group sees itself as a collection of different individuals but sees a marginalized group as a single collective entity. When terrorists destroyed the World Trade Centre in New York City and part of the Pentagon in Arlington, Virginia, the news filled up with the phrase "Islamic militants," painting several governments, millions of people and a major world religion with the same brush. The U.S. president stated that his country's retaliation "will make no distinction between the terrorists responsible and those who shelter them."[11] If the U.S. finds a government guilty of sheltering terrorists, this threat extends also to the millions of innocent people who live in that country. On the other hand, when Timothy McVeigh was convicted of bombing the Federal Building in Oklahoma City in 1995, no one referred to him as a "Christian militant." No one threatened to make war on the state or city where he lived. He was universally portrayed as an evil or deranged individual.

All groups are stereotyped to some degree, but those with power cannot be hurt by them as much as those with less power. Although the specific characteristics are different, all oppressed groups are undermined by damaging stereotypes.

The Structure of Violence

All oppressed groups encounter the mechanisms institutions use to keep us "in our place." We experience harassment, withdrawal of resources, slurs against our reputations, denial of promotion (or good grades, service or housing) for sketchy reasons. Some members of oppressor groups use violence to maintain their superiority. These tactics include threatening letters and phone calls, beatings, graffiti, vandalism and sometimes even murder or terrorism as a message to others who are thinking of standing up for their rights. There is little outcry when such tactics are used against oppressed groups compared to the public disapproval expressed when they are used against the privileged.

Oppressed groups also experience less obvious tactics used by people with power, such as tokenism, claims of liberal equality ("we're all equal now; you are asking for special rights") and funding competition (oppressed groups are forced to fight over artificially limited resources).

Assumptions/Slurs Concerning Sexuality

In my experience, every oppressed group has been assigned at least one false negative belief related to sexuality, usually the belief that the oppressed group is out of control or immoral sexually: "Black men want to rape white women," "Black women are sexier," "Indian women are a good lay and cannot say no," "People with a disability have no sexuality," "People with a mental disability are out of control and must be institutionalized," "Lower-class people breed like rabbits," "Gays are immoral," "All women want to be raped" and so on.[12] White South Africans held under house arrest for their anti-apartheid activities reported receiving letters from conservative South African whites accusing them of all sorts of unacceptable sexual practices (Paton 1982). Their "crime" was their opposition to apartheid, but their tormentors immediately interpreted it sexually, just as women who want more independence from their husbands are often accused of having an affair.

The connection between sexuality, particularly women's sexuality, and racism emerges again and again. In the anti-racism workshops I co-led, we would ask people to list words and phrases which contain "black" or "dark" and "white" or "light" (Bishop and Carvery 1994). We always got a mixture of expressions with a primarily racist history, such as "the black sheep of the family," and those with a primarily sexist history, such as "black witch" or "black cat." In Women of Crisis II by Robert Coles and Jane Hallowell Coles, a Aboriginal woman is quoted: "I'll never forget the nurse telling me that Indians are dark and we get our 'periods' before they do, the Anglos ... [Indian] children ... started bleeding early, because they are dark" (Coles and Coles 1990). Darkness and femaleness are linked in their portrayal as chaotic, fearful and evil.

I think this close connection between sexuality and various forms of oppression demonstrates the importance of sexuality to the spiritual and physical well-being of humankind and comes from the time when men began to take the control of their people's destinies away from women.[13] The ideas and values used to subjugate the female are applied to both women and men of marginalized groups — we are all seen as being closer to the earth and the animals and are, therefore, lower, more bound up with our bodies and sexuality — evil, seducing, insatiable and destructive. Women and marginalized groups are also accused of being sexually violent, although in reality it is the dominant group that more often acts out sexual violence.

I find it very interesting that there is at least one sexual myth about every oppressed group. I think it shows how strongly straight white men have been taught to equate controlling other people with controlling their sexuality. Do they believe that control of sexuality gives them control over future generations? Or perhaps this belief comes from the history of oppression, because the first human beings to use "power-over" were probably men subjugating the women of their own people.

Assumptions Concerning Treatment of and Access to Children and Efforts to Separate the Oppressed from Children, Even Their Own

I was amazed long ago to read a piece of historical fiction about the relationship between the Jewish and Roma (Gypsy) peoples in Europe during the years leading up to the Second World War, a relationship that grew from many years of shared marginalization. Unfortunately I have long since forgotten the title and author, but one particular point stayed in my mind — both Roma and Jewish people were accused of stealing and abusing children. It startled me because it is so similar to the accusations made against gay men, lesbians and witches. I began to watch for myths concerning oppressed groups and child abuse. I found many.

They divide into several types of myths. The first are the extreme ones — the oppressed group steals children, eats them, uses them as slave labour, sacrifices them in rituals or abuses them sexually. Once again, here is the oppressor group scapegoating marginalized groups, when it is the oppressor who steals the children of the oppressed group for slavery, both physical and sexual.

The same false accusations also appear in a more subtle form. For example, "women sexually abuse children as often as men do," or "gay men and lesbians recruit children." These myths turn up constantly in the media and in any meeting or radio phone-in show discussing child abuse.

Yet a third form of this myth denigrates oppressed people's ability to bring up their own children. As a consequence, young boys are removed from their mother's care to become "men" in boarding schools; the children of Indigenous people all over the world are placed in boarding schools run by the oppressor;[14] some charities that care for poor children offer no health care, nutrition, education or employment support to their parents;[15] social welfare systems take children from their natural parents and give them to higher-class foster parents who are paid a daily allowance several times the amount of the social assistance paid to the natural parents.[16] Black and First Nations children are placed in white adoptive homes when families in their own communities want them.[17] There are more Aboriginal children in foster care today than there were in the residential schools, even at their peak (Blackstock 2003; Blackstock and Trocmé 2005.

A fourth form has to do with the ideological rather than the physical separation of parents and children. The children of oppressed people are subject to constant messages, in school and the media, that their parents are not to be respected or emulated. Children of oppressed people are encouraged to despise their parents and scorn their parent's ancestry, history, dignity and struggles, in the interests of teaching them to identify only with their oppressors. When some members of an oppressed group begin to speak out about their experience, other oppressed group members counteract their messages, defending the oppressor group, whose perspective they have internalized.

For example, many Aboriginal people in Canada are currently describing the abuse they experienced in the Indian residential schools, while others are contacting[18] the public media to say that these stories are exaggerated or completely untrue. If the latter group were saying only, "my experience did not include abuse," they would not necessarily be speaking out of their internalized oppression. When, however, they try to silence and deny the experience being expressed by others of their own people, they are acting on behalf of the oppressor, whose interests they internalized long ago.

One way a dominant group can attempt to control an oppressed people's future is by controlling the education and development of their children. Going one step further, they can even try to control the oppressed group's bearing of children. An example is the massive and expensive efforts right-wing groups make to control children at the fetal stage. Their attempts to take decisions about childbearing out of women's hands cause pain and hardship for many women. The logic of their actions seems to be that the interests of women are opposed to those of children. However, the real welfare of future children is tied up intimately with that of women; only a group that is trying to take ownership of children away from their mothers could think that inflicting suffering on women is in children's best interests.[19]

In addition to the physical creation and ownership of the child, the oppressor must also be concerned with what influences the child's belief system, that is, by taking over the process of creating the adult from the child. The more the bearing and raising of their own children can be removed from the oppressed group, the more chance the oppressor group has of making a society in its own image and to its own advantage and keeping it that way. This is the corporations' intent when they aim their marketing strategies directly at children, as discussed in Chapter 4 (Bakan 2011).

Desire to Separate and Distinguish

The more the oppressor group can separate and distinguish itself from the oppressed group, the greater is its capacity to create and carry out policy, take possession of resources and build an ideology of oppression — all part of taking and maintaining control. The oppressed group has to make a choice, and most are split over it. If they decrease the separation and distinctions, they have a better chance of getting in on the privileges and resources reserved for the oppressor group. If they are involved in a process of liberation, playing down distinctions helps them focus on commonalities with other oppressed people. On the other hand, the more they can separate and distinguish themselves, the more chance they have of preserving an identity and spirit that will allow them to survive their oppression and move as a group towards liberation.

Specific Similarities

There are also particular similarities between some forms of oppression. For example, there is a specific similarity between Deaf people and gay/lesbian people. Both groups have a collective identity and culture that is not learned in the individual's family of origin. An estimated 95 percent of Deaf children are born and raised in hearing families; more than 90 percent of LGBT children are born and raised in heterosexual families. This situation often leaves scars on the individuals of both groups, as many have to break with their family to find positive role models and must struggle to build their self-esteem and counter the negative self-images they received as children. Both cultures have difficulty being recognized as cultures because they are not passed from parents to children but unite people that have no blood relation.

Distinctions within the Major Oppressions

The process of understanding the relationships among different forms of oppression is complicated by the fact that there are many different expressions of the major forms of oppression. These different expressions can become sources of competition or at least distrust. For example, in Nova Scotia the history and form of racism directed towards the African-Nova Scotian population is different from its expression towards the Mi'kmaw[20] people. The slavery and broken promises that brought African-Nova Scotian people here, killing thousands, was the result of racism. The appropriation of land and resources that pushed the Mi'kmaw people onto tiny, inadequate reserves, killing thousands, was also the result of racism. The two histories, however, are different.

As a result, the current generation of African-Nova Scotian and Mi'kmaw people apparently have different aspirations. The stated aim of most African-Nova Scotian organizations is a fair share of the resources controlled by white society, integration and an end to distinctions based on colour. On the other hand, most Mi'kmaw organizations say they aspire to sovereignty based on their Aboriginal right to the land that was theirs. Sovereignty means even clearer distinctions and the right to discriminate based on the time spent occupying the continent. Both groups recognize the power of racism and sometimes they can make common cause, but sometimes they cannot. Sometimes they react against one another because of cultural differences or because of their frustration with constantly being thrown together as "visible minorities" in programs that cannot fill the different needs of both groups.

Another example of variations in the same oppression can be found in the different ways heterosexism is experienced by gay men and lesbians. Because heterosexism is part of sexism, it affects men and women differently. Heterosexism as it applies to men is about five thousand years old. As described in Chapter 2, male-dominant, war-oriented societies use heterosexism to reinforce male ownership of women, male superiority to women and the relationship men require with one another in battle. Sexuality in such societies is related as much to conquest and ownership as it is to pleasure, so intercourse between men means that a man is conquered, possessed, lowered to the status of a woman. If he chooses this status, he insults the superiority of the male. Much can be achieved in shaping men for a war-making culture by encouraging hatred of those men who love other men. The literature of patriarchal peoples is full of heterosexism in reference to men.

Today, this legacy results in several expressions of heterosexism directed specifically at men. One is the fear that some young men, forming their masculine identity, feel towards gay men and act out in "gay bashing." Another is the variety of responses gay men have to women. Some cherish their "feminine" side and develop a deep understanding of and friendship with women; some develop a hatred of women beyond that of straight men; some find self-expression in women's clothes, or "drag," although it is not uncommon for "drag queens" to express hostility towards women.

On the other hand, there are very few references to women loving women in patriarchal literature before this century. This is because, until this century, most women in patriarchal societies were considered possessions of men and therefore had even less choice of sexual expression than gay men had. Lesbians suffered this lack of choice along with other women, and many feel oppressed by sexism as much as by heterosexism. Some of that sexism we experience from our gay brothers.

The concept of the lesbian only emerged during the early part of this century, as women began to develop independent lives and careers and therefore gain some space to express their sexual choices (Faderman 1981). Heterosexism as it is directed against lesbians is often indistinguishable from society's general resistance to women's independence. Men who batter their partners sometimes accuse them of being lesbians, simply because they have shown some resistance to male control of their lives. Women who take leadership in feminist organizations tend to be called lesbians for the same reason, no matter what their sexual orientation. Many people make no distinction between a lesbian and a feminist.

The oppression of lesbians grows directly out of our history as women in patriarchal societies and results in heterosexism taking a very different shape for us than it has for gay men. Our reactions, therefore, are sometimes not only different from theirs but in complete opposition. Hence, we see struggles inside LGBT organizations over issues like pornography, man-boy relationships and women-only space. Lesbians also resent having research and analysis of gay men automatically applied to us. Our community, culture and issues are often different from those of gay men.

The same type of situation occurs with discrimination based on disability. The experience of society's stigma is very different for someone in a wheelchair than it is for someone who has chronic pain. It is difficult to form an organization to defend the rights of all people with disabilities when the language of the Deaf must be visual and the language of the blind must be oral. It is difficult to build trust when Deaf people have a history of being perceived as mentally challenged and, consequently, some Deaf people want to distance themselves from those with a mental disability.

The web of oppression is complex. There are many points where marginalized peoples can work against each other and compete with each other. Those in power are always ready to foster these divisions. If we are going to be able to build the kind of solidarity that can change our society, we will have to be very clear on the different forms oppression can take and look through them to see our common interests.

notes

1. For more information on street children, see Thomas de Benitez (2011) and the website for the Consortium for Street Children <www.streetchildrenresources.org>.
2. For more information on re-evaluation counselling and its caucus groups, see Chapter 4, note 7
3. For more information on Deaf culture and community, see Cripps (2001) or visit the websites of Deaf Culture <www.deafculture.com> or the Toronto Deaf Culture Centre <www.deafculturecentre.ca>.
4. For more information on the role of the church in the survival and development of the African-Nova Scotian community, see Henry (1973: 122), Pachai (1987: 50–52), Walker (1980: 32–33, 42–43, 54, 107–108, 135–40) and Winks (1971: 53–58, 138–39, 339–51).
5. The word translated as "abomination" is the Hebrew "to'evah" or "to'ebah." It means "ritually unclean" or "idolatry" and refers to the rituals of religions other than Judaism. It carries a strongly judgemental connotation, therefore establishing a hierarchy of peoples and contributing to racism. See Coffin (1983: 2) and Barnett (1979).
6. For more information on the role of the church in the persecution of gay and lesbian people, see Grahn (1984) and Martin (1984: 342–43).
7. For a discussion of Aboriginal rights, see Richardson (1989) and the Royal Commission on Aboriginal Peoples (1996).
8. Thank you, Jackie Barkley.
9. This section was clarified during a conversation with Jeanne Fay. Thank you. Also see Muszynski (1991).

10. During the 1960s, when I began to develop an awareness of oppression, my first experience of being shocked by the Jewish mother stereotype was listening to the comedy sketches of Mike Nichols and Elaine May on their recording, *An Evening with Mike Nichols and Elaine May* (Mercury Records 1960). When I listened to Nichols and May's brilliant work again years later, I heard much more affection than oppression.

11. This quote can be found in any news source for September 11, 2001.

12. Andrea Dworkin connects racism and sexism in her analysis of the sexualization of Black and Jewish women in the United States and the sexual stereotypes of Poles and Roma (Gypsies) in pornography. See Dworkin (1981).

13. The literature on the witchhunts in Europe contain ample evidence of the linking of female sexuality with oppression. See Merchant (1980) and Starhawk (1982: 183–219).

14. More information on the Indian residential schools can be found in Chapter 4, note 13.

15. I encountered several examples of this when I was working for CUSO in West Africa in 1985.

16. In Nova Scotia since 2011, foster parents receive $17.50 per day for a child under nine and $25.43 for a child over ten to cover food and shelter, and an annual clothing allowance of $471 for a child under four, $777 for a child between five and nine, and $1088 for a child over ten. On top of this there is coverage for medical expenses, emergencies, initial placement costs, school supplies, recreation, babysitting, camps and clubs, dental care, diapers and formula, drivers' education, equipment and furniture, glasses, haircare, medical equipment, orthodontics, prescription and non-prescription medications, post-secondary education, special occasions such as birthdays, telephone calls, vacation, repair of damage caused by the child, a spending allowance for the child, travel and special talent needs <www.fosterfamilies.ns.ca/sites/default/files/pictures/Policy94.pdf>. A parent on social assistance receives a housing allowance of up to $620 per month, $133 per month for a child under eighteen ($4.37 per day), or $255 per month for a child between eighteen and twenty ($8.38 per day). Amounts can also be granted by workers for "special needs" if the item is essential to health and safety, the client assembles the right detailed documentation and the worker is satisfied that the client has exhausted all other avenues for assistance <novascotia.ca/coms/employment/income. Also see Dalhousie Legal Aid Service's Welfare Rights Guide <www.dal.ca/content/dam/dalhousie/pdf/law/DLAS/DLAS_Welfare_Rights_Guide.pdf>.

17. There is a huge collection of literature on Black and First Nations children in white adoptive and foster homes on the Internet. Use the search term "transracial adoption." Also see Johnson (1991).

18. See McDougall (1991). In this article three graduates of the Shubenacadie Indian residential school attack the school's critics. "'The Sisters of Charity deserved medals, instead of being criticized the way they were,' says Mrs. MacDonald. A lot of the negative stories are exaggerations or just plain lies, the three friends agree."

19. For an analysis of how women's interests are placed in opposition to their children's, especially at the fetal stage, by a society that does not value either women or children, see Mies and Shiva (1993: 87–88).

20. The Mi'kmaw people spell the name of their nation "Mi'kmaq" as a noun and "Mi'kmaw" as an adjective. See comments by Bernie Francis, Mi'kmaw linguist, in the introduction to the second printing of the first edition of Isabelle Knockwood's book *Out of the Depths* (1992).

Breaking Silence, Healing

I do not wish my anger and pain and fear about cancer to fossilize into yet another silence, nor to rob me of whatever strength can lie at the core of this experience, openly acknowledged and examined. For other women of all ages, colors, and sexual identities who recognize that imposed silence about any area of our lives is a tool for separation and powerlessness, and for myself, I have tried to voice some of my feelings and thoughts about the travesty of prosthesis, the pain of amputation, the function of cancer in a profit economy, my confrontation with mortality, the strength of women loving, and the power and rewards of self-conscious living.

> — *Audre Lorde,* The Cancer Journals *(1980: 9–10)*

Hello from all the years of pain that I and my sons endured and all the pain of a bruised body and spirit. I want to make people aware of what can happen to them and their children and their dreams. Only then will life have a meaning and the pain go away and the nightmare end. It has been almost ten years and for me the healing is not complete. There is still a lot to do and a lot to be said and I expect to be around to do that. I can not rewrite my past or forget it. By speaking out I can also help my-self and give my life a purpose and meaning and replace those old fears.

Fear and shame and failure are all the emotions that are experienced by a battered woman. I was born in a time when people did not reveal their personal problems. Emotions were kept inside, a secret. We all keep up appearances. And it is all part of early conditioning and very deep rooted. Battering and violence is not the taboo, speaking out against it is. It can only continue if we remain silent. I want to tell you to not be silent. Come forward. Be heard. The more that come forward the sooner we can change society's attitudes. Tell your story no matter how shocking. We must unite with one view. Do not cover up the bruises or your story.

> — *Jane Hurshman Corkum,*
> *"Presentation to the Dartmouth Task Force on Violence Against Women" (1991),*
> *as reproduced in the program for her memorial service, 2 March 1992.*

Chapter Six

Step 3
Consciousness and Healing

In Chapter 4, I offered an analysis of the cycle that perpetuates oppression. It can be broken at many points. I think, however, that there is one point where the cycle must be broken in order for any other break to last. This point is the unconscious pain buried in each of us: the pain that causes us to use old survival strategies, without question, when a new situation looks anything like an old one; the pain we project onto others and then punish them for it.

The oppression cycle makes it very difficult to organize the kind of social justice actions required to build a cooperative society. What makes justice possible is the amazing ability of human beings to grow in consciousness and heal. If unconscious pain is integral to the process of learning oppression, then consciousness and healing are necessary in the process of learning liberation.[1] Our means of liberating ourselves from oppression are organization and collective action, but without consciousness and healing, our organizations will fall apart and our actions will tend to lead towards a repetition of the very oppression we are trying to change.

Unconscious pain is both individual and collective. For example, African-descended people, whether they have experienced individual abuse or not, carry the memory of enslavement. Even when removed from the situation, peoples who have experienced oppression carry the scars. Jews, Roma, Palestinians, Armenians, Kurds, Aboriginal people and many others cannot just walk away from the injuries of their histories. European-descended people as well, whether or not we have personal memories of childhood abuse, carry the larger cultural memories of the centuries when mistreatment of women, children, racialized people and people who follow religions other than Christianity was an acceptable part of Western society. I believe that all descendants of those who went through the Inquisition, from 1300 to 1700 CE, carry fear, distrust and pain from that time, whether we are conscious of it or not. Starhawk calls the Inquisition "the abusive past of Western civilization."[2] In Chapter 4 I quoted the eleven-year-old daughter of Ann-Marie

MacDonald saying: "If you forget the past, it grows inside you." This is as true on the collective, historical level as it is in the life of an individual.

Consciousness and healing also operate at both individual and collective levels and come about through both individual and collective means. Consciousness in the individual can grow through such practices as journal writing, reflection, dream interpretation, reading, conversation, consciousness raising groups, meditation, therapy, counselling, silent retreat, ritual, research, observation and analysis. Sometimes consciousness comes unbidden when something is pointed out by others or emerges into memory through flashbacks, a powerful experience or finding out new information.

Collective consciousness comes through discussion, group study, collective action and group reflection. The ideological tools of the powerful, discussed in Chapter 3, are usually working to dim our consciousness or give us false notions of the reality we live in; on the other hand, they also are important sources of information for our growth in consciousness.

In both individual and collective healing, speaking out is vital. It is the courageous act of breaking out of secrecy, privacy and shame to contact others suffering similar pain that eventually leads to an understanding of the root causes. Speaking out becomes a collective movement, with important roles for writers, singers, artists and historical researchers. For example, women, and now men as well, speaking out about their experiences of childhood abuse have led to a movement dedicated to eradicating abuse and healing its survivors. Likewise, some historians and archeologists risked extreme academic discrediting and isolation to tell the stories I summarized in Chapter 2 — stories of peaceful, woman-centred early societies, the Enclosure Movement and the conquest of the Americas. By doing this, they provided the basis for a major transformation in the consciousness of white European and North American society. New consciousness offers an opportunity for healing.

As oppressive experiences — both individual and collective — are raised in one's consciousness, the pain that comes with them must be healed. On both the collective and individual levels this requires emotional expression with trusted people in deliberate healing settings, such as therapy, informal gatherings, self-expression and the arts. Healing can also come through organization and action. In both collective and individual healing, certain things taken away by oppression must be restored. These include participation in shaping our future, the ability to make decisions, sexuality, anger, grief, friendship, trust, self-esteem, love of our bodies, love of the earth, a sense of connection to one another and the ability to link together around common concerns.

Healing can sometimes lead to a violent backlash against those who expose the issues. Breaking the silence can carry great risk. Jane Hurshman Corkum, quoted at the end of the previous chapter, was a determined fighter against abuse of women and children. She courageously broke silence again and again about her own experience as an abused woman. The quotation appeared in the program for her memorial service. She was found dead of a handgun wound on the Halifax waterfront. The police concluded that she committed suicide, but few of her close friends and colleagues believe it (Some Angry Women 1992: 6–12). There were too many facts contradicting that conclusion, above all, the threats she received in the weeks leading up to her death. She was told to be silent or she would be silenced. Even if she did take her own life, it was a direct result of the years of abuse and the pressures put on her because of the outspoken public role she chose. She is one of many who have died, or suffered in other ways, for speaking out.

Backlash can also happen inside individuals and groups as the consciousness and healing progress. When a person is healing through counselling, for example, sometimes the process goes so far and then the old patterns of belief and behaviour cause the person to lash out violently and irrationally, as if the old patterns are cornered and fighting for survival. At the beginning of Chapter 4, I spoke of two experiences of groups that operated in a cooperative, consensus fashion for two years, then broke up suddenly, violently and irrationally. Both groups were unusually powerful in their ability to create a setting in which people progressed quickly with their own healing. The sudden breakup may have been the phenomenon of "cornered patterns" on a collective level. It was truly as if "power-over" itself lashed back, terrified and fighting for survival. Perhaps this is what a "demon" is — the practices of "power-over," deeply rooted in people's scars. When there is an attempt to "exorcise" these patterns, from an individual or a group, the patterns fight back, almost as if they had a life of their own.[3]

Every person has to find their own way to consciousness and healing. Sometimes it is important to work at it in a solitary fashion or with a few trusted others; sometimes the process requires healing through activism or group dialogue. Both are necessary. Without individual healing, a person might destroy the groups they join; without group healing, individual healing reinforces the private isolation that is the basis for "divide and conquer." Sometimes the process will seem to leap ahead; at other times there will be a plateau that appears to stretch on forever. Healing involves times of deep despair and pain; there are also times of joy and humour. The path always involves courage, honesty, self-examination and listening, but it is different for everyone.

Those who work for justice must understand the differences in our healing paths. I get very angry when we waste our energy accusing each other of being "wrong" in our search for consciousness and healing. This sort of conflict is especially common between those who are, at that time, in need of solitary or inner healing and those who are currently healing through collective action. The activists accuse the personal healers of "navel-gazing" while the personal healers accuse the activists of using action as a way of avoiding self-awareness. There may be truth in the accusations, but labelling any path to healing as wrong only contributes to the divide-and-conquer strategies of the powerful.

I believe consciousness and healing make the difference between a person or group that achieves a measure of power and uses it against others who are less powerful, and a person or group that uses power to work towards building a new society. Consciousness and healing melt the seals keeping the blueprint of oppression locked inside individuals and organizations.

notes

1.   When I use the term consciousness, I mean the concept of *conscientização*, as developed by Paulo Freire, Amilcar Cabral, Ivan Illich and others. See Freire (1970) and Smith (1978).
2.   Starhawk made this statement in a speech in Halifax, NS, on February 10, 1991.
3.   The idea that "demons" are a collective expression of the damage we have experienced, certain cultural settings (like a violent ethos combined with heavy alcohol consumption) or our unrecognized basic animal nature are explored in Wink (1992) and Jung (1966).

Chapter Seven

Step 4
Becoming a Worker
in Your Own Liberation

The spiral of human liberation has been well documented.[1] It begins with breaking the silence, ending the shame and sharing our concerns and feelings. Story-telling leads to analysis, where we figure out together what is happening to us and why, and who benefits. Analysis leads to strategy, when we decide what to do about it. Strategy leads to action, together, to change the injustices we suffer. Action leads to another round of reflection, analysis, strategy, action. This is the process of liberation.

Sandra Butler (1978) speaks of healing as a journey from victim to survivor to warrior. Some dislike the word "warrior," but few have walked their own healing path without reaching a stage where further progress requires taking action to change the situation which caused the injury in the first place. This is the point where people become workers in their own liberation.

Reaching this transition does not mean that healing is complete, nor is it the end of private, individual healing; rather, a new stage is reached and a new need is felt. Healing requires taking action to save others from experiencing what you experienced. The task becomes more than recovery of yourself and your own life. It becomes necessary to find the power to change old and deeply rooted oppressions. Where is this power found?

There is a saying that comes from an old pagan tradition of Europe: "Where your fear lies, there lies your power also" (Starhawk 1987: 9). Fear is often a guide to the areas in which the dominant society has particularly crushed and controlled you, and the reason you have been particularly crushed and controlled in these areas is because they are the sources of your power.

One of our sources of power as women is our ability to bear and nurture new human life. Men in power have made great efforts to control our bodies and our reproductive ability. The "medicalization" of childbirth by mostly male doctors that began in seventeenth-century Europe only started to be reversed in the last decade of the twentieth century. Childbirth and menstruation have been surrounded with fear and loathing, and the tradition — common in female-positive cultures (Göttner-Abendroth 2009, 2012; Sanday 2003) — of women being together at these times has been misinterpreted as men pushing women out of their company because they are "dirty."[2]

Sexuality is a source of power in itself, apart from its relationship to reproduction. Sexuality is a source of deep connection between people and wholeness within an individual; it triggers a release of emotion and creativity. Any society held together by hierarchical oppression must repress and limit sexuality, make it a fearful, filthy thing, link it with violence and turn it into a sign of ownership rather than pleasure and joy. It is particularly effective to turn sexuality into a private shame, into something that divides people from one another, disguising our similarities, by making us hide our deep feelings from one another. In their film *Not a Love Story*, Bonnie Sherr-Klein and Linda-Lee Tracy (1981) claim that part of the Nazi strategy was to flood conquered countries with pornography, encouraging individual shame to separate people and reduce organized opposition.

Anger is a source of power. Anger should be an expression of our will directed against injustice. Anger, in this society, however, has been turned into violence without analysis, an excuse for more repression. We tend to believe anger is something to be feared and controlled, in ourselves as well as in others. People in our culture, especially women, are afraid to be angry because they believe that no one will associate with them anymore, that they will be isolated and written off as "hysterical." Women are even told it will "spoil your looks."[3]

Sharing grief is a source of power that brings us very close to one another. Some other cultures that are closer to the earth, themselves and each other, have wailers at funerals to encourage the expression of grief. Later, the wailers prompt story-telling about the deceased, laughter and celebration of the memories.[4] In Western culture, grieving is not condoned. We stand in frozen politeness, talking as if we were attending an afternoon tea rather than a funeral, ashamed if we "break down." Children are told not to cry at a funeral because they might disrupt others' composure. Western funerals are a great boon to tranquilizer manufacturers.

Our bodies are a source of power. They carry us through our tasks and actions, give us pleasure and warnings, tell us directly the state of the earth we live on and provide us with a wonderful thinking, feeling, moving, sensing instrument for carrying out our will in the world. Our experiences of oppression teach us to hate our bodies for their gender, their colour and their connection to nature.[5] If we can love and appreciate our bodies, we can regain a source of power.

Friendship is also a source of power. Oppression maintains itself by putting us in competition with one another, encouraging us to distrust and distance ourselves from each other. Friendship is crushed by sexism and heterosexism, which try to convince us that closeness to another person can only be defined in sexual terms. Recovery of friendship gives us back the power of trust, equality, connection, value and respect and gives us the ability to become conscious, heal, organize and act together.

A great source of power for all people is the process of linking our common problems and concerns. This requires breaking the bonds of shame and talking about our deep feelings. This is the process of confession, of "coming out," the beginning of consciousness. It is the source of the healing power of self-help groups, peer support and counselling. Every time it happens, another movement for social change begins, because people are linked in struggle again and we lose our shame. No wonder the churches would rather we confessed singly, privately, to a priest, or that we repeat a formula printed in a prayer book.

In developing the systems that keep us controlled and oppressed, those who have benefitted all along have zeroed in on the sources of people's power and concentrated their violence there. No wonder we feel fear whenever we approach one of these areas: our bodies, sexuality, friendships, grief, anger, shame. No wonder so many of us fear having any kind of power. No wonder fear can act as a guide to finding those areas of life where we have lost our history of collective power.

The next question is: What kind of power do we want? Many of the sources of power I list above are sources of "power-with," wisdom and authority. These are our key tools for building a new society, but are they enough, considering the extent of "power-over" we have to deal with?

When we are organized, we also have some means of gaining influence with those who have "power-over." These means include lobbying, advocacy, demonstrations, hunger strikes and many, many more. But what about "power-over"? Do we want that? Can we make changes without it? Can we use it without becoming addicted to it as so many others seem to be?

Followers of Gandhi would probably say no, we must use only the forms of power we want to see used in the society we are creating.[6] I would like to be able to argue, but it seems to me that we must, at some points in our liberation, use "power-over." Sometimes there is little choice. Meeting young Nicaraguans who fought for their liberation convinced me of that. Their only other choice was to wait for death.[7]

In theory, cooperative people could use "power-over" for a certain specific purpose if they were conscious and had healed themselves to the point that they would not become addicted. The use of "power-over," like any addiction, hooks a person's unhealed, buried pain. I cannot imagine, however, that any of us are that conscious or healed. Perhaps all we can do is surround our use of "power-over" with as much consciousness and healing as possible and devise checks and balances, held by a number of people, to be sure it is employed for the purpose originally intended and then discarded afterwards.

I say this because of the first experience I described in Chapter 4. I watched while a single person, using the tactics of "power-over," destroyed a workplace where consensus, a form of "power-with," had been working very well. As department coordinator, I had the means of "power-over" in that situation, given to me by the hierarchy of the larger organization within which we were working, but I was afraid to use it. I believed at that point that any use of "power-over" was wrong by definition. As a result, I watched a single source of hierarchical power destroy a well-established experiment in "power-with." I saw for myself how vulnerable a consensus process can be when even one person wants control. The department had been doing very good work and growing within the organization. I allowed it to become so weakened by internal struggle that we could barely keep up with our daily tasks. Then, when the organization decided to close the department, blending our work into a larger unit, we could not organize ourselves to resist. I lost my job and eventually the department's mandate was cut altogether.

Thinking back on the situation, I wonder if I could have taken control of the department in a traditional, hierarchical manner until the situation was dealt with, then returned it to its consensus-based method of operating. There would have been problems, of course, caused by this course of action but the department would not have been in a weakened internal state when it was hit by an external attack. It could have continued doing useful work. It would have been important to be open with everyone about what I was doing and why. I learned from this experience not to fear my own share of "power-over" nor to consider its use wrong in all circumstances.

I also struggle with the power I have over children. I try to use consensus as much as possible with the children in my life, but sometimes it is necessary for an adult to control the situation for the health and safety of all concerned. I do try to communicate what I am doing and why, but all the same, I use my power over children.

While weighing these choices, it is very important to remember that "power-over" breeds "power-over," no matter what we do to prevent it. Its use must be a last resort. For real change, we must develop new and creative ways to use "power-with" and "power-within."

As a community development worker, I found the challenge was always how to support the empowerment of individuals and groups in such a way that they would value and practise "power-with" rather than grab "power-over." Because "power-with" is not generally understood or supported in our culture, oppressed people sometimes form organizations and learn skills only to turn and dominate someone less powerful. Sometimes when individuals learn to speak up and stop disempowering themselves, they begin to dominate their group, using nepotism and manipulative tactics to maintain their power. "Power-over" is the only model they see.

The image I have for the work of empowering oppressed people is one of trying to walk on a muddy ridge between two plough furrows. You pull yourself up on the higher soil, only to slide over into the next trough. Another image would be one of those little games, encased in plastic, where the object is to put a ball bearing into a depression in the cardboard base. Too little speed and the bearing falls short; too much and it scoots over. The challenge is to support the empowerment of people, but with healing and consciousness as part of the process, so that the power they learn is used in a cooperative fashion. It is also important to remember that the community development worker is not in charge; the people involved are. We can encourage new leaders, provide information and teach skills, but in the end, the use of the power gained is decided by the recipients. The surrounding society, which values competition and reinforces the wounds people have experienced in the past, is still the environment in which we function.

This, then, is the process of liberation — moving from consciousness and healing, individual and collective, to the analysis and strategy-building required to change society. As I explained in Chapter 4, I believe we must experience oppression in order to learn how to participate in oppressing others. I also believe that the opposite is true; we must be engaged in working towards our own liberation in order to become allies to others in their process of liberation. I explain my view of this connection further in the next chapter.

notes

1. See Chapter 1 note 3.
2. A colleague, Jean Arnold of New Brunswick, spent several years living with the Shoshone people in Wyoming. She talked about how hard the women worked and how much they, and she, looked forward to the quiet, restful time they would spend in the "women's lodge" during their menstruation. Unfortunately, in many post-colonial societies, this practice has been interpreted as negative. Women are banned because they are "unclean" or dangerous at this time. For a discussion about how women begin to be seen as dangerous to men during a transition from a female-positive to a patriarchal society, see Starhawk (1987: 50).
3. For excellent commentary on the socialization of women's anger, see Lerner (1985).
4. My first introduction to the tradition of wailers was a conversation in 1978 between a Cree elder, Stan Cuthand of Saskatchewan, and a visiting Maori judge from New Zealand's Maori courts. They compared many aspects of their culture, including their way of mourning. This was an exciting discovery for me, raised as I was in a tradition that represses grief. For a written description of wailers and other grieving traditions in various cultures, see Counts and Counts (1991).
5. Katherine Gelday has made a dramatic film about how women's body image is eroded in patriarchy, *The Famine Within* (Gelday 1990); see also Orbach (1978).
6. See Raghavan (1973).
7. This information comes from personal conversations with young Sandinista soldiers in Nicaragua in March 1980. During the long war that led to the revolution in July 1979, children served as look-outs, message-runners, bomb-makers and graffiti-writers for the anti-Somoza forces. They also threw bombs under tanks, since they were too small to be seen by the tank's drivers. As a result of this activity, Somoza's troops were ordered to shoot children on sight. This put many young people in a position where their choice was to wait for death or join the Sandinista forces (see also Guillén 1979). For a general background history of the Nicaraguan Revolution, see Kinzer (1991).

Racism and Sexism

Gay Pride Week, 1990

This morning I attended a workshop on racism. I went to listen to the speaker's experiences and to struggle with his reality from a position defined by my basic assumptions about being an ally: that is, he knows, I don't; I'm here to listen and understand and become an ally through contributing my effort and resources to the struggle in ways he defines and controls.

Then, this afternoon, he fought against a group of lesbians struggling to have some woman-only time in our gay and lesbian club. We tried to explain that we, as women, are excluded by the way men behave, express and display their sexuality, and use space. In the presence of darkness and liquor, they awaken frightening memories for many of us. We don't want prime time at the club, just some time to be among our own and not have to be squeezed into the leftover corners and feel afraid, again.

I know the issue for him is exclusion because of his (and many others') history of being turned away from, beaten up in or asked to leave white bars.[1] I understand that it looks like any other exclusion to him, but it's not. We are not white bar owners who don't want Black people in our establishments. We are women trying to struggle against the omnipresent domination of men. He couldn't hear us. Ready to accept our willingness to be allies in the struggle against racism, he was not ready to be an ally in the struggle against sexism.

I can't then say, "I won't be your ally anymore," like a child on a schoolyard. We're talking about peoples and history, what my people have done to his, and his gender has done to mine, over hundreds of years. It's not him or me as individuals. I must be an ally in the struggle against racism simply because I see it. If he cannot see our relationship as also man to woman, there isn't much I can do. My hope that all of us can engage with each other to end oppression fades a little.

note

1. There is a long history in Halifax of African-Nova Scotian people being harassed in and excluded from bars. This problem led to violent disruption on the streets of the city during July 1991. The speaker at this anti-racism workshop was a leader for years in the efforts of African-Nova Scotians to have equal access to bars.

Chapter Eight

Step 5
Becoming an Ally

In the early 1990s, I co-led a workshop called "Unlearning Racism" with Valerie Carvery, a friend and colleague who is African-Nova Scotian.[1] When you begin to teach something, you find out what you do not know. This workshop was truly a learning adventure for me.

Leading anti-racist education is akin to tip-toeing through a mine field. Sometimes we could feel the group carefully skirting a possible blowup; at other times, we stepped on the mine. When this happened, there was an angry backlash from some white participants. We conducted the workshop five times before we made it all the way through without the process being derailed by conflict.

Following one of our most explosive workshops, we began to list the different reactions of the white participants to this process of unlearning racism. Later, the descriptions began to fit into three rough groups: 1) the "backlashers," who deny the existence of racism while making racist statements and expressing outrage that they are forced to listen to stories of racism; 2) the "guilty," who personalize the issue and become defensive and paralyzed; and 3) the "learners" or "allies," who use any opportunity to learn more and then act on what they learn.

Some of the people who took part in our workshop did so because they belonged to an organization that contracted us to lead it, but most came voluntarily as individuals, out of their own interest and concern. As a result, despite saying to myself that my sample was skewed, on some level I was under the impression that quite a large proportion of the population is willing and able to learn to be allies.

Years later, however, I was engaged to develop and teach a mandatory one-day workshop on employment equity for provincial civil servants. Teaching people who were forced to be present was a far more gruelling experience.

Going through my notes from my five years of teaching mandatory equity classes, I estimate that approximately 5000 individuals attended these courses. In roughly one out of five sessions, there was enough blatant, nasty bigotry to dominate the tone for at least part, and sometimes all, of the day. Usually one group was chosen as the target, often depending on the work done by the participants. If the unit in question dealt with low-income people as part of their work, poor bashing would be the order of the day. If their work involved natural resources, Aboriginal people became the target. Responsibility for prisons and schools brought out bigotry against both Mi'qmaw and African-Nova Scotian people. Attacks on women and LGBT people could pop up anywhere. In two or three sessions each year these appalling attitudes came from a majority of participants, but more often they were expressed by a vocal minority confident that they had the right to dominate everyone's experience of the day. Sometimes it was clear that the bigotry was a game played to derail the session and test the limits of the teacher. Sometimes participants who are members of the groups under attack told me during breaks, at lunchtime or after the session how frustrated, frightened and angry they felt. Many more must have felt the same but kept it to themselves. In some cases the aggressive negativity appeared to be intended as a threat to the minority employees.

Out of the 5000 or so people I taught during that five-year contract, I can literally count on one hand the number of people — five individuals — who had an understanding of the structural nature of oppression and what it means to be an ally.

A large majority of the people I met during these courses were well-meaning but in active denial that any form of oppression still exists. If they understood that some aspects of oppression persist, they tended to think it can be dealt with quickly and easily by education and good intentions, and they certainly did not see themselves as perpetrators. I began to distinguish between this group and the outright bigots, dividing the people I formerly thought of as "backlashers" into "backlashers" and "deniers." The two groups require a different teaching approach, which I discuss in Chapter 9.

What "backlashers" do is repeat the worst stereotypes about oppressed groups. Theft, dishonesty, corruption, laziness, greed, manipulation, whining, excuses, over-sensitivity, "playing the race card," domination of the oppressor group, sexual perversion and violence are declared to be "just the truth." If contradicted, this group insist that they've experienced it personally or know someone who did.

Deniers say things like: "That all happened a long time ago," "I've never hurt anyone different from me," "It's a theoretical problem," "I feel silenced by Black/gay/etc. people; I can't say anything right," "My brother worked in Jamaica/a gay bar/the North End and said there it's the other way around," "Women/Black people/gays/etc. treat men/white people/straight people/etc. worse than the other way around" (or "Women/Black people/gays/etc. treat each other worse than men/white people/straight people/etc. treat them"), "You're talking about a few bad apples; don't blame the whole barrel," "Don't jump on me, I was just asking a question," "It's just human nature to discriminate against someone who's different," "If only they didn't ..." "Some of my best friends are Black/gay/poor/etc.," and above all, "I'm not racist/sexist/heterosexist/ableist/etc."

The two groups' statements sometimes overlap, but there is a difference in the level of anger and aggression. "Backlashers" try to commandeer the session and dominate the conversation. They are out to attack marginalized group members, present or not, the teacher, and anyone who defends either. When they discover they cannot get away with direct attacks, they try to disrupt the session. Favourite tactics are texting on their cellphone, resisting participation with surly silence, carrying on side conversations, organizing games such as tic tac toe out of the teacher's line of vision, vandalizing flipcharts and handouts, deliberately breaking the rules or cheating during simulation exercises, repeating the same point over and over again whatever the explanation or response, inserting nasty comments just quietly enough that the teacher can't hear and laughing. When the teacher asks to have the comment repeated, they will say something like, "You don't want to know," followed by another laugh. A great deal of time is wasted in boundary-setting and, even if they grudgingly respect the limits teacher sets, the atmosphere of the session becomes negative.

The deniers can become angry but not to the same degree. Often they are more confused or frustrated. Many are open enough to explore new information in a curious, or at least honest, way.

Neither group sees the collective, structural aspect of oppression or their own privilege. Both take too little personal responsibility.

The "guilty" also fail to see the collective, structural aspect of oppression but they take on too much personal responsibility. They feel crushed, powerless, unable to move. They sometimes think the person or situation that made them aware of the problem disempowered them and they react with anger. They often seek forgiveness from someone they see as a representative of the oppressed group. Privilege is often invisible to the "guilty" group, too, or if they see it, it just adds to their immobilizing guilt.

"Backlashers" and "deniers" do not understand the meaning of oppression for those who experience it; the "guilty" are all too aware of it, but they are inclined to react as if nothing can be done. "Backlashers" and "deniers" tend to think the current North American model of "democracy" is working and people could solve their problems if they "just pulled themselves up by their bootstraps." The "guilty" also believe there is democracy here and that they, as voters and citizens, have the power. If something is not working, it must be their fault.

Members of the "ally" group, on the other hand, are much more critical of the real power structures of North America and the world. They look at things from a "structural" perspective. They have an understanding of themselves as part of a people or various peoples. They understand that if something is done to another member of their own group, it could just as easily happen to them. For example, they understand that if a woman is raped, it is not because she asked for it, dressed seductively or went where she should not have; it is because she is a woman and it could happen to any woman. Likewise, "allies" understand that, as part of various

Reactions of the Privileged to the Oppressed

	Backlash	Denial	Guilty	Ally
Underlying assumption	Like the *status quo*	There's no such thing or, if there is, I'm not part of it.	We've done terrible things to other people and must make up for it.	Our society is structured around oppression.
Purpose	Preserve the *status quo*	Deny there's a problem	Comfort, friend-ship, forgiveness	Personal/insti-tutional/societal transformation
Whose problem?	Oppressed	What problem?	Mine	All of us, espe-cially those who have power and privilege
Who has power?	Whoever is strong and smart enough to get it	Democracy, therefore everyone does	Democracy, therefore I do	A small elite
Who has privilege?	No such thing, society functions on the basis of merit	No such thing, society functions on the basis of merit	I do, and I feel terrible about it. I try not to exercise it.	Those on the domi-nant side of any form of oppression.
Attitude to own oppression	No such thing, society functions on the basis of merit.	No such thing, society functions on the basis of merit.	I'm more/ less oppressed (hierarchy of oppression)	Committed to the struggle against it, this struggle is complementary with all others.
Important question	What do these people want, anyway?	What problem?	Will they see me as …?	Of course we're all racist/sexist…; what can we do to change it?
Dominant emotions	Anger when *status quo* disrupted	Puzzlement/surprise	Anger/ guilt/helplessness	Acceptance of struggle with all the emotions involved
Reaction to allegations	Action against op-pressed to restore *status quo*	Denial	Guilt	Take allegations seri-ously, listen, learn
Typical statements	Insist on truth of negative stereotypes	"That was a long time ago." "I feel silenced." "Sometimes it's the other way around." "I'm not …" "Some of my best friends are …"	"You can trust me." "I need you to forgive me." "I'll do whatever you want me to."	"What's your experi-ence of oppression?" "I don't expect you to trust me." "What can we do to change this?"

oppressor groups (white, male, able-bodied, heterosexual, middle or above in the class structure) they did not individually bring the situation about and they cannot just reach out with goodwill and solve it. They understand that they must act with others to contribute to change. They believe that to do nothing is to reinforce the *status quo*; if you are not part of the solution, you are part of the problem. Many "allies" still drive themselves too hard and try to do too much, but they do understand that they are part of something much larger and older than they are. They take responsibility for helping to solve problems of historical injustice without taking on individual guilt. Most look for what they can do, with others, in a strategic way and try to accept their limitations beyond that.

A structural understanding of power relationships is rare in our society. The political/economic/ideological system that keeps power in a few hands has been very successful in developing methods of childrearing and education that ensure North Americans do not understand power and how it works.[2] Those who do understand have usually worked their way to their insights through their own experience, reflection and efforts to work towards social change.

"Allies" are distinguished by the following characteristics:

- their sense of connection with all other people;
- their grasp of the concept of social structures and collective responsibility;
- their lack of an individualistic stance and ego, although they have a strong sense of self, perhaps *because* they have a strong sense of self;
- their sense of process and change;
- their understanding of their own process of learning;
- their realistic sense of their own power;
- their grasp of "power-with" as an alternative to "power-over";
- their honesty, openness and lack of shame about their own limitations;
- their knowledge and sense of history;
- their acceptance of struggle;
- their understanding that good intentions do not matter if there is no action against oppression; and
- their knowledge of their own roots.

These are the characteristics of allies; they are also characteristics that mark people who are well advanced in their own liberation process.

Because of the connection I see between the experience of powerlessness and the need to find safety through controlling others, I believe that an experience of oppression is necessary for a person to learn to be an oppressor. Margaret Green's account of her anti-racism therapy groups strongly supports this connection. She tells a story about a woman working on her difficulty welcoming new immigrants who came to the advice centre where she worked:

I suggested she try welcoming me. As a Jew and a foreigner I could never have enough of it, I explained, and besides, no one had ever welcomed me to England anyway. She tried. She was extremely timid and tentative. I asked if she had ever been made to feel welcome. She burst into tears; no, of course she hadn't. There was no warmth for her in her family; she had always felt unwanted. (1987: 194)

After this and several other examples, Green concludes: "One of my assumptions is that no one would ever willingly choose to take on the role of oppressor if they themselves had not been systematically oppressed" (195).

Because of my observation that people who approach other oppressed people as allies are those who are involved in their own process of liberation from oppression, I also believe that one must be in the process of liberation from one's own oppression to become an ally in another's liberation. Green's experience again supports mine. She says:

> You cannot be proud of other cultures and delight in their richness if you are not proud of your own. By "proud" I don't mean the defensiveness which hides feelings of shame and inferiority and I don't mean that one doesn't question certain aspects of one's culture. A sense of one's own rich roots is however essential if one is to meet on an equal level with a person from a different background. (196)

I don't mean to suggest that everyone who experiences oppression becomes an oppressor and everyone engaged in their own liberation becomes an ally. Far from it. What I am saying is that I don't believe it is possible to become an oppressor without experiencing oppression nor become an ally without being involved in your own experience of liberation.

Learning about Yourself as an Oppressor

The process of learning about your own oppression is different from learning about yourself as an oppressor. The former process clearly has experience as a base; it is a transition from experience to consciousness through reflection.

When learning to see yourself as an oppressor, the experience is by definition hidden from you, because part of the process of becoming a member of an oppressor group is to be cut off from the ability to identify with the experience of the oppressed. It is this lack of empathy, this denial that anyone is hurt, that makes oppression possible. When the oppression is not part of your own experience, you can only understand it through hearing others describe their experiences, along with a process of analysis, imagination and drawing parallels.

Many people resist beginning the process of becoming an ally because it is so difficult and painful. Is it more difficult and painful than your own liberation? I think so. I have found it much harder to understand and accept myself in my oppressor roles than in those where I am the oppressed.

The righteous anger of understanding one's own oppression releases a great deal of energy and propels the process forward. Facing fear often releases energy and produces a major shot, first of euphoria, then of good, solid self-confidence. The process of bonding with others dealing with the same oppression creates a deep level of sympathy and understanding, a growing pride in one's recovered identity and a shared language that is as satisfyingly secret as the "pig latin" of childhood.[3] There can be lightning fast communication among women in a room or among lesbians in a room. There is laughter or a flurry of glances, a smile, a comment with a double meaning, and you know "you" all understood and "they" did not.

Coming to understand your identities as an oppressor is often an enervating process. It means being shut out from someone else's secret language; it involves accepting your inheritance of a shameful and evil past. There is guilt, which drains energy. There is always that unsettling knowledge that you cannot see what is going on as clearly as the oppressed group can. The oppressed always know a great deal more about the oppressor than the oppressor knows about the oppressed.

Understanding one's own position as an oppressor, without being completely immobilized, also requires a balance between understanding oneself as an individual and as part of a collective reality. This balance is rare in the culture we live in. Modern Western thinking is extremely individualistic. Our ties to the land and our own history, community and culture have been severed. With so little understanding of ourselves as part of a collective entity, it becomes very difficult to figure out our own responsibility for patterns larger than ourselves.

Failure to understand collective structures leads to what Kate Kirkham calls "overpersonalization." In her article "Teaching About Diversity: Navigating the Emotional Undercurrents," she says:

> Many majority group members do not move quickly or comfortably back and forth between their individual identity and their identity as a member of a racial or gender group in this society. If they do think of themselves as a member of a group, it is often associated with negative emotions: feeling stereotyped or threatened, etc. Therefore, majority group members may enter a discussion less prepared to sort out what is being said about the behavior of numbers of whites (or men) as experienced by others and the impact of their own individual behavior. ... When asked to respond to the question of who really is racist and/or sexist, many majority group individuals in my research and teaching experience, assume: "If I didn't intend something as racist or sexist then it is not racist/sexist." In other words, the general criteria they use in testing for racism/sexism is an overpersonalized one. They believe that personal motive determines the presence of racism or sexism in interactions. (1988/89: 51)

How to Become an Ally

Having written that title, I must now admit that I cannot tell anyone exactly how to become an ally. I can, however, use my growing analysis of the process and my experience to offer some guidelines. Most people in our society do not yet see the connections between different forms of oppression or even have a general sense of how oppression works. Therefore, we still find ourselves dealing in most instances with one form of oppression at a time, and in a given setting, we are either in the role of oppressed or ally. I hope these observations will be as useful to you as they have been to me when I find myself in the ally role.

1. It is important to be a worker in your own liberation struggle, whatever it is. Learn, reflect on and understand the patterns and effects of oppression, take action with others, take risks, walk towards your fear to find your power.
2. Try to help members of your own group understand oppression and make the links among different forms of oppression.
3. I cannot overstress the need to listen. Listen and reflect.
4. Remember that everyone in the oppressor group is part of the oppression. It is ridiculous to claim you are not sexist if you are a man or not racist if you are white and so on. No matter how much work you have done on that area of yourself, there is more to be done; the oppressive messages that surround us, unconsciously absorbed, constantly undo some of our efforts. All members of this society grow up surrounded by oppressive attitudes; we are marinated in it. It runs in our veins; it is as invisible to us as the air we breathe. I do not believe anyone raised in Western society can ever claim to have finished ridding themselves completely of their oppressive attitudes. It is an ongoing task, like keeping the dishes clean. In fact, the minute I hear someone claim to be free of the attitudes and actions of a certain oppression (as in "I'm not racist") I know they have barely begun the process. Humility is the mark of someone who has gone a way down the road and has caught a glimpse of just how long the road is.

    There is a parallel here with the principles of the twelve-step addiction recovery process. Just as the twelve-step programs teach that the process of healing from addiction is never finished, so it is with the process of unlearning oppression. A white person never becomes non-racist but is always a "recovering racist," more often referred to as "anti-racist."

    There is another reason members of an oppressor group are always oppressors, no matter how much individual learning we have done: until we change the politics and economics of oppression, we are still "living off the avails."[4] We would not be where we are, doing what we are doing, with the skills and access we have, if we did not have the colour, gender, sexual orientation, appearance, age, class or physical abilities we have. Resources and power continue to come to us because we are members of the dominant group in relation to the particular form of oppression where we seek to be allies.[5] So, until we succeed in making a more humane world, yes, we are racist (or ageist, or classist, or heterosexist and so forth). Understanding this is part of learning to think structurally rather than individually. It is part of avoiding overpersonalization of the issues.[6]

5. Although every member of an oppressor group is an oppressor, this does not make you a "bad" person. Self-esteem does not have to mean distancing yourself from the oppressor role; it can come instead from taking a proud part in the struggle to end oppression. This involves learning to separate guilt from responsibility. Guilt is appropriate in situations where we have personally made bad choices or done harm. In relation to oppression, this means taking on the whole weight of history as an individual. Responsibility, on the other hand, means accepting your share of the challenge of changing the situation. Members of oppressor groups spend a great deal of energy in denying responsibility for oppression. What would happen if all that energy could be put to work figuring out how to end it?

6. Remember that in the oppressor role you cannot see the oppression as clearly as the oppressed group can. When people point out your oppressive attitudes or language to you, your first response should be to believe it. Ask questions and learn more about the oppression going on in that particular situation. Try not to leap to your own defence in one of the many ways oppressors use to deny responsibility for oppression. Self-defence is an overpersonalized response.

It is true that you will likely meet members of the oppressed group who want to claim that every little thing is oppressive and use it as a focus for their anger. You will also perhaps find members of the oppressed group who try to use your efforts to unlearn oppression to manipulate you. It is all part of the process — their process. The point is not to defend yourself; it will not work anyway. If you can deal with your own defensive feelings, you can turn the situation into a discussion in which you, and perhaps everyone else, will learn more about the oppression, and you will be less vulnerable to manipulation. The defensiveness, or guilt, is the hook for the manipulation.

Also, if you can use your own experience of liberation to understand the anger of the oppressed, you will be able to accept it as a member of an oppressor group, not as an individual. Leave their process — working through their anger — to the oppressed group. Give your attention to your own process — becoming an ally. Then we can all participate in the process we share, ending the oppression.

7. Count your privileges; keep a list. Help others see them. Break the invisibility of privilege.[7]

8. If you hear an oppressive comment or see an example of oppression at work, try to speak up first. Do not wait for a member of the oppressed group to

point it out. Sometimes this draws a response of "Oh, I don't mind," "It was just a joke" or even anger directed at you from a member of the oppressed group. That person may be speaking out of their internalized oppression, or you may be off base. Just accept it, if you can; admit it is not your experience. More often you will find members of the oppressed group grateful that they did not have to raise the issue for a change.

9. You must be patient and leave room for the greater experience of members of the oppressed group, but there are also limits. If it becomes clear over time that you are being used or mistreated, say something and/or leave the situation. Here is an example: a group is interested in having you present as an ally for reasons of their safety or your contacts, legitimacy or resources, but is not ready to offer you any information or support. The message might be: "Just do everything we tell you and don't ask questions."

Another common assumption is that allies will do all the work on the margins— moving chairs, cleaning up, taking minutes, childcare and making coffee. This may well be appropriate. When men began to support feminist groups in these maintenance tasks, it was an important statement of solidarity and education about gender roles. On the other hand, these symbolic expectations can go too far. I was once in the role of white ally in a group of racialized people where I was expected to do all the photocopying and secretarial work. I felt quite torn about this, since the setting was a workplace where I had the lowest job status of anyone in the group and was the only one without a secretary. Indeed, after I was laid off, the members' secretaries did take over the support tasks I had been doing. I considered raising the issue for discussion, but the group was working under pressure. I did not feel entitled to take up its time.

It is also hardly fair for the members of the oppressed group to direct all their anger, over a long period of time, at a well-meaning would-be ally. This is not reasonable treatment for anyone. It is fair for you to ask them to decide: are they willing to reflect on how they treat you or do they want you to leave?

10. Try to avoid the trap of "knowing what is good for them." Do not take leadership. They are the only ones who can figure out what they need to do and developing their own leadership strengthens their organizations. It is fine to add thoughts or resources to the process by asking questions of the individuals with whom you have already built up some trust and reciprocal exchange, who will not take it as coming from an authority greater than themselves just because you are a member of the oppressor group. It is not all right to take time at their meeting or public gathering to present your own agenda or to suggest in any way that they do not understand or see the big picture.

11. Never take public attention or credit for an oppressed group's process of liberation. Refuse to act as a spokesperson, even when reporters gravitate to you because they are more comfortable with you or curious about you. You

should speak in public only if members of the oppressed group have asked you to speak from your point of view as an ally or to take a public role on their behalf because speaking out will be too dangerous for them.

12. Do not expect every member of the oppressed group to agree; does your group agree on everything?

13. Learn everything you can about the oppression — read, ask questions, listen. Your ignorance is part of the oppression. Find people in the oppressed group who like to teach and who see value in cultivating allies in general or you in particular. Ask them your questions. Do not expect every member of the oppressed group to be ready and willing to teach you. When you are in the ally role, you have privileges and comfort in your life that members of the oppressed group do not have because of the oppression; do not expect them to also give you their time and energy so that you can learn about them.

14. Support the process of unlearning oppression with other members of your own group. Do not usurp the role of communicating the experience of the oppression; that belongs only to members of the oppressed group. You can, however, share with other members of the oppressor group the journey of becoming an ally; you can help break through others' denial and ignorance of the oppression. Members of your own group might hear you when they cannot hear a member of the oppressed group.

15. Remember that you will probably have to go out of your way to maintain your friendships and connections with members of the oppressed group. Our society is set up to separate different groups. Without a little extra effort, you will live in different parts of town and never cross paths. On the other hand, do not fall over backwards. It is not good to ignore the friends and support base you have already established because you are spending all your time working at the barriers or becoming a "hanger on" of the oppressed community in an inappropriate way.

16. Try not to look to the oppressed group for emotional support. They will likely be ambivalent about you, happy on one hand to have your support, annoyed on the other at your remaining oppressor arrogance, your privilege and the attention you get as a member of the dominant group. Their energy is needed for their own struggle. This does not mean you will not receive support from members of the oppressed group, sometimes more than is warranted. For example, look at the praise men get for doing housework when women still do the vast majority of it. Don't expect the oppressed group to be grateful to you or trust you.

17. Be yourself. Do not try to claim the roots and sense of connection that a history of oppression can give to a community if it is not your own. Do not become what the Mi'kmaw community calls a "wannabe." Dig into your own roots. The oppressive history of the group you belong to is a burden you carry. Search out the history of allies from your group as well. Dig even deeper than

that. Every group started out as a people with roots in the earth somewhere. Find your own connection with your people's history and the earth. If it is impossible to trace, find appropriate ones and rebuild roots and connection in the present for yourself, but do not try to steal someone else's; you cannot anyway.

18. Be yourself. Be honest. Express your feelings. Do not defend your internalized oppressor attitudes; say that it hurts to discover another piece of it. Do not sit on your doubts (except in public gatherings or meetings where you are an observer); ask them of someone you trust. The key word is ask. Assume that you are a learner; good learners are open.

Margaret Green provides a brief summary of the process of becoming an ally in matters of race:

> There is usually a dawning realization that being an ally to a person of colour involves knowing a great deal about one's own background, remembering with pride one's own history of resisting injustice as well as one's participation in the history of racism. It involves being able to listen and tolerate the differences between people, expecting to make mistakes, knowing that people of colour will be angry with you to the point of what appears to be unreasonableness, and learning to take it. It involves also knowing that people who view you as an oppressor may try to mistreat you — but this you need never accept. (1987: 204)

Dr Lynn Gehl , an Algonquin-Anishinaabe-Kwe author and Indigenous rights activist, has written the following, beautifully compact "Ally Bill of Responsibilities."[8]

Responsible Allies:

1. Do not act out of guilt, but rather out of a genuine interest in challenging the larger oppressive power structures;

2. Understand that they are secondary to the Indigenous people that they are working with and that they seek to serve. They and their needs must take a back seat;

3. Are fully grounded in their own ancestral history and culture. Effective allies must sit in this knowledge with confidence and pride; otherwise the "wannabe syndrome" could merely undermine the Indigenous people's efforts;

4. Are aware of their privileges and openly discuss them. This action will also serve to challenge larger oppressive power structures;

5. Reflect on and embrace their ignorance of the group's oppression and always hold this ignorance in the forefront of their minds. Otherwise, a lack of awareness of their ignorance could merely perpetuate the Indigenous people's oppression;

6. Are aware of and understand the larger oppressive power structures that serve to hold certain groups and people down. One way to do this is to draw parallels through critically reflecting on their own experiences with oppressive power structures. Reflecting on their subjectivity in this way, they ensure critical thought or what others call objectivity. In taking this approach, these parallels will serve to ensure that non-Indigenous allies are not perpetuating the oppression;

7. Constantly listen and reflect through the medium of subjectivity and critical thought versus merely their subjectivity. This will serve to ensure that they avoid the trap that they or their personal friends know what is best. This act will also serve to avoid the trap of naively following a leader or for that matter a group of leaders;

8. Strive to remain critical thinkers and seek out the knowledge and wisdom of the critical thinkers in the group. Allies cannot assume that all people are critical thinkers and have a good understanding of the larger power structures of oppression;

9. Ensure that a community consensus, or understanding, has been established in terms of their role as allies. Otherwise, the efforts of the people will be undermined due to a lack of consultation and agreement;

10. Ensure that the needs of the most oppressed — women, children, elderly, young teenage girls and boys, and the disabled — are served in the effort or movement that they are supporting. Otherwise, they may be engaging in a process that is inadequate and thus merely serving to fortify the larger power structures of oppression. Alternatively, their good intentions may not serve those who need the effort most. Rather, they may be making the oppression worse;

11. Understand and reflect on the prevalence and dynamics of lateral oppression and horizontal violence on and within oppressed groups and components of the group, such as women, and seek to ensure that their actions do not encourage it;

12. Ensure that they are supporting a leader's, group of leaders', or a movement's efforts that serve the needs of the people. For example, do the community people find this leader's efforts useful, interesting, engaging, and thus empowering? If not, allies should consider whether the efforts are moving in a questionable or possibly an inadequate direction, or worse yet that their efforts are being manipulated and thus undermined, possibly for economic and political reasons;

13. Understand that sometimes allies are merely manipulatively chosen to further a leader's agenda versus the Indigenous Nations' communities', or organizations' concerns, and when this situation occurs act accordingly;

14. Do not take up the space and resources, physical and financial, of the oppressed group;

15. Do not take up time at community meetings and community events. This is not their place. They must listen more than speak. Allies cannot perceive all the larger oppressive power structures as clearly as members of the oppressed group can; And finally,

16. Accept the responsibility of learning and reading more about their role as effective allies.

How to Work with Allies When You Are a Member of the Oppressed Group

When the shoe is on the other foot, that is, when you find yourself in a situation where it is your oppression under consideration, the same principles are in operation, but they are applied a little differently. Here are some guidelines, from my experience, for the situations where you are a member of an oppressed group dealing with allies.

1. Make a clear decision about if, why, when and how you will work with allies. Do you want to work with allies at all? What can allies offer you that you would find useful? It is easy to know what you do not want members of the oppressor group to do; figure out what you do want them to do. Are there certain times, places, meetings, tasks and functions where allies would be useful and others where their presence would be inappropriate? Be clear and conscious about your degree of openness to allies. Make sure everyone agrees on what is appropriate or at least can live with the decision without undermining the people who come in as allies. Working with allies brings a certain kind of struggle; be sure you are ready to enter into it.

2. Allies need support and information. Decide before you begin working with them what you can offer. There needs to be someone in your group who has the patience for teaching allies more about the oppression you are dealing with. If the group is unwilling to provide support and information, you will be using your would-be allies in an unethical way; for example, asking them to speak out in public because they are more likely to be taken seriously while isolating and ignoring them in meetings.

3. Be wise and canny about who is really an ally. If you end up with members of the oppressor group who are acting out of guilt, trying to replace lost roots, taking centre stage or telling you what to do, you will have more frustration than help. Also, beware of people who have no consciousness of their status as a member of the oppressor group or who are unaware of their own oppression in other areas.

4. Do not lump members of the oppressor group together, thinking of them as all "white" or "straight" or "male." Remember that everyone is or was also a member of an oppressed group and that people identify more with the parts of themselves that have been oppressed. You may see a woman as white when

she thinks of herself as Jewish, or you may think of a man as male when he identifies himself primarily as gay.

5. You must listen too.

6. Be kind. Allies are taking a risk, exposing themselves to a situation that is bound to be painful at times.

7. Try to be clear about who is the enemy. There are lots of people who hate you and want to oppress you, punish you and keep you in your place. Many deny that your oppression exists. There are the rich and powerful who are creating, sometimes deliberately, more of the oppression you suffer daily. Allies are usually well-meaning people without a great deal of power in the system. They are more vulnerable to your anger because they lack power and because of their very desire to be an ally. Do not waste resources fighting with them.

8. Be yourself, be honest, express your opinions, be open. Working with allies is all part of a learning process for you too.

Working for Liberation and Becoming an Ally: Using the Lessons Back and Forth

A person who is involved both in struggling for liberation as an oppressed person and in becoming an ally to other oppressed groups has a wonderful opportunity to learn by constantly drawing parallels back and forth. For example, when I want to figure out what I should do in a situation where I am the only white person, I begin by asking myself what I would want a man to do if he were the only one in this situation with a group of women. I do not necessarily do what I would want that hypothetical man to do, but thinking about it provides some guidelines.

Likewise, my own experience as an ally has given me a great deal of insight into the value of allies to the groups where I work on my own liberation. I observe the groups I belong to interacting creatively with allies or mistreating allies, and I can use my own experience as an ally to understand what is going on and figure out what to do about it. My own experience as an ally has also taught me how oppressed groups often overlook the information and insights allies can give them, especially when it comes to building a strategy for action.

Balance and Clarity

For each guideline I have written in this chapter, I can think of a time when the advice would be misleading. I know sometimes the guidelines almost sound contradictory. That is because the essence of the path to becoming an ally is balance and clarity. One must balance patience and confrontation, flexibility and limits, boundaries and allowances, learning and opinion, humility and self-confidence, your own oppression and others' struggles. Clarity comes from observation, reflection and analysis in a specific situation. In the light of this process, the complexities of the relationships between oppressed groups and their allies can resolve into beautiful, clear patterns. There is even sometimes a feeling of being "crystal clear" inside, a "knowing," when you see what to do and know what will happen when you do it.

Criticism of the Ally Approach to Privilege

In the mid-1980s, when I first heard the term "ally" used to describe people with privilege taking action to end the oppression that gave them their privilege in the first place, I embarked on a long search, over several years, before I found others discussing and writing about it. Now the word is common and has, of course, its detractors as well as its promoters. This is to be expected; the process of challenging systems of oppression and privilege and creating something better is massively complex and filled with conflict. Like many other words that we use to define our struggles, "ally" is a magnet for disagreement, even among those who use the term in an anti-oppression context, let alone where it has been adopted by more liberal approaches such as diversity education.

Many of the critiques I have read are thoughtful and grounded in experience familiar to most of us who work at anti-oppression education and organizing. For example, there is this description of a workshop from an essay by Michelle O'Brien on the *Colours of Resistance* website (2003):

> It was a mostly white group. A few people of color in the room started talking. What the people of color said was fairly complex and subtle, and included a few criticisms. All the white people in the room start freaking out inside. None of us know what to say. Then a white person, clearly remembering some antiracism workshop of some sort, starts bringing up how we should focus on our white privilege, dealing with the racism in our movements. A few other white people perked up, recognizing the language involved, and launch into a lengthy discussion that seems straight out of a white-ally meeting. The statements of the people of color in the room got boxed into the narrow confines of this workshop rhetoric, and the people of color get erased completely. A dozen utterances of 'our racism' later and all the white people started actually believing the room had only white people in it. The people of color got totally ignored, now totally excluded from the discussion. Whatever challenge or threat they might have posed to white people's arrogance was thoroughly contained, managed and diffused. They were reduced to just the crude caricature of workshop rhetoric. And all the white people, clearly, were feeling great about being so on the ball about racism.

I immediately recognized the workshop she describes, not because I was there, but because it is like a play performed in different theatres by different actors, all repeating the same lines. How easily we revert to our defensiveness when we are in the dominant role, grasping at new ideas and language to relieve ourselves of old guilt, once more blocking out the voices of the people we oppress.[9]

Besides this point — that identifying as an ally allows members of the dominant group to feel better, take back control of the conversation and avoid action, critics of the ally approach talk about two further problems: the idea of an ally is too individual and it has become a self-defined identity (Anonymous 2011; O'Brien 2003; Thompson 2003).

Some writers suggest a change of language, returning to the tried and true "solidarity," or the related but not quite parallel phrase "bearing witness." Clearly, I think the word and concept of ally is useful, or I would not be writing a third edition of this book, but how can we learn to resist bending it to serve our persistent pursuit of comfort, immediately and at all costs?

It seems to me the guidance we need lies in the very points of critique levied against the concept of ally: it is not intended to be an individual, self-defined identity designed to relieve guilt. On the contrary, it refers to a collective process of taking responsibility for privilege, guided by those who are the target of that form of oppression and firmly rooted in a structural analysis.

It is not, of course, surprising that those of us who are products of Western capitalism continually fall into seeing ourselves as individuals in a world made up of other individuals. We live in a culture that has little room for anything else. Our bodies cycle and recycle every bit of soil, air and water that exists. Our location in history makes us inheritors of the role our people have played in all the centuries that have gone before. Our consumption, employment, pension funds, taxes and investments tie us to the violence and racism of every colonial system on earth. In fact, when I consider how embedded each of us is in the world's history and structures, it is hard to believe that there is any such thing as an individual,[10] but this vast web of connections is, for the most part, invisible to us.

Likewise we have been taught to deny that our thinking, emotions and behaviour are largely unconscious. All that matters in our culture is the rational, conscious part of our mind, particularly our intentions. Becoming an ally means stepping out of this liberal individualism, recognizing that we can never be separate — physically, emotionally, historically, ideologically, politically or financially — from the complex, self-perpetuating system of oppression and privilege. This is the heart of a structural analysis.

In Western culture, an identity is an individual naming or self-naming with a tendency to be static: "I am a ..." An ally is not an identity, but an endlessly unfolding struggle for equity. Just as an alcoholic must accept that they will never not be an alcoholic, an ally never "arrives." One cannot *be* an ally, but is always *becoming* one, part of a larger process, and not anywhere near the centre of it. It is likewise not for us to name ourselves allies, because the point is to contribute to a struggle defined and named by those who are the targets of that particular form of oppression.

As for guilt, to repeat a point made earlier in this chapter, it is an appropriate

Be A Better Ally In 3 Easy Steps:

response to an action we chose, had control over or at least influenced by commission or omission. In the context of a structural analysis of oppression and privilege, responsibility is far more appropriate. We are not talking about something we did or choices we made, but rather something we've inherited and can't refuse, something that continually gives us dividends from past history. As an Aboriginal participant once said to me during a workshop: "You have a daily-interest account in the Bank of Colonialism." We look for ways to change it because, as Alice Miller says in the quote that introduces Chapter 4 , we see it and know it is wrong. Action is the only way we can be true to ourselves. If taking action makes us uncomfortable or even asks a price of us, it is never as serious as the price paid by those who are the targets of that particular form of oppression and it is not constant. Allies have the privilege of taking breaks, and I see nothing wrong with doing that from time to time, since part of becoming an effective ally is that we are also engaged in our own liberation from the forms of oppression where we are the targets and cannot take breaks — also, because we are in this for the long haul. I also see nothing wrong with responsibility feeling better than guilt, as it has for me since I first saw the difference. It is not about what allies feel but what we do.

There is a truly simple, three-point guide to resisting our tendency to twist the concept of ally into a comforting individual identity, a cartoon that has circulated around Facebook and the Tumblr blog website for several years, to the point where I have not been able to trace it back to its original creator.[11] The title is "Be a Better Ally in Three Easy Steps." It shows a chair with an arrow pointing to the seat, a sign that reads, "Shut up" and a hand cupped around an ear.

notes

1. Valerie, an outstanding educator and community worker, died on January 25, 2014, while I was working on the third edition of this book <atlanticfuneralhomeshalifax. sharingmemories.ca/siteContent/memorial.html?personId=248639&source=mem list>. She is sorely missed by her family, friends and community. Our workshop was based on exercises adapted from CUSO (1988), Katz (1978) and Obedkoff (1989). See Bishop and Carvery (1994).

2. See Miller (1981, 1983, 1986).

3. "Pig latin," the way we spoke it as children involves moving the first letter to the end of every word. "Struggle against oppression becomes "truggles gainsta ppressiono."

4. "Living off the avails" is the charge brought against pimps who live on the earnings of prostitutes they control.

5. See McIntosh (1990) and Jensen (1998, 1999).

6. Dartmouth, Nova Scotia, playwright Wendy Lill has explored how systemic racism emerges through individuals despite a positive attitude, pleasant personality and kind motives. See her powerful plays *The Occupation of Heather Rose* (1987) and *Sisters* (1991).

7. See note 5.

8. Dr Gehl offers other reflections on becoming a responsible ally and a list of resources for allies on her website <www.lynngehl.com>.

9. Robert Jensen writes about the use of ally language to defend racist behaviour in "I know I am racist but…" (2002).

10. There is a great deal of psychological, sociological and neurological research to back this up. A good starting point is Hood (2012).

11. I got as far as the website *Winnemen Wintu Voice* <http://winnememwintuvoice.tum-blr.com/post/52339685343/muddypetticoats-dancing-with-diversity> where there is an attribution trail for this cartoon, but there were too many missing links to trace it back to its source. If you are the creator of this brilliant cartoon and see this book, please get in touch. I and many others would like to give you credit for your work.

How Not to Be an Ally —
An Open Letter to the Young Man Who Spoke at our Memorial Rally on December 6th

On the evening of December 6, 1990, several hundred people gathered in Halifax's Grand Parade Square to remember the fourteen women killed at L'École Polytechnique in Montreal a year earlier. Their murderer had yelled at them that he hated feminists. Over the days leading up to the anniversary, the media had reported on men taking over microphones at similar memorial rallies to shout abuse at the women present, even to threaten them with a fate similar to the Montreal women. Some women stayed home from the December 6 rally out of fear; those who came were watchful and tense. The invited speakers were all women. During the rally, a young man took the microphone, obviously uninvited. Later I wrote this entry in my journal:

Dear young man: I know you meant well when you took the microphone, uninvited, and spoke to us at the December 6 rally in memory of the women who died in Montreal a year ago. Your "contribution" added the only sour note in an amazingly powerful and expressive series of events that evening. You provided a crystal clear example of how not to be an ally to an oppressed group.

Your first error was your disrespect for the women who organized the rally. If you wanted to speak, why didn't you find the organizers and arrange with them in advance? That would have given the group the opportunity to think about it together and make a decision about when and how you might, or might not, fit in. Instead, you put one woman, the one holding the microphone, on the spot, forcing her to make a complex decision instantly and alone. You also spoiled the careful ordering of the speakers, which had been working beautifully.

Your second mistake was your complete insensitivity to the meaning of the event and the deep emotions and painful experiences that underlie it. Women have been subject to male violence and abuse for five thousand years. We all carry a deep fear of it somewhere inside us. The events we were recalling that night bring that fear very close to the surface. Also, the news all week had carried stories of men taking over the microphones at similar events and yelling abusive insults at the women present. When you took the microphone, in a manner that made it obvious to everyone there that your speech was unplanned by the organizers of the event, I'm sure almost all the women present tensed up completely, as I did. I immediately started calculating the distance between us, as I was standing on the steps near you and could have tackled you and grabbed the microphone if your intent was abusive. Massive fears welled up inside me with thoughts of who else might be there. Were there other men present considering violence? If you roused them, or if I took action to stop you, would they react with their voices, hands, even weapons against the women present? Is there a copycat in the house? I discovered later that I was not the only woman nearby who was going through exactly the same series of thoughts.

Finally, why did you have to speak at all? You went on far too long and said very little. Do you not think we know what we need? Do you not know we need to see our own kind at the centre of attention at an event that is about our oppression? Do you not respect our need to speak and listen among ourselves, to channel our emotions and share our thinking, in reaction to an event that touched us deeply? Can you not stand back and listen respectfully for even a brief time; can't you accept that you cannot share our experience? I cannot imagine going to the front and taking the microphone at an event where Black people are working through something of importance to their liberation — or people with disabilities, or immigrants, or francophones, or Jews, or Aboriginal people. To be present as an ally is a privilege, and the role of an ally is to listen and learn and trust that the people who are central to the event know what they need. When they trust you and know you well enough, they will ask you to do something specific to support their efforts.

You made all of these errors before you even opened your mouth. Then there was what you said. No, we will not take what Marc Lepine did with "a grain of salt." We can't. And yes, some men are our allies, but not when they take centre stage at our event to spill out their misplaced defensiveness.

Perhaps you really do want to be an ally. I'm glad, but you have some learning to do. First, you must sort out your own business — your pain at facing yourself as a member of an oppressor group, your confusion between individual and collective responsibility, your inability to distinguish between support and patronizing and, above all, your need to set aside your ego and LISTEN.

I hope to see you around again, quietly listening at the edge of the crowd.

Chapter Nine

Notes on Educating Allies

Much of my work for the past forty years has been in the field of adult education, specifically popular education. The term "popular education" is a translation from the Spanish "*educación popular*." Although it was developed in all of the Southern continents — Africa, Asia, Latin America, the Caribbean and the Pacific Islands — it made a specific journey to Canada from the grassroots organizations of Central American during the 1970s.[1] Its aim is to overcome the internalized oppression that marginalized people have learned from our oppressors and give us the analysis and action tools to move toward liberation.[2] It is based firmly in a structural and historical understanding of oppression, where people are seen as part of larger systems, products of history and rooted in a class system that makes us unequal in our access to power, legitimacy and resources.

By contrast, liberal education assumes that if we increase the knowledge and change the attitudes and behaviours of individuals, then organizations, institutions and society as a whole will also change. This is, in general, the approach of "diversity education" and "cultural competence," although the naming of educational approaches can be quite flexible. Sometimes a teacher or facilitator who refers to what they do as "diversity education" or "cultural competence" will turn out, on close inspection, to be taking a structural approach. Sometimes the individual educator is taking a structural approach within a program named "diversity education" by the institution within which they work. On the other hand, it is common for someone who refers to what they do as "equity" or "anti-oppression" education, terms that usually indicate a structural approach, to be working from a liberal perspective.

There is nothing wrong with building skills and knowledge in individuals, as "diversity" and "cultural competence" approaches seek to do, as far as it goes. Skill-building is an important component in the growth and development of allies. The problem is the assumption that this activity by itself will change larger structures.

Popular education assumes that our institutions and culture can change only if we fundamentally change their patterns of status, power and resources, and this can happen only through collective organization and action informed by reflection. The process can be illustrated as a spiral, moving from experience to reflection, then to analysis, strategy and action, beginning again with the experience gained from taking action. (See the spiral diagram later in this chapter).

As I began to think about my own role as oppressor as well as my experience of being oppressed, I joined many other educators experimenting with popular education, designed to dismantle oppression, adapting it to "unlearn" our role as oppressors. Sometimes called "unlearning oppression," "anti-oppression education" or the "pedagogy of the oppressor" (in reference to Paulo Freire's seminal work on popular education, *Pedagogy of the Oppressed* (1970) (Curry-Stevens 2005; Schacht 2001), I tend to think of it as "educating allies."

What Is the Process of "Unlearning" Oppression?

My years of teaching would-be (and wouldn't-be) allies has given me many opportunities to observe how we think as oppressors. In Chapter 8, I explained my division of workshop participants' responses roughly into four groups; "backlashers," "deniers," "guilty" and "allies."

The allies are already engaged in reflection and action, on a journey of liberation from their own experiences of oppression while taking responsibility for their privilege in the areas where they have it. For this group, the classic spiral of popular education works well. They are, however, a very small group of people. As I said in Chapter 8, of the approximately 5000 individuals I taught during five years of leading mandatory employment equity courses for provincial civil servants, I met five individuals who fit into this category, although many others, particularly if their education was in the field of nursing or social work, knew the language of "structural oppression," "privilege" and "allies" but did not firmly grasp the concepts.

The challenge is to lead the backlashers, the guilty and, by far the largest group in the Canadian context, the deniers to the point of becoming allies. In order to define the route through the barriers that stand in the way, it is necessary to understand what those barriers are.

As I said in Chapter 8, backlashers like to repeat the worst stereotypes of oppressed groups and insist they are "true," that they have seen the behaviour in question personally or others close to them have witnessed it. Backlashers are deeply committed to individualism. Their approach to anyone different, let alone belonging to an oppressed group, boils down to what American anti-racism writer jona olsson calls "the three crown jewels of U.S. social propaganda: the Rugged Individual, the Level Playing Field, and the Bootstrap Theory" (1997). Their thinking is also deeply dualistic: "us" and "them," "normal" and "other," "natural" and "unnatural," "good" and "bad." In order to move toward becoming allies, they first need to have this binary approach to the world broken down and their view of oppressed and oppressor groups expanded to see humanity and complexity in both.

This is very difficult for them, because their own sense of identity and "rightness" often comes from seeing themselves as "us" in opposition to "them." They need to see the complex web of oppression and privilege and understand their involvement in it. For that, they need to see the structural nature of oppression. In order to get around their extreme resistance and familiar "logic," these learning tasks must be accomplished by surprise, including humour, which they do not expect in these circumstances (other than the nasty, aggressive form of humour they use in their attempts to control the room).

Backlashers will also usually distrust your leadership and, since they have not chosen to be present, they will resent being forced to attend. Humour and surprise help overcome their resistance. Facilitators must also pass the test of being honest, knowledgeable and completely unflappable.

For the guilty, individualism takes the form of too much personal responsibility, an overblown sense of their own power, or rather, the power they think, in theory, they should have. This group suffers from a feeling of helplessness. They need to grasp the structural and historical nature of oppression to get a more realistic view of their place in it. This will aggravate their sense of helplessness, because the centuries-old dance of oppressor and oppressed can be overwhelming. In order to accept themselves as actors in a more realistic way, they need to see that our task is to do what we can in whatever realm of influence we have, joining with others for impact and support. They need to know that the struggle toward a more humane and compassionate world has gone on before them and will continue after them. They need activist role models.

Those who react to oppression and privilege with guilt also tend to have a strong notion of "good" and "bad." Dualistic thinking assumes that one is either racist/sexist/heterosexist/etc. or not. If the guilty come to understand they are part of an oppressor group, therefore they must be racist/sexist/heterosexist/etc. and "bad." Like the backlasher group, the guilty need their dualism expanded into more humanity and complexity. They need to separate guilt, which rightfully belongs to the realm of conscious choice, from responsibility, which includes action to change circumstances handed to us by history and structures outside our personal control

The largest group, the deniers, are, understandably, viewing the world through a liberal ideology — understandably, because liberalism is by far the dominant ideology in Canadian society. In Chapter 1, I described the liberal approach to the world, which stresses common humanity and good intensions, ignores the ongoing impact of history and conceives of the world as made up entirely of individuals. A liberal worldview is so strongly individualistic that the systemic structures of our collective life, particularly wealth and power, are invisible. (See Chapter 1 and "Liberal" in the Glossary).

A liberal worldview is also dualistic, with much focus on "good" and "bad" individuals, strongly identified with "good" and "bad" intent. When they come to understand the structural nature of oppression, the response of deniers can be that they are, therefore, "bad" people, or being labelled as such, which can lead to defensiveness and reinforce their denial. The defensiveness/denial often takes the form of defending intentions: "I'm a good person; I didn't mean to hurt anyone; therefore I can't be racist/sexist/heterosexist/etc." This group, like the backlashers and guilty, need to have their dualistic notions replaced with a more complex worldview. They often also need to learn how much of human action is based in unconscious biases and attitudes, so that they can grasp how little intention has to do with it and take responsibility for their own privilege without seeing themselves as "bad" people. This group, in particular, cannot move forward without grasping the structural nature of oppression.

If the session is mandatory, deniers will sometimes resent being forced to attend because they don't feel they need it and have other pressures on their time. Very early in the session, they must be surprised by what they don't know. Some of the same exercises that catch the attention of the backlashers with surprise and humour also work to pique the interest of the deniers, letting them know there might be something for them to learn from the session.

Given my understanding of the three main groups I find among the participants in ally education, I cannot overemphasize my belief that when ally education is effective, it is because it successfully challenges the three key blocks in participants' thinking: their ahistorical, individualistic and dualistic worldview. It does this by leading them to understand the *structural nature* of oppression.

Having come to this conclusion several years ago, I was delighted to discover *The Emperor Has No Clothes: Teaching about Race and Racism to People Who Don't Want to Know* by Tema Okun (2010). Okun is an anti-racism educator with experience in both community-based organizations and the National Louis University in Chicago, where she teaches in the Department of Educational Leadership. Building on a thorough analysis of our "normal" and invisible "white supremacy culture" and the dynamics of "privileged resistance, she lays out a process for a fundamental cultural shift away from racism. Her prescription centres on changing three deeply held elements of North American cultural belief: the right to profit, individualism and binary thinking.

Okun defines the right to profit as the cultural valuing of money over human life, making the growth and metastasization of cancer capitalism, as portrayed by John McMurtry (2013), possible (see Chapter 2). Because the global system of private wealth and power is an evolution of colonialism, the exploitation of the peoples of Africa, Asia, North and South America to benefit the people of Europe, it has white supremacy for its foundation.

Individualism, according to Okun, grows from the right to profit, embedding in us the notion that we are separate from community, culture, our species and our planet; that what we do or don't do does not affect anyone else; that we can get rich without making someone else poor; and that our personal experience defines reality. Individualism makes it almost impossible for us to see larger structures of wealth and power, oppression and privilege. It also makes it possible to believe that oppression is a matter of intent: if I don't intend to participate in racism, then I'm not racist.

Binary thinking, Okun's third cultural keystone, is also an outgrowth of colonialism/capitalism, in that it divides what and who is valued from what and who is not, who has the right to own from who is owned, the side we are on from the side we fight against. This simplification of, and therefore ability to control, the world, unfortunately traps us in an understanding of ourselves as either good or bad, right or wrong, making it extremely difficult to grasp the complexity of the systems of oppression and privilege in which we live.

Much of what Okun says about the right to profit complements my analysis in Chapters 2 and 3, describing how oppression came about and how it is held in place. Her emphasis on individualism and binary thinking matches mine on individualism and dualism. I have adopted ahistorical thinking as my third cultural barrier, that is, Western culture's failure to understand how history has shaped structures that continue to operate, giving privilege to some at the expense of others. In order to overcome oppression, the past must be confronted and healed. Remember the quote from Ann-Marie MacDonald's eleven-year-old daughter in Chapter 4: "If you forget the past, it grows inside you," a saying as true for cultures, nations and institutions as it is for individuals. Yet one of the most frequent objections of backlashers and deniers is: "That's all in the past; they should just let it go." Okun places the history of colonialism at the heart of her analysis of the right to profit.

We have carved up the concepts and named them a bit differently, and yet we are talking about the same educational task. My feeling while reading Tema Okun's work was delight and recognition, not only at this similarity in our understanding of the cultural underpinnings of oppressor thinking, but in many other aspects of our teaching practice as well. *The Emperor Has No Clothes* should be required reading for every educator working against oppression.

Returning to the three key ideas that block people from becoming allies as I have named them, individualism, dualism and an ahistorical worldview, leading potential allies past these barriers requires that they grasp the concept of a structural worldview. The next question, obviously, is: how?

Part of the task is the content of ally education. It must successfully communicate the concept of a structural worldview to people who have been conditioned all their lives to see themselves as individuals in an ahistorical, binary reality. The second piece is facilitation, learning to approach the backlashers, guilty and deniers skillfully with exercises and discussion designed to overcome their particular blocks to becoming allies. But before discussing either, I want to talk about the context of ally education. No matter how effective the content or skilled the facilitation of ally education, it cannot be effective without a larger organizational context of structural and cultural change.

The Organizational Context of Ally Education

When educators picture education, we tend to see a group of people gathered in a room for a course or workshop. This is sometimes all we, as teachers and facilitators, are given to work with, and if the course is long enough, an academic term for example, there is enough space, time and commitment for ally education to take place. All too often, however, organizations want a quick fix, a day or weekend of "sensitivity training" or "diversity training." One of my teachers called this kind of session "hit and run" education.[3] When equity education is attempted without being grounded in a larger, longer campaign for organizational change, in my opinion, it does more harm than good. Even if we do accomplish some positive change in that group of people on that day, there are no structures in place to reinforce and carry it forward and the potential to trigger destructive backlash.

A true effort to make cultural change in an organization involves a very long timeframe, measured in years, sometimes decades. Resources are required, not only to make change activities possible, but to signal to everyone that this effort is valued by the organization at the highest levels. Such an effort has at its core a group of committed individuals who are allowed the time to reflect, learn and plan, with the organizational power to implement those plans. The aim is to transform the way power and resources are used in and by the organization — that is, structural change — moving it toward greater equity and collaboration. New management and leadership skills must be developed, and all must be held to account, including the highest levels in the hierarchy.

Such change is possible. My work with provincial civil servants was guided by the Diversity Roundtable, representing all of the departments, support units and unions. For a time, conditions within the civil service were such that they were able to make some important changes, including employment equity and respectful workplace policies, education and criteria for management training and hiring, supported by the uppermost levels of the organization. Later, it seemed to me, the loss of some key people and collisions with barriers, particularly in some departments, caused the momentum to fade. I was not close enough to the situation to know why, or even if my perception is accurate. However, my point is that during my work under the guidance of the Diversity Roundtable, they referred repeatedly to the cultural change that had been accomplished in the organization by the inter-departmental committee working on issues of health and safety. This campaign, over a couple of decades, had transformed the civil service into a workplace where there was universal awareness of health and safety and universal support for correcting problems that came to light.

If courses and workshops are not grounded in a long-term, committed organizational effort to achieve change, they can generate, at best, token change. The organization checks "diversity" off its list, posters appear on walls and the "right" books are purchased for resource shelves. People pick up "politically correct" language, helping them pass as open-minded and tolerant without really grappling with the continuous, structural, collective nature of unlearning oppression. This can lead members of oppressed groups to trust them when they shouldn't, and it becomes more difficult to identify the real sources of injustice.

At worst, "diversity" education out of context can create a backlash in which the most vulnerable people, the very minority employees the program was designed to support, are further victimized. In the presence of bullying, corruption and poor management, justice is not possible. All the "education" does is erode the fragile ledge the "different" employees or other participants in the organization are standing on, "blowing their cover," as the expression goes, making it more difficult for them to "play along" in whatever way they must to survive in the organization. They become scapegoats for their colleagues' anger over the pressure to take part, particularly if the "education" is mandatory.[4]

Mandatory diversity/equity education is controversial (Kalev et al. 2006; Bell et al. 2008; Bregman 2012). It carries great risks, as described above, generating backlash, exposing already vulnerable people to increased bullying and harassment, making it possible to claim that what can be done has been done and disguising the roots of the inequity that continues to plague the organization. It is a pale cousin when compared with the depth of organizational cultural change that can be generated by voluntary education in a setting where people have the motivation to take part (Velasquez 1998). However, I strongly believe that mandatory education has an essential place in organizational efforts to achieve equity, especially in the early stages. Later it can take its limited place alongside voluntary education. Mandatory education makes it clear to all employees that the organization places a high value on its equity policies and practices and that everyone in the organization will be held accountable to them. It can make talking about equity less scary by "breaking the ice" and introducing respectful language for discussing the issues. It can establish basic concepts and reach those who need it most, those who would never volunteer to take part given the choice.

Mandatory education can backfire completely if it is not compulsory at all levels. While working with provincial civil servants, I frequently heard: "If this is so important, why isn't our manager here?" I admit I would rather have participants challenge me over the absence of their manager than deal with a hostile manager. When it is the managers undercutting the intent of the session, everyone else follows their example or at least stays silent. On the other hand, when a manager is present and taking the session seriously, even with high resistance in the group, the tone is respectful. Some of my best sessions took place in departments notorious for their harassment and rough culture, but we had a skilled and thoughtful manager modelling the line between honest questioning and destructive bullying.

In order for mandatory education to contribute what it can and minimize the risks, it must have a well-thought-out place in a much larger campaign for organizational change and it must be competently designed and facilitated by teachers skilled and experienced in this type of education. A teacher who does not thoroughly grasp the concepts and demonstrate being an ally in their own actions, who does not have the skills to deal with the deep emotions that will be stirred up, who panics under attack or who gives up control of the room to the backlashers can solidify oppressive attitudes, contributing to backlash against the most vulnerable people involved.

If you are considering leadership of ally education and are not completely clear on the concepts involved or do not have the skills and experience to deal with attacks and strong emotional reactions, please do not experiment. Find an appropriate opportunity to learn or apprentice with someone more experienced. The aphorism "every little bit helps" does not apply in this case. The risks are such that doing nothing is sometimes the better choice.

Computerized Equity Education

I am associated with several organizations that have made the decision to put their mandatory equity courses online. This is convenient for employees and volunteers, who can complete the program at their leisure and the organization saves the money it would otherwise spend on space, equipment, travel and a facilitator. However, in my opinion, this type of exercise should not even be called an equity course. All it does is give learners the briefest of introductions to the organization's equity policies in a way that is quickly forgotten.

When adult educators begin to design a workshop or course, the first thing we are taught to think about is objectives. What are we trying to teach? Learning objectives come in categories: do we want learners to remember information, explore their emotions, master skills, change their behaviour, change their attitudes or take action on something? Computers and the Internet can be useful tools for communication between teachers and learners, especially if there is distance between them, but in the automated online courses some organizations are using to save money on equity education, there is no teacher. Students read, watch or listen to content and then take tests that are marked by the computer. This type of education can introduce information, although education research says it is not remembered for long. It can offer an opportunity to explore emotions, attitudes and behaviour, introduce a skill, point to resources or suggest action to those who are ready and willing to go farther on their own. It cannot provide the kind of surprise and challenge that makes cracks in the worldview of learners stuck in backlash, guilt or denial, nor can it provide the reflective process required to plant new seeds in the soil exposed by the cracks. It cannot change attitudes and behaviour in the unready or unwilling. It cannot move an organization toward equity or erode the barriers in the way. On the contrary, this type of exercise makes a huge statement that equity is a low priority for this organization, an afterthought.

The Basic Structure of Popular Education

Let us assume that you have a sound context for educating allies: a community or organization with a long-term commitment to developing a structure and culture of equity. Let's also assume that you have the skills and experience to facilitate this type of education. Now it's time to design your workshops or course. What will it look like?

The basic structure of popular education includes: naming ourselves (Who are we?), reflecting on our experience (What's happening?), analysis (Why is it happening?), strategy (What are we going to do about it?) and, finally, action. The next round begins with naming experience again (What happened as a result of what we did?), analysis (Why did it happen that way?), strategy (What are we going to do next?), the next action, and so on. The process can be illustrated as a spiral:

Spiral Model of Learning

Reflection
* feelings
* reactions
* hopes
* fears
* challenges
* surprises
* contradictions

Analysis
* history
* power structure
* dynamics
* patterns
* trends
* context
* leverage points
* actors
* interests
* allies/enemies

Action
* do it!
* becomes the next experience for reflection

Placing Ourselves
* class
* race
* sex
* age
* language
* sexual orientation
* religion
* ability/disability
* national origin
* values
* assumptions
* ideology
* learning style

Strategy
* implications
* goals/objectives
* planning for action

Naming Ourselves

Popular education does not assume that we are individuals on a "level playing field," as liberal education does. We come to our gathering with different genders, skin colours, abilities, ages, education, backgrounds, genetic heritages, classes and class origins, ideologies and beliefs, sexual orientations and access to power and resources. Popular education is never impersonal or "objective." In a short learning experience, a workshop for example, there may not be time to do much reflection on who we are, but our differences will have an impact on our collective learning experience nonetheless. In a longer timeframe, a course for example, it is important to build in reflection on who we are, coming back to it from time to time, deepening the exploration with each round. In a shorter time, it is important to at least learn everyone's name and something about that person — why they are there, what they are looking for from the session, some hopes, fears and expectations. Even the act of hearing each person's voice breaks the ice for their contribution later.

In any session longer than a day, and many educators would say any session regardless of length, it is important to discuss ground rules. What do people expect from one another? What does respectful interaction look like? What is the line between honest self-expression and disrespect? What will happen if someone is not keeping to the agreed-upon ground rules?

In the Toolkit (the Appendix), you will find a small selection of exercises appropriate for "Naming Ourselves." Many others can be found in the at the end of the Toolkit section.

The Naming Ourselves part of a session is especially important for denier and guilty participants, who need to deepen their analysis of who they are in their structural context; however, when a group or a significant part of it is hostile, the Naming Ourselves component gives the backlashers an opportunity to set the tone. When teaching mandatory sessions, I began cutting this section quite short, just a brief go-around of introductions and expectations, so that I could move as quickly as possible into "Reflection on Experience" with an exercise that included humour and surprise.

Reflecting on Experience

In popular education as it was originally conceived, the subject of reflection is the experience of oppression. As explained in Chapter 8, although we are taught not to recognize our experience of being oppressed, it is there to be observed, because oppression can be seen, heard and felt by those who are its targets. The experience can be hidden under layers of fear, shame and denial, as discussed in Chapter 6, and making it visible can be painful, but the end result is relief, healing and new sources of power and support.

Our experience as a member of a dominant group is much more difficult to see. For one thing, a basic feature of the oppression is that we are cut off from our ability to empathize with those we oppress. If we are aware of it at all, we tend to get defensive or write it off as not very serious — "They are just whining" or "playing the race card." For another thing, the privileges that we obtain from oppressing others are invisible to us. For a third thing, oppression is structural. We derive benefits from being male or white or straight or able-bodied without taking any personal action against a woman, a racialized person, an LGBT person or a person with a disability.

As mentioned earlier, direct discussion of our experience as members of oppressor groups can only be done with experienced allies. Learners who fall into the backlasher, guilty or denier groups have internalized "scripts" filled with stereotypes about "us" and "them." Any attempt to simply talk about the experience of privilege in our lives encourages participants to insist on these stereotyped responses more strongly. When you expect that a substantial proportion of participants will fit into these three groups, which is almost always the case in Canada, the experience component must be built into the session and contain an element of surprise. Examples of exercises to accomplish this, such as "Barnga," "Step Forward; Step Back" and simulated reversal exercises, are in the Toolkit section in the Appendix.

An important principle of popular education is that the teacher or facilitator is also a learner. It is typical for a facilitator to share the agenda before beginning and negotiate the process along the way. Research has demonstrated that life-changing learning can result from leaders making themselves vulnerable and expressing their own struggle with their role as oppressor or oppressed (Griffith 1982). Making yourself vulnerable in a session however, is appropriate only when reflecting on an experience of oppression or working with experienced allies. In the presence of guilty or denier participants, it causes confusion and defensiveness and leads to unproductive arguments and tangents. In the presence of backlasher participants, it can be a disaster. They tend to have a "power-over" mentality, which does not hesitate to take advantage of the leaders' vulnerability and use it to control the session.

Analysis

After reflecting on the experience of oppression, it is important to move on to exercises designed to help the group understand what oppressive structures are and how and why they are put in place and maintained. There are many tools for this process: drawing diagrams, making human sculptures, acting out skits, doing research, putting yourself in the position of someone responsible for creating an oppressive society (as in the example used in Chapter 2).

In my experience, there is a temptation to skip over analytical work, perhaps because it is a critical, intellectual process, and we live in a society where many people have been put down and shut out by those who use only this method of teaching or make it into a competitive activity in our schools and universities. Do not skip over it. Analysis in small groups can be exciting and revealing and provides an essential basis for the steps that follow. I describe two of my favourite exercises for analysis in the Toolkit section, and there are good instructions for many others in resources such as those listed at the end of that section.

If you plan to present content — a talk, video or some other form of presentation — the analysis segment of the process is the place to do it, building on the participants' discussion during the naming, reflection and early analysis pieces of the process. It is at this point in an educating allies workshop that I make a presentation on the structural nature of oppression. By this time I always have a great deal to work with, picking up on the usually liberal analysis that participants have produced and using their own words to expand their understanding. The Toolkit section includes "The Iceberg," my favourite handout and talk for accomplishing this.

Strategy and Action

Popular education is not complete without action. The Toolkit includes a handout with steps for planning a strategy for action. Participants who will be taking action together can work through all or part of it and bring their plan back to the rest of the group. At the very least, look at what changes people want to make, who has the power to make those changes, who should be involved and what leverage points are available to the participants to move the process forward.

If people take part in a session as individuals, they must work out their action plans on their own, but they can share them and make contracts to call one another at some point in the future to ask how each other's plans are coming along. When people take part as members of groups or are all part of one organization, the process of building a strategy for action is a more complex and satisfying one. The plan can be very specific and can include determining different roles for different people and setting dates for meetings to evaluate progress and adjust the plan.

In my experience, the strategy and action component of popular education can be used in the process of educating allies only when the participants have chosen to be present. They can be experienced allies or members of the guilty group. In fact, strategy and action are particularly important for the guilty group. Deniers can move on to strategy and action only once they have ceased to be deniers. Backlashers should not be led into strategy and action at all. The strategies and actions they think about are not what any anti-oppression activist would want to encourage. If you are able to surprise some of the backlashers into catching a glimpse of what oppression is and feels like, challenge their stereotyped thinking and introduce them to the concept of the structural nature of oppression, in my experience you've done very well and should leave it at that.

Part of the strategy and action component of a session can include teaching participants skills for identifying and responding to oppression. Sample exercises can be found in the Toolkit and Resource sections. If participants are working toward specific action, this is an opportunity to learn the skills they might need to carry it out. If the session is more general and participants will not be taking specific follow-up action together, the strategy and action component of the workshop can consist almost entirely of skill-building exercises followed by reflection on how the skills might be applied in their life, organizations or work.

Reflection, Evaluation, Closure

When the time available for a workshop or course is very full, as educating allies sessions always seem to be, it is tempting to not save enough time to close properly. This is a mistake. The closing process ties together the loose ends, gives a sense of completion and helps participants become conscious of their learning and take the experience away in a useful form.

Reflection is a time for participants to go back over the session and talk about what they learned.

Evaluation means collecting feedback from the participants, aloud or in writing, that will help improve the session the next time it is offered.

Closure should be quick and energetic, something to get people on their feet, say a final word and feel a clear ending to the process. There are many tools for this.

A Note on Emotional Responses

As explained in Chapter 4, at the core of our roles both as oppressor and oppressed is the unhealed hurt of our own experiences of oppression. As a result, any educational activity designed to unlock these experiences, no matter how academic, will also arouse strong feelings. For those who experience the oppression under discussion, the frustration comes from the defensive, angry or guilty reaction of those who don't. It can be yet another experience of oppression. For those who are in the dominant group in relation to the oppression under discussion, there is frustration because of their difficulty in seeing the oppression, as explained in Chapter 8. In "Teaching About Diversity: Navigating the Emotional Undercurrents," Kate Kirkham of Brigham Young University talks about this source of emotional response on the part of dominant group members when race or gender are discussed in a university classroom:

> Individual majority group members do not hear or see in their day-to-day interactions the very examples the minority person offers as proof of the existence of racism or sexism. Certainly majority group members do not pass on stories to each other about what they did to contribute to sexism in their organization. The research on sexual harassment, for example, has recorded that it is a few of the men who do most of the harassing. The problem is that the behaviors of many of the men may not make it obvious who is the one who will later harass. Several men may "enjoy" a sexist joke but only one may continue his "enjoyment" of sexism by harassing women he works with in the organization. However, the men that allow the joke, all "look" like potential harassers. The men may individually (i.e., personally) dismiss or tolerate the joking without seeing how it fuels the one or two men who will continue to bring inappropriate sexual conduct into the workplace. The women who hear or hear about the joking may be weary of all those who allowed it. The men who allow joking, language or inappropriate discussion of women's appearance to occur at one point in time will not be present later when the behavior of other men becomes even more severely sexist. (Kirkham 1988/89: 53)

Kirkham's example illustrates the frustration of a discussion on gender or race for members of the dominant group, particularly if they understand human relationships to be personal only and fail to see the structural elements. Another of her examples, also mentioned previously, shows this gap in understanding even more clearly:

> When asked to respond to the question who really is racist and/or sexist, many majority group individuals, in my research and teaching experience, assume: "If I didn't intend something as racist or sexist then it is not racist/ sexist." In other words, the general criteria they use in testing for racism/ sexism is an overpersonalized one. They believe that personal motive determines the presence of racism or sexism in interactions.
>
> An example of this assumption is present in the pattern of reactions of a majority group member in a graduate organizational behavior course during a discussion of racism and sexism in the workplace. Every comment made by a woman or minority student in the class was responded to by him (as soon as he had a chance) as if they had been directing their comments to him personally therefore indicting his intentions. He resented this and kept saying so with increasing emotional intensity. With some assistance, he identified the core reason for his reactions. He became aware that he was using what he thought was intended as the only legitimate criteria. If the point someone was making did not fit what he thought was intended in an example, then it was not an example of racism or sexism. Because he was emotionally defending what he thought were personal and unfair accusations, he could not broaden his understanding of racism and sexism. Once he realized that others were using criteria that included intended and unintended outcomes of behavior, he could better understand their examples.
>
> An additional insight came from the above class discussion and indicates the usefulness of surfacing underlying assumptions that trigger emotions in a discussion. Many of the majority group members, who had been quick to label a minority group member as over-sensitive, became more aware of how their own version of over-sensitivity was showing up with just as much emotional conviction behind it. (51)

I once asked a colleague how he became an ally to women. He said: "I finally understood that I may not be a perpetrator of violence against women, but I'm a perpetuator."[5] Many others have not yet taken this step from understanding oppression in personal terms to understanding it as a structural reality. The result is that they cannot hear the structural reality discussed without feeling accused of something terrible and reacting with either guilt or anger.

When the setting is one in which deep feelings are expected, the framework and skills will most likely be in place to deal with emotional responses when they emerge. For example, in Margaret Green's work with women exploring their racism, the setting was a therapy group and Green herself is a therapist (Green 1987). This is an ideal situation, with concepts, tools and skilled facilitation specifically designed for exploring the emotion and painful memories that underlie oppressive behaviour.

In other settings, the emotions connected with the topic may not be as easily integrated into the discussion. As Kate Kirkham illustrates in her article quoted above, she uses classroom discussion to explore the underlying assumptions students have about the legitimacy of the subject, their definitions of racism and sexism, their concept of what constitutes "proof" that racism and sexism exist and their methods for defining what is a problem and how big or small a problem it is. As she says in her article: "Ferreting out the core assumptions ... enables the emotional intensity to be more richly explored for all involved in a discussion" (49).

Whatever tools you have for processing the emotion in your educational setting, you will be called upon to use them when you enter the arena of educating allies. If you are not confident of your skills in handling emotional response, get some training before trying any experiments. As explained above, you can easily do more harm than good by venturing into ally education without the proper tools.

Knowing What to Say

One of the issues for facilitators of ally education is knowing what to say when participants make comments that come from a guilty or denier perspective, and even more so when the comment comes from a hostile backlasher. With experience, you develop a collection of effective responses that are appropriate and comfortable for you and specific participants.

For example, when working with people, particularly men, who come from an outdoor, hunting and fishing culture, the target of attack is often Aboriginal people because of conflict over hunting and fishing rights. The specific stereotypes in their negative comments are based on the symptoms of poverty and cultural destruction in Aboriginal communities. I found an image that worked very well in this situation, borrowed from Malidoma Patrice Somé, a teacher, author and Elder of the Dagara people of Burkina Faso. In *The Healing Wisdom of Africa* (2002), he says:

> Readers may be wondering how this harmonious picture of villagers chanting and singing together as they shape pots or grow yams fits with the more common picture they have been shown of African children starving and of the grim specter of death bearing down upon tribal communities. What I must emphasize here is that the energy required to sustain the harmony we are talking about is so delicate that it can easily be destroyed by the slightest intrusion, and such intrusion has clearly taken place through colonialism. Africa today is not what it used to be. ...
> These images have cemented a certain stereotype of Africans, a stereotype

created by the destruction wrought through colonialism. When colonialism, old or new, disrupts the energy working like an umbrella to protect people, the people under the umbrella will be exposed to the elements. Like fish in a lake whose water has suddenly evaporated, the fish will die. The great problem is that the fish have been brought to public attention after the drying of the lake; beholders may not remember the fish as it was or could have been in a full lake. (69)

The image of fish dying in a drained lake resonates so well with people used to the outdoors that I have had participants refer back to it, interrupting their own negative stereotypes, half expressed, with a comment like, "Oh yeah, the fish in the empty lake."

Another example comes from the fact that I am a lesbian. When the target of participants' hatred is LGBT people, I can sometimes stop the attack in its tracks and bring about a more positive learning discussion simply by coming out. Occasionally this does not work and the rest of the session can then be a difficult challenge.

In learning how to respond well to negative comments, I appreciate the work of Dr Ishu Ishiyama, who teaches education and counselling psychology at the University of British Columbia. He developed a workshop model called "Anti-discrimination Response Training" (2006). Its purpose is to build participants' skills in what he calls "active witnessing," or responding constructively to remarks and situations of racism, discrimination and disrespect. During the workshop, participants watch vignettes and practise responses. I have never had the privilege of attending one of Dr Ishiyama's workshops, but there is a sample trainer's manual online <static.diversityteam.org/files/79/a-r-t-trainers-manual.pdf?1268182977> and a friend shared a workshop handout with me. What I find useful is the organization of different possible responses into categories. Here are some examples:

> Assertive Interjections ("I don't mean to put you on the spot, but I can't remain silent.");
> Personal Emotional Reactions ("I don't feel comfortable with what you just said.");
> Naming the Racism or Discrimination ("Maybe you don't mean it, but that sounds like a racist remark.");
> Disagreement ("I disagree.");
> Questioning the Validity of the Statement ("Always? Everyone?");
> Pointing out the Hurtful or Offensive Nature of the Comment ("If you said that to me, I'd be really upset.");
> Putting the Offender on the Spot ("Are you really saying that women aren't as smart as men?");
> Empathic Confrontation ("Would you mind sharing with me what led you to say this?");
> Supporting the Victim ("I want you to know you're not alone.");

Approaching External People ("We need your advice and guidance. This is what happened today…");

Approaching Co-witnesses ("Did you hear what I heard?").

For someone like me who does not think quickly on my feet, having these categories in my head helps me select a response I think might be effective in the circumstances.

A Note on Homogenous and Mixed Groups

It makes sense that members of an oppressor group should work together to overcome our problem. We should avoid taking any energy away from the group we oppress by making them listen to our ignorance or asking them to teach us. Some have used such settings very effectively, particularly because being away from those we oppress allows for completely open exploration of attitudes without fear of hurting someone. Margaret Green, in her method of working with women to unlearn racism, demonstrates such work at its best (1987).

The pitfall of all-oppressor groups, however, is that they can easily slip into being too comfortable. Good education treads an important line between being too comfortable and too threatening. The facilitator of an all-oppressor group must be careful to create an educational design that presents challenges to the participants.

When I first decided to deal with my own racism and contribute to the struggle against racism by developing a workshop, I began by talking with several African-Nova Scotian colleagues and friends about the idea. All but one opposed the idea of a white facilitator leading an all-white workshop on racism. They felt that the misconceptions white people hold about Black people and our tendency to deny racism would go unchallenged. It is hard for us to see our own racism, no matter how long we have been working at the process of unlearning it.

Because of these tendencies to develop blind spots and too much comfort in oppressor-only groups, mixed groups do work well for educating allies. However, it is very, very important that the members of the oppressed group present understand the purpose and process of the workshop and agree to take part. If possible, they should be paid or honoured in some way as resource people.

Another way of dealing with the inequalities between oppressor and oppressed in a workshop might be to design two parallel processes that interact. Members of the oppressed group work on the questions from their point of view; for example, "What are the stages you have gone through in coming to understand your oppression?" Members of the oppressor group work on the questions from their point of view; for example, "What are the stages you have gone through in your process of becoming an ally?" Later both groups report and reflect together.

A third method is to design a session intended to look at several forms of oppression and how they interact. Small groups or individuals reflect on their oppression, all using the same questions. Later they make presentations and all session participants reflect together on the relationships among oppressions. Oppression/Privilege Reflection, described earlier, is an example of such a process. I have never tested this idea. Years ago a diverse group of anti-oppression activists in Halifax designed a two-day version of this workshop, but could not find enough participants and resources to carry it out.

When workshop members are reflecting upon an invisible form of oppression, there is no way at the outset to tell who is or is not a member of the oppressed group. In this case, always assume you are working with a mixed group and make sure your language is inclusive. It also works well to make a rule at the outset that members of the oppressor group must hide their identity. In a heterosexism workshop, straight people learn a great deal from having to hide their wedding rings, change pronouns when talking about their partners and refrain from saying, "of course, I'm heterosexual, but. ..." It is very important to reflect on this experience later in the workshop.

Homogenous or Mixed Leadership Teams?

The questions that come into play when deciding about homogenous or mixed groups of participants all play a part in decisions about the leadership as well. There is a spectrum of opinion, from those who believe the leadership should be made up only of those who experience the form of oppression in question, through those who prefer mixed teams, to those who believe that the oppressor group should be working on their own problem separately. There are advantages and disadvantages to all of these options.

Leadership by the oppressed group in question can be limited by lack of understanding of the processes potential allies must go through and the risk and pain involved. Also, there is always the question of whether the energy required could perhaps be better used in the struggles of the leaders' own people, rather than in educating allies. It is easy as well to put participants in a position of "damned if they do, damned if they don't." For example, when I participate in heterosexism workshops, I want participants to express their oppressive attitudes so that I can work with them in the learning process, but sometimes I do not want the pain involved in hearing those sick old clichés once again.

On the other hand, leaders from the oppressed group have direct experience of the oppression to communicate, and the experience in a workshop of reversing the usual roles of oppressor and oppressed can raise responses which provide rich opportunities for reflection.

Leadership by and for an oppressor group has the same problems as a homogenous group of participants — the facilitators can reinforce misconceptions and the process can become too comfortable. However, it is very important for members of the oppressor group to take responsibility for the oppression and to push one another to make changes without asking the oppressed group to spend energy on them once again.

Mixed leadership has the benefits of both — the communication of experience and challenge of having members of the oppressed group in leadership; and the comfort and knowledge of becoming an ally that members of the oppressor group can provide. A mixed team can model a respectful working relationship for participants. One potential drawback is that the leadership team can become so involved in their own struggle to maintain a good working relationship across divisive histories that attention to the participants' needs can suffer.

Reflections on Educating Allies

I have done many different kinds of adult education in the past forty years. No two sessions are ever alike, but I have found nothing as unpredictable as educating allies. Even if the sequence of exercises is exactly the same, the workshops are totally different experiences. Difficult emotions are involved: hostility, guilt, denial, fear, embarrassment, pain. The experiences being communicated are powerful. Both of these things can also be said for sessions where people are working on their own form of oppression, but for some reason the mix in a group of allies is more complicated and explosive. As I have experimented with ally education, the process has gradually become more predictable to me, although there are still many surprises. I expect this learning to continue far into the future.

Educating allies is also a very satisfying form of education. Bridges are built on the spot, goodwill and risk-taking are obvious, communication takes place across the barriers of centuries, and experiments are initiated which have immediate importance in the process of building a new, more cooperative society. According to my analysis, this is exactly what we must do if we can hope for a future on this planet. Any degree of new learning or successful experimentation that unfolds during these sessions gives me great hope.

notes

1. The story of this migration of an educational approach can be found in Arnold and Burke (1983) and Arnold, Barndt and Burke (1985).
2. The basic principles of popular education can be found in the work of Paulo Freire (1970, 1972, 1973).
3. Thank you to Hélène Moussa for this term. She used it many years ago and I have used it ever since.
4. For a more detailed description of tokenism and the backlash process, see Bishop (2005).
5. Thank you John Hugh Edwards.

Chapter Ten

Step 6
Maintaining Hope

> My heart is moved by all I cannot save.
> So much has been destroyed.
> I have to cast my lot with those who,
> Age after age, perversely,
> With no extraordinary power
> Reconstitute the world. (Rich 1978)

The Dream

People change. Sometimes the process involves two steps forward, one step back, or even two back, but people do change and heal and grow. People change individually and collectively, transforming structures along the way. It does not even require a new generation, raised differently, to see change in a society.

When the United States invaded Grenada in 1983, I was working for an international development agency and had the privilege of speaking at length with those who had experienced firsthand the four years when Grenada was led by the New Jewel Movement.[1] Some were Canadians, some Grenadians. During that cooperative, truly democratic period, they said people's everyday behaviour changed. Even at the level of fighting in bars or needing police to break up tussles at soccer games, people began to reflect the sense of common destiny and responsibility they felt. Ordinary events became peaceful. Violence against women declined dramatically in response to stiffer punishments and employment for all women in their own cooperatives. Prostitution disappeared.

When the coup and invasion of 1983 restored foreign domination, exploitation and extreme divisions between classes, the whole thing reversed immediately. Violence returned as a daily occurrence. Women were on the streets again, without shelter or employment, working as prostitutes, fleeing violence in the workplace and at home. As this example shows, it is not just individuals who change within a society, nor does social change take generations. Whole societies can change, rapidly, for better or worse.

What we have learned can be unlearned. The question is, can it be unlearned in time, before the rich and powerful own the entire world and destroy it, before the depth of our "oppression training" makes us passively stand by and watch, or even assist in the destruction.

Idealism

Whenever I have spoken publicly about social justice, I get the response, "But that's idealistic." It is always said negatively, as a condemnation. People actually mean: "You are a fool because it's impossible," or "You are hopelessly näive." They are mistakenly opposing "idealism" and "realism." Idealism means a belief in the power of ideas to affect human life. Its opposite is materialism, the belief that material reality shapes ideas. If you believe in the power of ideas, idealism is realistic.[2]

Hope

The other common response is: "Where do you get your hope?" The two responses are related. When I hear either, I know I am once again up against the North American concept of hope. In mainstream North American culture, hope is defined as a static thing. It has to do with outcomes, laying bets, guessing right, investing. You decide what you think will happen and invest your time, energy and money there. Then, if you are right, you win; if you are not, you lose. If you say what you think will happen out loud to many people, everyone will admire you if you win and despise you if you lose. For example, there is some evidence that when the results of opinion polls are made public just before an election, they influence the vote. If this is true, it suggests that Canadians may care more about being on the winning side (and the resulting patronage) than about political parties, issues or any other aspect of the "democratic" election process. This is an example of static hope.

Static hope reinforces consumerism and the "win/lose" assumption of financial investing. It leads people to conclude that if they have no proof that the world will change, they might as well spend their time being as happy and comfortable as possible, that is, accumulating as many material things as possible. These concepts of "happy" and "comfortable" are also static, as is this understanding of the purpose of material things.

Static hope has difficulty living with ambiguity. It does not want to "dwell on" problems at length and in depth, or "dwell with" them, admitting that some are too complex to solve in a short time, in our lifetime, or perhaps ever. Static hope wants "solutions" (Jensen 2007).

Guessing the eventual outcome, competing to win and wanting immediate solutions, that is, static hope, is irrelevant to allies. A person becomes committed to social justice, including the processes of liberation and becoming an ally, out of a living concept of "happy" and "comfortable."

To people whose dreams have been crushed and whose roots have been severed, a life of living happiness, comfort and peace looks like a discouraging, painful struggle. And, while it can be a discouraging, painful struggle, such a life also fills a person up; it is deeply satisfying. Living happiness, comfort and peace opens horizons, brings dreams and insights, expands vision and creates patterns, connections and networks. At the worst moments, a person committed to social justice has to fall back on: "Well, if I stop struggling, I'll become part of the problem, and I couldn't stand that." At best, the process brings great joy and companionship.

In fact, for people who are connected to their own emotions and dreams, to all other life and the earth, there is no choice. Again, I quote Alice Miller as she explains that for people who have full, spontaneous access to their emotions, resistance to social injustice is simply a matter of being themselves.

> Rejection, ostracism, loss of love and name calling will not fail to affect them; they will suffer as a result and will dread them, but once they have found their authentic self they will not want to lose it. And when they sense that something is being demanded of them to which their whole being says no, they cannot do it. They simply cannot. (1983: 84–85)

It is for those separated from themselves that work towards social justice is an intellectual choice, a matter of duty, morals and conscience:

> Morality and performance of duty are artificial measures that become necessary when something essential is lacking. The more successfully a person was denied access to his or her feelings in childhood, the larger the arsenal of intellectual weaponless the supply of moral prostheses has to be, because morality and a sense of duty are not sources of strength or fruitful soil for genuine affection. Blood does not flow in artificial limbs; they are for sale and can serve many masters. (85)

There is a choice for these people. They can stay "safe." No wonder they see those who stand up to injustice as naïve and "idealistic."

Hope is also something we can deliberately build into the structure of social change organizations. Our efforts must include intellectual processes like critique, clear thought, analysis, strategy, choices, judgement and making distinctions. We also must have affirmation, acceptance, tolerance, pleasure, joy, humour, release, creativity and fun. If there is too much intellectual work, participants burn out and lose hope. Too much intellectual work can also result in making judgements and distinctions within the group, with some members putting others down. On the other hand, if there is too much openness and fun, the group can be at risk of becoming confused and co-opted, unable to stick to the harder tasks of the struggle or adjust the course when the situation changes.

An effective social justice group, whatever its purpose, can only maintain its hope if a balance of these two ways of functioning is established. Unfortunately, such a balance is difficult. Splits often occur along the line between the two. Some people find others too serious or critical and feel attacked by the kind of judgements that can be made or implied in analytical thought. The "intellectual" group thinks the "fun" group is not serious enough, just not interested in being on the "political cutting edge." It is also difficult for some to give up anger as the drive behind the impulse to work for social change. Humour, fun, warmth, vision and love are all motivations for social change too, but our culture, particularly "the left," is much more familiar with anger.

The other common reason for burnout in social change organizations is conflict. Just like in a relationship or a family, the members of a group in conflict must have the courage to name the problem and deal with it, with a skilled outside facilitator if at all possible.

I believe human beings have a need to bond and struggle together. In our society this need has been interpreted as competition and co-opted by business, politics and professional sports, even by war. When some men remember their experiences in war, the memories might be terrible, but they also recall those years as the "best time of my life." War offers soldiers the satisfaction of bonding in struggle; this is not part, in any real form, of most of North American society. The co-opted versions, like sports and video games, divert our attention away from the real bonds and struggles, those that will decide our future as a species on this planet.

Commitment to social justice means beginning a completely unknown journey — a journey that can unfold only one step at a time, with confusion and danger along the way, and where the end is a mystery. It is a very difficult journey for any-one to enter if their upbringing and education denied them love and security or their scars make insecurity unbearable. The childrearing and education structures of our society seem to be designed to make as many people as possible carry these limitations. On the other hand, for someone who has worked at healing the scars, finding their own love and security, the journey is very familiar. They have already been on a similar unknown path.

My first reason for attempting this journey is the dream. This dream is a deep, driving force in me, and I know many others share it. The dream is a vision of a world I would like to live in, a world based on cooperation, negotiation and universal respect for the innate value of every creature on earth and the Earth herself. This is a world where no one doubts that to hurt anyone or anything is to hurt yourself and those you love most, a world where everyone works to understand what the effects of everything we do will be on future generations.

The activities leading us into this dream are already underway, by millions of people, in millions of different forms. There are small, courageous experiments happening everywhere, based in local conditions, but aware of the whole world. Our recovery of hope — full-colour, three-dimensional, hard working, clear thinking, wildly radical, living hope — is our key to liberation.

notes

1. For more information on the story of Grenada and the New Jewel Movement, see Marcus and Taber (1983) and Payne, Sutton and Thorndike (1984).
2. I am using "idealism" the way it is used in everyday conversation, not with the more exact meanings developed over time by the Idealist school of philosophy.

Glossary

Below I explain my understanding of many of the terms I use in this book.

able-bodied: See physical or mentally challenged/disabled/able-bodied.

ableism: A social/political/economic/ideological system that allows physically, socially, perceptually, mentally and emotionally able people to exclude, marginalize and exploit people with disabilities.

Aboriginal, Native, Indigenous, First Nations, Métis: The Aboriginal, Native or Indigenous peoples of North America are those peoples who were here before European settlement, for example, Mi'kmaq, Maliseet, Cree, Innu and so on. The term First Nations refers to people who have legal status under the *Indian Act*. Métis people are descended from male French voyageurs and settlers and Aboriginal women. The term is accepted legally for the Métis Nation of Western Canada, contested for others, such as the Acadian-Mi'kmaq/Maliseet descendants of Nova Scotia, New Brunswick and Prince Edward Island.

Just as Black people's term of self-definition moved from Coloured to Black, many Aboriginal people have abandoned the term Indian as oppressive, although it is still the legal term in Canada and some Aboriginal groups have reclaimed it as a term of pride. Like the complex naming and self-naming of other peoples, there is conflict around all of these terms. I generally use Aboriginal as an inclusive term, First Nations when I mean Aboriginal people with legal status under Canada's *Indian Act*.

Aboriginal rights: Basic justice requires that the original inhabitants of a land must be able to continue to live on it and make a living from it. This right cannot be taken from them by intruders or conquerors. The original inhabitants should also be able to continue their own culture, language, spiritual practice and traditions.

adultery: In a patrilineal social system, men and women are considered married permanently. If either has sexual intercourse with anyone else, they have stepped outside of accepted social bounds and have "committed adultery." The punishments were traditionally much more severe for the woman because the original purpose of patrilineal marriage was to control inheritance by knowing with a doubt the father of a child. If a married woman had intercourse with another man, she might be carrying an "illegitimate" child. In matrilineal cultures, where it is only necessary to identify a child's mother, marriage is a social and economic structure not tied to sexual exclusivity. Adultery is not a problem and there is no such thing as an "illegitimate" child.

adultism: A social/political/economic/ideological system that allows adults to exclude, marginalize and exploit children.

African-Canadian/African-Nova Scotian: See Black/African-Canadian/African-Nova Scotian/people of colour/racialized people/visible minorities/immigrant people/white people.

affirmative action: A policy or action designed to "level the playing field" for those who are disadvantaged by structural/historical oppression. Affirmative action is not, as a common myth would claim, "reverse discrimination." When the goal of equity is accomplished, the affirmative action is no longer valid.

ageism: Ageism is a social/economic/political/ideological system where some have privileges or experience discrimination because of their age. It can work against a person for being too young or too old, and sometimes a person can be too young in one situation and too old in another at the same time.

ally: A member of a dominant group who works to end a form of oppression which gives them privilege. For example, a white person who works to end racism or a man who works to end sexism.

analysis/synthesis: The process of coming to understand a situation requires both analysis and synthesis. Analysis means taking the situation apart and looking at its pieces; synthesis is the opposite — taking the various pieces and fitting them together into one picture.

anglophone/francophone: Anglophones speak English; francophones speak French. In Canada, the struggle between these two groups, dating from the English conquest of New France in the eighteenth century, is a major feature of the political landscape. People from other countries sometimes do not understand this, and English dictionaries from countries other than Canada often do not even contain the words.

anti-oppression (anti-racism, anti-sexism, anti-heterosexism, etc.): An approach to work, communication, policy and education in a diverse setting that takes wealth, power and historical, structural inequity into account.

anti-Semitism: A social/political/ideological system that allows others, particularly Christians and Muslims, to exclude, marginalize, exploit, exile and kill Jews. A form of ethnocentrism, sometimes included in the term racism.

assimilation: When a conquered people "melt" into the dominant society, becoming indistinguishable, they have been assimilated.

backlash: When those working toward equity try to push an organization or other established system beyond token change, those in leadership must choose between the pursuit of structural change or an attempt to return to the *status quo*. This latter response is called backlash and has certain typical features, such as scapegoating, mis-naming the problem, shooting the messenger and enhancing token measures to create the appearance of change. The backlash process is described in detail in Bishop (2005).

bigotry: Persistent, intolerant belief in a worldview or hatred of a group of people.

BCE/CE: Before the Common (or Christian) Era and the Common (or Christian) Era. A way of dividing time using the traditional year of the birth of Jesus as year 1 CE. Years in the Common Era are counted forward; that is, 1920 CE comes before 1950 CE. Years before the Common Era are counted backward; that is, 1920 BCE comes after 1950 BCE.

bisexual: See lesbian/gay/bisexual/heterosexual

Black/African-Canadian/African-Nova Scotian/people of colour/racialized people/visible minorities/immigrant people/white people: The language of racism is very complicated. Sometimes racism is used to refer only to systemic oppression based on colour; sometimes other forms of oppression based on language or religious tradition are included. Sometimes the term is applied to individuals as well as structures and systems, as in "That person is racist." For purposes of clarity in this book, I use racism to refer only to colour-based structural oppression. When I mean ethnic, language or religious oppression, I say so. I do not refer to individuals as "racist," "sexist" or the name of any other oppression except in questions designed to promote discussion in workshops. When individuals are spoken about, it is more appropriate to use words like "bigoted" or "prejudiced."

The words for groups who suffer from racism are complex as well. Some have roots in insulting terms invented by white people; others have developed out of the pride and liberation struggles of the people they name. Sometimes a name which is used with pride in one generation becomes an insulting term in another, and a new word emerges. Sometimes one sub-group develops a term of pride and other sub-groups are not comfortable with it. For example, in Halifax "Black" is still the most common respectful word used by Black people and their supporters and has been since the 1960s. The phrases "African-Canadian" and "African-Nova Scotian" are emerging to replace it, with African-Nova Scotian referring to the community that came from a particular history of settlement in our province. For some, "African-Canadian" and "African-Nova Scotian" represent a new surge of energy in the fight against racism; others are not yet comfortable with them. For some who are now elders in the community, even "Black" is uncomfortably new. Their term of pride is still "Coloured," and two organizations continue to carry the name — the Home for Colored Children and the Nova Scotia Association for the Advancement of Coloured People.

When speaking to someone you know, it is important to use whatever term they prefer. Otherwise, "Black" is generally acceptable, or "African-Nova Scotian," if you are speaking to or of a member of that community. In this book

I try whenever possible to use the terms claimed by communities themselves — "Roma" rather than "Gypsy," "Innu" rather than "Montagnais," "Anishinabe" rather than "Ojibwa," and so on. When I do use a word with racist roots, it is because I do not know any better. I hope any person or community I insult in that way will forgive and inform me.

In my experience, "people of colour" is generally considered a respectful term and many use it to make stronger connections among all who suffer from colour-based racism, but some African-Nova Scotian people object to the phrase. "Visible minority" is often used as a neutral or legal term, but some object to it because it is a phrase that is clearly from a white perspective; that is, those who are different from white people and therefore visible to us. "Racialized people" is a more recent term used to refer to all people who are targets of racism. Its strength is that it underlines the fact that the concept of race is a social/political invention; there is no such thing as race.

The term "immigrant" usually refers to people who suffer from colour-based racism in North America because of their Asian, Latin American, African, Southern European or Middle Eastern origins. We tend to forget that white people are immigrants here too. As a result, I tend to use "recent immigrant" or "new Canadian."

capitalists/workers: When I use the words capitalists and workers, I am making a classic Marxist distinction between the owners of the means of production and those who sell their labour to the owners. The situation in Canada is very confusing. Many people in Canada own capital — a rental unit, a piece of land, shares in a company — and some professional workers are much more comfortable and hold much more power than some owners of the means of production, such as farmers, woodlot owners and fishers. The situation becomes a little clearer when you consider the fact that the means of production apparently owned by farmers, fishers, and woodlot owners are in fact largely owned by the banks. In spite of the confusing line between capitalist and worker in Canada, I think the distinction is an important one to use in understanding the underlying power structures that shape our lives.

CE: See BCE/CE

class: As explained above, class lines in Canada are very confusing. Our society is stratified and increasingly unequal. People at different class levels have extremely unequal levels of access to resources, voice in the political system and even control over their own lives. However, drawing the lines is not easy. Class is not simply a matter of income but of power and influence. Power and influence are a function of money, culture, colour, class, gender, birth, education and social and political position. When I use class in this book, I am referring to our different levels of access to power in Canadian society; I do not try to be precise about defining what the classes are. See also middle class.

competition/cooperation: Competition is part of a worldview where every person is a detached individual who gets ahead of or falls behind others according to merit, luck, ability or ruthlessness. Competition is almost a religion in North America, something that is seen as an absolute good. Cooperation, on the other hand, is part of a worldview that sees everyone and everything as connected, where no individual can get ahead or fall behind without everyone moving forward or falling back.

There is a spectrum of cooperation. On one end, negotiation can be a way for two parties to agree on something they want, while agreeing to give up other things they want. On the other end are collective methods of organization such as consensus decision-making, non-hierarchical organizations and communities that share everything.

There is a type of friendly rivalry that does not count as competition in the way I am using the word. For example, a group of children in a berry patch decide to see who can pick the most berries in half an hour, or an educational workshop includes a game that pits small groups against each other. The difference between friendly rivalry and competition is that competition results in one person or group being counted as superior to another or obtaining more rewards than another. Friendly rivalry on the other hand results in more benefits for everyone. All of the children can eat more berries because of their picking race. All participants in the workshop learn more because of the rivalry included in the learning game.

connection: See separation/connection

conquest: Conquest involves using power over another person or group of people in order to control what they have — their resources, land, skills, knowledge, labour or reproductive ability. The power used can be economic, political, social, military or ideological.

cooperation: See competition/cooperation

cultural competence: The skills required to live, work and communicate well in a diverse group of people.

Deaf/hearing: Deaf people who identify with their own highly developed culture and language call themselves "Deaf," with a capital "D." The privileged group responsible for their oppression are "Hearing." When the reference is simply to someone who can or cannot hear, they are called "hearing," "deaf" or "hard of hearing" for people whose hearing is limited.

diagonal oppressions: The horizontal form of oppression is class. Cutting across classes are the diagonal oppressions of race, gender, age, ability, sexual orientation and so on. They affect everyone who is a member of a certain group, but more or less according to their class. See "Class and Other Forms of Oppression" in Chapter 5.

disabled: See physically or intellectually challenged/disabled.

discriminatory harassment: Persistent, ongoing communication (in any form) of negative attitudes, beliefs or actions towards an individual or group which might reasonably be known to be unwelcome, with the intention of disparaging a person or group. Forms include name-calling, jokes or slurs, graffiti, insults, threats, discourteous treatment, and written or physical abuse. It may be either subtle or blunt (Hamilton 1995).

diversity: People with many differences living, working and communicating in positive way. Often used in a liberal sense, without recognizing historical structural inequality.

DNA: Deoxyribonucleic acid is an acid within the nucleus of a living cell. It contains the genetic code and carries inherited characteristics from generation to generation.

economic: This refers to anything having to do with money or wealth. Economic power is the use of money or wealth to get what a person or people want. See money/income/wealth.

elite: The small group of people at the top of the class system are the elite; they benefit from the labour, abilities and resources of everyone else.

employed/unemployed: Most people in Canada are dependent on employment for their livelihood. This creates a great difference in class between those who currently have a job and those who do not. The employed are not the source of oppression of the unemployed, but the employed have many privileges that the unemployed lack.

employment equity: A specific form of affirmative action aimed at employment practices such as recruitment, training, hiring, remuneration, staff retention, etc. In Canada, employment equity legislation is aimed at four groups generally under-represented and under-paid in the workforce: Aboriginal people, people with disabilities, visible minorities and women.

equality/equity: See hierarchy/equality/equity.

ethnocentrism: An inability to see and accept that other ways of viewing reality and acting exist and have validity outside of the norms and values of one's own culture. It is often unconscious and stems from a lack of exposure to the inner workings and values of other cultural groups. Judging other cultures using the standards of one's own culture. Seeing one's own culture as better than other cultures (Agger-Gupta 1997).

exploitation: When a person or people control another person or people, they can make use of the controlled people's assets, such as resources, labour and reproductive ability, for their own purposes. This is exploitation. The exploiters are those who benefit, and the exploited are those who lose.

feminist: There are many lively debates among feminists about exactly what a feminist is. I am part of these discussions and I have my opinions about what does and does not form part of a feminist ideology. However, for the purposes of this book, details are not necessary. I use the simplest possible definition: a feminist is a woman working against sexism.

First Nations: See Aboriginal, Native, Indigenous, First Nations, Métis.

francophone: See anglophone/francophone

gay: See lesbian/gay/bisexual/heterosexual

gender/sex: Sex refers to the physical characteristics of a person which make them male or female. Gender makes a person male or female through a collection of socially defined traits — appearance, attitudes, roles, preferences, work and so on. A patriarchal society has two rigid gender definitions and can be disrupted when a person of one sex displays the gender traits of the other. Other types of societies have more fluid definitions of gender. According to a two-spirited friend, some First Nations cultures had five or seven genders, with two-spirited people forming the middle group, half female and half male in their characteristics. See lesbian/gay/bisexual/heterosexual, transgendered, heterosexism/homophobia, transsexual and two-spirited.

GLBT: See LGBT

healing: Physical healing involves getting rid of damaged tissue and contaminants from the body and building new tissue to replace what has been injured. Emotional healing involves getting rid of pain, fear and anger through appropriate expression to supportive listeners and building new, healthy patterns of living to replace the old self-protective ones. Spiritual healing includes physical and emotional healing, with the addition of throwing out all the beliefs and images forced upon a person for purposes of control and replacing them with life-loving beliefs and images coming from deep inside and deep in the roots of the individual's culture. Since an individual person cannot be fully healthy in a sick society, all of these forms of healing eventually demand that the person become involved in a collective healing process, that is, in building a healthier society.

heterosexism/homophobia: Heterosexism refers to the structures of society that favour one kind of loving — between one man and one woman in a monogamous marriage with children — over all others. Heterosexism oppresses gay, lesbian and bisexual people, transgendered people, two-spirited people, single people, one-parent families, unmarried couples, childless couples and anyone else who does not fit the ideal mould. Homophobia is an individual reaction of hatred, fear or discomfort toward gay, lesbian, bisexual and transgendered people acted out through discrimination and violence.

heterosexual: See lesbian/gay/bisexual/heterosexual, heterosexism/homophobia, transgendered, transsexual and two-spirited.

hierarchy/equality/equity: Hierarchy is a social arrangement where some have more status, wealth and power than others. Equality and equity refer to a social structure based on everyone having equal value and equal access to power. In fact, equality or equity require a different definition of power from that used in a hierarchy. The aim of equality is that everyone receives the same treatment and has exactly the same degree of power at all times. Equitable social systems are more flexible and mobile, with different people taking different forms of power at different times, although the goal is to have it all even out over time; no one is allowed to exploit another. Equity does not assume equal treatment, but rather structures that give each person what they need to thrive. An approach that aims for equality has a problem with affirmative action, which gives extra support to those facing structural/historical barriers until those barriers are overcome. An equity approach has no difficulty with this concept.

homophobia: See heterosexism/homophobia

human rights: An international movement based on the belief that all individuals have a claim to the resources and benefits available to humankind and a certain quality of life, including life, liberty, security of person and property, education, health and well-being, privacy, nationality, citizenship and access to public services, employment, just and equal pay, trade union representation, freedom from slavery, torture, arbitrary arrest, exile or detention, equal protection before the law, the right to be presumed innocent until proven guilty, the right to consenting marriage, freedom of movement and residence, thought, conscience and religion, opinion and expression, assembly and association and freedom from discrimination. The Universal Declaration of Human Rights was adopted by the United Nations in 1948. Arising out of the experience of the Second World War, it was written by a Canadian, John Peters Humphrey, director of the United Nation's newly created Division of Human Rights, and championed by Eleanor Roosevelt. Canada has human rights legislation at the national and provincial levels designed to protect individuals' human rights by finding remedies to specific cases of discrimination.

ideological: This is the element of society that has to do with ideas — what people believe, value and understand to be true and real, right and wrong, acceptable limits. Ideological power is the ability to shape what people think, believe and value.

illegitimate children: These are children whose parents were not legally married when they were born. The concept only exists in patriarchal societies, because marriage in such systems exists to ensure control over the fathering of children. In other societies, it is the mother who is more important and, consequently, all children are legitimate.

immigrant people: See Black/African-Canadian/African-Nova Scotian/people of colour/racialized people/visible minorities/immigrant people/white people.

income: See money/income/wealth.

Indigenous: See Aboriginal, Native, Indigenous, First Nations, Métis.

intellectually challenged or disabled people: See physically or intellectually challenged/disabled.

intercourse: This takes place when a man enters another person with his penis. This is an extremely important act in patriarchal societies because it defines who has been conquered by that man and therefore belongs to him. For women and children in Western societies, it defines who is "pure" and "undefiled" and who is not. Again, in societies that are not patriarchal, the entry of a man's penis into another person's body does not have the same power to define social relations.

internalized oppression: Oppressed people usually come to believe the negative things that are said about them and even act them out. This is called "internalized oppression." No other form of liberation can get very far unless the participants in the struggle are also freeing themselves from these negative beliefs about themselves.

LGBT: An abbreviation of lesbian, gay, bisexual, transgendered. Sometimes a second "T" is included for two-spirited people and/or "Q" for queer. See lesbian/gay/bisexual/heterosexual, heterosexism/homophobia, transgendered, transsexual and two-spirited.

lesbian/gay/bisexual/heterosexual: As with feminism, there are lively debates among people of all sexual orientations about what exactly defines lesbians, gay men, bisexuals, and heterosexuals. Again, I have my own opinions, but they are not particularly important for understanding this book. Put very simply, lesbians are women who relate, emotionally and sexually, primarily to other women. Gay men relate intimately primarily to other men. Bisexual people are men and women who relate with equal depth to either men or women. Heterosexuals are men or women who relate intimately primarily to people of the opposite sex. See heterosexism/homophobia, transgendered, transsexual and two-spirited.

leverage point: A lever makes it possible to move objects many times your own weight. Most people have used a simple lever, such as a pry bar or long plank with a stone under it. Likewise, in a social justice strategy, a "leverage point" is an opportunity for a person or group with less power to move someone or something with more power. A certain piece of legislation, a good contact in places of power, and fortunate timing can all be leverage points.

liberal: Individually, every person has their own particular ideological system; that is, beliefs, values, worldview and so on. Individual ideological systems can be grouped into collective ideological systems using certain key traits. One of these is the way of thought generally called "liberal."

Historically, liberal ideology comes from the time of the "liberal" revolutions — French and American — that overthrew monarchies and brought a merchant "middle" class to power. It was originally defined as an economic theory by Adam Smith in *The Wealth of Nations*, published in 1776. The key principle was no government intervention in economic matters. Wealth, according to this theory, comes from "free" enterprise, "free" competition and "free" trade. After 1870, liberalism was modified by thinkers who believed that it was appropriate for government to regulate economic matters to a certain degree and intervene in the social realm to prevent conflict. In the 1930s, this form of modified liberalism, as defined by John Maynard Keynes, inspired the "New Deal" of the Franklin Roosevelt government in the United States. Since about 1975, however, many powerful political and economic players have worked to return liberalism to its roots. Generally called "neoliberalism," this philosophy promotes a "free" market with no state intervention, cutting of expenditures for social services, deregulation, privatization and elimination of the concept of "the public good." Because of the changes liberalism has gone through during its 250-year history, the term is now sometimes confusing, with different connotations in Europe and the United States.

When I use the term in this book, I am referring to an ideological system defined primarily by its belief in individuality. Equality of individuals in this way of thinking is a given, something already achieved or achievable with some reform. Liberal systems put a great deal of emphasis on individual freedom and negotiated common solutions to common problems. However, because liberals see people and groups as basically equal, the negotiations often fail to recognize the unequal resources and power of different parties. Liberal societies are shaped by those who have power, money and historical advantages, because it is assumed that they get their way through merit. Liberals are reluctant to recognize historical and structural inequalities.

In a liberal democracy, decisions are made by majority vote. This system totally ignores the patterns of who votes and who does not; who can purchase the means of influence and who cannot; who has historical reasons to believe they will be heard in the process if they take an active part and those whose history has taught them not to bother because they will not be heard anyway; and other inequities in the process. Liberals believe in tolerance of all differences, views and opinions, with no judgment. In fact, liberals often deny differences all together. This makes liberals wonderful, kind, accepting friends and relatives, but it also means that the more powerful forces in a liberal society are free to increase their power without being judged or limited.

Liberal ideology is the dominant one in Canada. To the right of liberal thought is the conservative minority, who believe in a God-given hierarchy that is the only "right" way to run a society. To the left is the progressive, or radical, minority who believe that equality is yet to be achieved and requires radical systemic change. Sometimes the conservative and radical minorities in Canada are more comfortable with each other than with the liberal majority, in spite of their opposed views — at least both groups have a sense of right and wrong that can be defined. Liberals are much harder, if not impossible, to pin down. The experience of social change workers in Canada is often one of "trying to nail jelly to the wall."

liberation: When an oppressed or exploited group or individual moves to change their situation, they are participating in a process of liberation. Sometimes the goal is to reverse the exploiting roles, sometimes it is to change the whole system of exploitation into one of cooperation. Both are still called liberation in common English. When I use the word I mean only the struggle to change exploitation to cooperation.

marginalized/margins: Groups that have a history of oppression and exploitation are pushed further and further from the centres of power that control the shape and destiny of the society. These are the margins of society, and this is the process of marginalization.

matrilineal: A social system where children trace their ancestry and take their name from their mother.

mentally challenged: See physically or mentally challenged/disabled/able-bodied.

Métis: See Aboriginal, Native, Indigenous, First Nations, Métis.

middle class: I usually put the term "middle class" in quotation marks because I am deliberately using the term inaccurately. According to Marx, the middle class is made up of those who own wealth such as land, factories and rental properties. In other words, the middle class is the capitalist class. However, many Canadians use the term vaguely. Most often we use it when referring to white-collar workers, people with a university degree or people whose income is above the poverty level but below "rich." In anti-poverty work, "middle class" has come to mean those who have an education and/or a job and are, at least for the time being, out of poverty. The "middle class" are those who can be allies to those living in poverty. In this book, I am using the term in this way.

military: This refers to armies, police and other armed forces. Military power is the use of armed forces.

misogyny: See sexism/misogyny

money/income/wealth: Money or income is the amount of currency a person has or gains from employment or another means such as interest, inheritance and grants. Wealth is money invested in the means of production, that is, money invested in order to make more money.

monogamous: Sexuality within a monogamous relationship is limited to two people. Within a patriarchal system, monogamous relationships between one man and one woman are the only acceptable kind. See heterosexism/homophobia.

multinational or transnational corporation: A multinational or transnational corporation (often abbreviated to simply "multinational" or "transnational") is a large company or group of companies operating in more than one country. They often have vast economic power, which they use to obtain political, military and ideological power. In this century multinationals have achieved power beyond the control of any individual government. In fact, they control some governments and heavily influence others. They are the most powerful institutions in the world today. See Chapter 3.

mythology: A collection of beliefs and stories about the past or about a group of people in the present. These beliefs and stories are a powerful part of ideology.

native: See Aboriginal, Native, Indigenous, First Nations, Métis.

North: See South/North

oppression/oppressor/oppressed: Oppression occurs when one group of people uses different forms of power to keep another group in a powerless position in order to exploit them (or an individual keeps another in a powerless position for the same purpose). The oppressor uses the power; the oppressed are exploited.

pagan: A person who follows one of the old earth-based religions. The term comes from the Latin word for "countryside" and developed during the centuries when European cities and educated classes had become Christian, but the rural people still followed the old ways.

patriarchy: Put most simply, patriarchy is a system where males are dominant.

patrilineal: A social system where children trace their ancestry and take their name from their father.

people of colour: See Black/African-Canadian/African-Nova Scotian/people of colour/racialized people/visible minorities/immigrant people/white people.

people with disabilities: The large and varied group known as people with disabilities includes people who suffer from completely different forms of oppression. Those who move with the aid of wheelchairs face different types of discrimination from those who suffer chronic pain, those whose mental abilities are different from the majority or those who are Deaf. Therefore, different disability-based oppressions should not be thrown together, when advocating for services. Any joint action among the various groups must be organized carefully, as a coalition rather than one group with completely common interests. However, for purposes of analyzing the underlying patterns of oppression, I have put all the different forms of disability-based oppression together, because I feel that they all have a common base — a society with war-making at its heart, therefore placing a high value on physical ability. Friends who suffer from this form of oppression have taught me that it is important to say, "people with disabilities" rather than "disabled people." The latter suggests that people with disabilities are not complete as people.

physically or mentally challenged/disabled/able-bodied: Physically or mentally challenged or disabled refers to a person whose oppression is based on a physical or mental difference. The able-bodied are those who are privileged by oppression of the physically challenged. I do not know a word for those who are privileged by oppression of the mentally challenged. I use the phrase physically or mentally challenged or disabled as well as the older term, people with disabilities.

political: In Nova Scotia, when people use the term "political," they are usually referring to a connection with a political party. I use the word much more broadly, including any activity that gives a person or group more or less voice in the process of making decisions that affect the society we live in.

politically correct: In the 1970s, this was a self-deprecating term used by people involved in social change. By the 1990s, the term had a negative connotation of "holier than thou." It has become a backlash term, intended to reduce struggles for justice and equity to a matter of enforced false politeness.

popular education: Also called "action/reflection learning" and "conscientization," this is a "school" of adult education based on a socialist understanding of class and oppression. It is directed at people who are marginalized from the resources and benefits of society. Its aim is to help people question the worldview that they learn from the oppressor, replacing it with analysis and action for social change based on the experience of the oppressed.

Unlike most other forms of adult education, the action component is integral. Learning in popular education is depicted as a cycle or spiral including experience, reflection, analysis and action. The spiral is illustrated in Chapter 9. Developed in Africa, Latin America, the Caribbean, Pacific Islands and Asia, popular education came to North America primarily through voluntary international development and solidarity organizations. See Chapter 9.

prejudice: See racism/prejudice

private ownership: Private ownership refers to an individual owning and controlling the means of production, that is, land, factories and so on. The objects a person owns and uses in everyday life — clothes, a bicycle, a house, a car, a piano and the like — are not included in private ownership. These are one's personal property.

racialized people: See Black/African-Canadian/African-Nova Scotian/people of colour/racialized people/visible minorities/immigrant people/white people.

racism/prejudice: Racism is structural oppression based on colour. The term can be used to include oppression based on language or religion, but I have used other terms for these — language-based oppression, religious oppression and anti-Semitism. Racism is a social/political/economic system that privileges white people. The form practised by individuals is racial prejudice.

queer: A relatively new term for LGBT people, not acceptable in all settings, but catching on quickly. As a writer, I think this may be because it reduces a long string of words — lesbian/gay/bisexual/transgendered/transsexual/two-spirited — to a single syllable.

reverse discrimination: The perception that employment equity or political correctness is causing members of the traditionally dominant cultural group (historically Euro-Canadians or even more specifically, white Anglo-Saxon males) to be discriminated against. Often this is a perception of opportunity denied or of minorities unfairly hired or promoted over more qualified white candidates (Agger-Gupta 1997).

reproductive capacity: The ability to produce the next generation. One of the purposes of sexism is to give men control over women's reproductive capacity.

resources: Resources are what people need to accomplish anything. They include land, food, forests, fish, money, skills, information, knowledge, social mobility and so on.

Roma or Romany people: A wandering people of Europe, originating in India, now spread all over the world. They have been severely oppressed by white European-descended people for centuries and still are today. The outsiders' name for them is Gypsies.

separation/connection: Separation is the basis for oppression, competition, conquest and hierarchy. It is the belief that people are independent, and actions can be taken in isolation, without affecting everyone and everything. Connection is the opposite. It is the belief that everything is linked — nothing can happen to one that does not affect all. It is unthinkable to oppress or exploit another person in a system of connection.

sex: See gender/sex Sexism is the political/economic/social/ideological system that privileges men and oppresses women; misogyny is hatred, fear and mistreatment of women by individual men.

sexual orientation: This refers to a person's emotional, physical and/or sexual attraction to people of their own or the opposite sex. See gay/lesbian/bisexual/heterosexual, heterosexism, transgendered, transsexual and two-spirited.

South/North: The world is divided into South and North as a result of centuries of colonialism. The Northern countries, particularly in Europe and North America, are industrialized and predominantly white; the Southern countries, particularly in Asia, Africa, Latin America, the Caribbean and the Pacific, live by selling raw materials and are populated predominantly by racialized people.

"South" is replacing the earlier descriptor "Third World." Third World began as a proud self-naming. It was adopted by twenty-nine post-colonial states at the African-Asian Conference in Bandung, Indonesia, in 1955 to express their determination not to be drawn into the Cold War divisions of East and West (Singham and Hume 1986; Mortimer 1980). However, the term was picked up by North Americans and made into a hierarchy — First World (the capitalist North), Second World (the socialist North) and Third World (the South). As a result, many people of the South have rejected "Third World" along with "underdeveloped," "developing" and "less developed." All of these terms deny the process by which the North deliberately "un-develops" the South through oppression and exploitation.

standardization: Societies centred around industrial production and war need to establish sameness — in trees, crops, manufactured goods, administrative systems and people — for purposes of automation and control. This is one of the sources of all forms of oppression, particularly that of physically and mentally challenged people.

straight: This is a common slang term for heterosexual people.

street children: In both the South and the North, there are children (as well as adults) who are destitute and homeless. They survive as best they can by petty trading, drug dealing and prostitution. These are "street children." There are millions of them in the world today, testimony to the low value placed on children in the world's dominant political/economic/ideological system. See Chapter 5, note 1.

struggle: Struggle refers to the ongoing efforts of oppressed people to achieve liberation.

synthesis: See analysis/synthesis

tokenism: A dominant group sometimes promotes a few members of an oppressed group to high positions and then claims there are no barriers preventing any member of that group from reaching a position with power and status. The people promoted are tokens and the process is called tokenism. Tokens can also be used as a buffer between the dominant and oppressed groups. It is harder for the oppressed group to name the oppression and make demands when members of their own group are representing the dominant group. An organization can place tokens in competition with one another, with some characterized as "good" and others as "bad." This is a way of reinforcing the behaviour the institution requires of those who would assimilate (Kanter 1977, 1993).

The term "token" can have a negative connotation, implying criticism of oppressed group members who choose or are forced into token positions. As Tim Wise says, the criticism should be applied to the game, not those forced to play it (2009).

Tokenism can also refer to the adoption of "politically correct" terminology and appearances to disguise the lack of change to structures of wealth, power and status.

I made an extensive analysis of tokenism in the sequel to this book, *Beyond Token Change* (2005).

transgendered: This is a term that includes a wide variety of people who do not fit clearly into the male/female gender division of Western patriarchal culture. Some people included in this group are transsexuals (see definition below), cross-dressers/transvestites, drag queens, androgynes (people with physical traits of both male and female) and intersex people (people with primary sex characteristics of both male and female, that is, chromosome, hormone or genital features, formerly called "hermaphrodites"). Transgendered people can also be referred to as gender variant or queer.

transsexual: Some people have a strong sense that they have been born into the wrong body. Their identity is female, but their body is male, or the other way around. Such people are referred to as "transsexual." Some choose to live publicly as the gender indicated by their body, some choose to dress and live as the gender of their identity, despite the sex of their body. Some pursue medical treatment, such as hormones and surgery, to change their body to fit their identity. Transsexual people suffer from the oppression of heterosexism. They can share in some issues with gay/lesbian/bisexual people, but in other cases, their issues are separate.

two-spirited: In the belief systems of some First Nations, there are more than two genders. Some have seven genders, some nine. Each of these genders involves a different combination of the characteristics Western society defines as "masculine" or "feminine." In the middle of this range of genders are people who are equally "male" and "female." These are the "two-spirited" people. In many Aboriginal cultures, two-spirited people were held in high esteem. In some, they were thought to have particular spiritual gifts and were trained to be spiritual leaders and healers. In many cultures, not only North American Aboriginal, but all over the world, two-spirited people had or still have particular roles, for example, as caregivers for children. Some two-spirited people are what the mainstream culture would define as gay/lesbian/bisexual, but not all. A two-spirited nature encompasses much more than just sexual orientation. It is a complete gender identity. (This information was given by Tuma Young, a two-spirited Mi'kmaw gay man, at a workshop on two-spirited people, Atlantic Gay/Lesbian/Bisexual Conference, Halifax NS, 1993. See also Roscoe 1988.)

unemployed: See employed/unemployed.

violence: I use the word "violence" in the broadest sense, that is, any action by a person or group that causes harm or is against the interests of any other person or group. The extreme form of violence involves physical force, but there are more subtle means as well — threats, damage to self-esteem, humiliation, cruel humour, withholding resources, ignoring needs, making someone invisible, providing and controlling addictive substances.

visible minorities: See Black/African-Canadian/African-Nova Scotian/people of colour/racialized people/visible minorities/immigrant people/white people.

wealth: See money/income/wealth.

white people: See Black/African-Canadian/African-Nova Scotian/people of colour/racialized people/visible minorities/immigrant people/white people.

witch: Witch comes from the Anglo-Saxon word "wicce." Some authors say wicce means "to bend or shape," others say it simply means "wise." A witch is a spiritual leader in European pagan traditions. Witches can be male or female. Witches were once healers and female witches acted as midwives. Many people accused of being witches were imprisoned, tortured and burned to death during the witch hunts of the fourteenth to eighteenth centuries. Most of those who were persecuted were women. After this time, pagan traditions went underground and witches became a Halloween caricature of evil. Halloween itself is a remnant of the European pagan tradition. The last day of October was celebrated as Sahmain, the end of the year, the time when the "veil between the worlds" was at its thinnest. Both the tradition and the witches are now re-emerging. See the case study on the Enclosure Movement in England in Chapter 2.

Appendix

Toolkit

This toolkit provides a small selection of group exercises which I have used for many years in ally education. They are "tried and true," and I give you advice from my experience on what they can and cannot accomplish. Some of the exercises come from specific resource books and websites where you will find many other ideas and techniques for ally education. I list a few at the end of the Toolkit section. The three handouts illustrated in this section — "Flower of Power," "Iceberg" and "Building a Social Change Strategy" — along with the "Spiral" illustrated in Chapter 9, are available in a full-page format on my website <www.becominganally.ca>.

Flower of Power, Powerline and Step Forward, Step Back

History: Flower of Power was invented by Enid Lee (1985) and further developed by members of the Doris Marshall Institute in Toronto (Arnold et al. 1991: 87). I learned Powerline from Eileen Paul of Resourcewomen. Step Forward, Step Back exists in many forms and places. The version I use comes from the website "Organizing for Power, Organizing for Change" <organizingforpower.org/anti-oppression-resources-exercises>.

Use: These exercises are useful in the Naming and Reflection components of the popular education process and work with both willing and unwilling participants.

Description: Flower of Power is a handout, illustrated below. Each participant receives a copy. In the centre of the flower, various forms of oppression, such as sex, race, ethnicity and age, are listed. The inner petals are blank. Participants fill in their own social identity in relation to each form of oppression listed in the centre — are they male or female; white or racialized, LGBT or straight; have they suffered from ethnic oppression. In the original exercise, the outer petals are also blank; working together, participants fill in the group they think are dominant in our society in regard to each oppression. If the time for the exercise is short or if you suspect the group will spend all their time arguing about which group is dominant and miss the point of the exercise, the outer

Flower of Power

petals can be filled in before the flower is photocopied for the participants.

After the inner and outer petals are filled in, it is helpful to have participants colour in the sections where their inner and outer petals match with one translucent marker or highlighter, the pairs where they do not match with another. This makes the participants' experiences of oppression and privilege in different parts of their identities stand out vividly.

Powerline is an alternative to Flower of Power. Participants are asked to imagine a line drawn down the middle of the floor. One side has power and privilege, the other side is oppressed. As different forms of oppression are called out, people go to one side of the line or the other. For example, when the issue is sex, men go to the privileged side of the line, women to the oppressed side. When we are considering ethnicity, those who have experienced oppression by another ethnic group go to one side, and those who have experienced being in a dominant ethnic group go to the other. There are sometimes people in the middle who have experienced both or neither side of a given form of oppression.

In Step Forward, Step Back, participants begin on the same line drawn across the room. They step forward or back in response to a series of questions. For example, step forward if your family owned their own home, or step back if your family taught you that police are something to be feared.

A note of caution applies to all three of these exercises. People often have to, or prefer to, keep their identities in some of these categories hidden. Don't ask participants to step forward or back, or to one side of the line, on issues such as sexual orientation, addiction, psychiatric diagnosis or childhood abuse. It works to mention the category as one that has an impact on people's experience of oppression or dominance and explain why you are not asking people to move in response to the question. I have had people upset because this approach denied them the opportunity to "come out," but most are grateful and the point is made regardless.

Flower of Power works best when group members are intellectually oriented and all have literacy skills. Powerline and Step Forward, Step Back are more active, bring laughter and energy into the workshop and avoid the question of who in the group cannot read and write the dominant language. Flower of Power provides more room for learning about which groups are dominant in our society; Powerline gives less room for this discussion and is useful when you think a group is likely to spend all of its time debating who is dominant, diverting attention from the primary lesson of the exercise, that is, that we all have experience on both sides of the line. As mentioned above, the discussion of which group is dominant can also be avoided with Flower of Power if the inside spaces are already filled out before the flower is copied for the participants. Step Forward, Step Back can provide the surprise necessary to begin engaging hostile participants.

All three exercises give a good starting point from which participants can reflect on their experiences on both sides of the line and the lessons learned on each side that can be useful when one is on the other side. The group can focus their discussion around the questions: "What did you learn from filling out Flower of Power/participating in Powerline/Step Forward, Step Back?" "What are your experiences in the areas where you are a member of the oppressed group?" "What are your experiences when you are a member of the dominant group?" and "What have you learned from your experiences of oppression that could be useful to you when you are the oppressor trying to become an ally?"

In my experience, these exercises quickly bring out participants' readiness to learn to be allies. People who are already allies will have no problem with the premise of the exercise, moving quickly into reflection. People with a liberal worldview will argue with the exercise's structure-based ordering into oppressed and dominant groups. People who are guilty will use the information that surfaces in the exercise to be hard on themselves. Deniers will become angry about sorting themselves into oppressor and oppressed. Backlashers will resist the process altogether. Regardless of the response, the exercise serves to introduce the basic concept of structural dominance and oppression and can stimulate a discussion of our different group histories and identities.

Differences

History: Differences was created by the brilliant Tiagi (Sivasailam Thiagarajan) and is included in *Tiagi's 100 Favourite Games* (2006).

Use: Differences works in the Naming component of a session, with willing or unwilling participants.

Description: In the Differences exercise, participants answer the question "I am a(n)..." ten times, listing their responses on a piece of paper. These are placed on a central table, written side down. Each person picks up someone else's list and, using a handout of categories such as "age," "activity level," "gender," "language," "profession" and "marital status," places each response in a category. Together the group gathers information on what category was most common for a first response, what categories were most common overall, which identities are associated with dominant or oppressor groups, whether dominant or oppressor identities were more common on people's lists, etc. The exercise provides information for naming the makeup and attitudes of the group and can lead to reflection on membership in oppressed or dominant groups.

Barnga

History: Barnga is another simulation game developed by Tiagi (1990).

Use: This is one of my favourite exercises for the Reflection component of a workshop. It is fun and produces an amazing number of insights in just forty-five to ninety minutes. It works with a range of approaches from cross-cultural communication to anti-oppression. Above all, it provides the kind of laughter and surprise that can turn a hostile group of backlashers around and get them started on the right foot early in a session.

Description: Barnga, named after a West African town where Tiagi learned a powerful lesson in cross-cultural collaboration, is based on a card tournament. Because the impact of the exercise depends entirely on surprise, if I give it away, your experience will be spoiled should you have the opportunity to take part. I hope you do have this opportunity, but even if you do not and need a dependable exercise for all groups, especially hostile ones, order the game manual from Intercultural Press, P.O. Box 700, Yarmouth, ME 04096 USA.

Oppression/Privilege Reflection

History: This exercise emerged from various facilitation teams I have been part of.

Use: This form of Oppression/Privilege Reflection, as its name suggests, is useful in the Reflection component of a session. It can follow Flower of Power, Powerline or Step Forward, Step Back and works only with willing participants.

Description: At the beginning of the exercise, people are asked to form small groups of two to six members who experience the same form of oppression. This can be done in an open "marketplace" style, where one person might call out "Who would like to work with me on language oppression?" and another person, or several others join them. When the groups are formed, each gathers around a sheet of flipchart paper to answer the question: "I know I am in the presence of _____ (the form of oppression chosen) when ..." For example, "I know I am in the presence of body image oppression when someone makes a nasty comment about my dress size." The group should label their page with a heading at the top and fill in as many indicators of that form of oppression as they can fit on the page.

When the groups have filled their pages, put them up on the wall with enough room between them to fit in another set of flipchart sheets. Ask each group to share what they have written. If there is time, allow them to expand upon their points and answer clarifying questions from the rest of the group.

After all the groups have spoken, ask the participants to form new groups, also with two to six people in them, based on shared membership in a dominant group. Again the "marketplace" method can be used. This time, ask the groups to complete the sentence: "What privileges do we get from being _____?" For example, "What privileges do we get from being white?"

When they have filled their pages, have them put them on the wall between the pages that are already there. If there is a pair, put them together; for example, if you have a page for oppression based on disability and one for the privileges of being able-bodied, put them side-by-side. Again, ask each group to present their page, expanding and answering clarifying questions if there is time.

When all the pages have been presented, put up three flipchart pages labelled "Oppression" "Privilege" and "Both." Ask the group to identify patterns that they see in the sheets on the wall. For example, a pattern under the heading "Oppression" might be "Stigmatization, assumed to be bad and inferior." A pattern under the heading "Both" might be "Rigid boundaries, no shades of grey." Under the heading "Privilege," the participants in a 1996 workshop saw one pattern as: "See yourself more (in the media, etc.) but recognize yourself less!" Take time to discuss the patterns. When there are as many patterns identified as you have time for, ask the question: "What can we learn from our experiences of oppression that helps us become allies when we are in the dominant group?"

Simulated Reversals

History: Blue Eyes, Brown Eyes was developed for a grade three class by Iowa teacher Jane Elliot in response to Martin Luther King's assassination in 1968. It has been used by her and many others in different settings all over the world ever since (Elliot 1971, 1985, 1995].[1] The Poverty Game (Monkman et al. 1983) was developed by a group of low-income single mothers in Dawson Creek, B.C. Imaginary Journey comes from Cooper Thompson's *A Guide to Leading Introductory Workshops on Homophobia* (1990).

Use: Simulated reversals are exercises that put the participants from a dominant group briefly and partially into the shoes of those who suffer that form of oppression. They belong in the Reflection component of the workshop and work equally well with willing and unwilling participants. Unwilling participants will react with anger. Help them see that the injustice they have briefly tasted is the full-time experience of the oppressed group.

Description: Sometimes just listening to members of the oppressed group tell stories about their experience can be a reversal in itself, since it is unusual for members of the oppressor group to listen to the stories of the oppressed. Participants sometimes react with anger and a feeling of being "silenced," "made powerless" and "forced to listen." These responses provide an excellent opportunity to help participants understand that these experiences and feelings are common for members of the oppressed group. Listening to stories can also bring out feelings of guilt. It is important to reflect on this response, making clear the distinction between feeling guilty (bad, wrong — a liberal response) and taking responsibility for changing a structural inequality that is not your fault but gives you unfair privileges.

Other reversals take place in structured simulation exercises. An excellent example is the Blue Eyes, Brown Eyes simulation for understanding racism. The Association of Black Social Workers of Nova Scotia has used this exercise effectively in their racism workshops. When participants arrive, they are divided according to eye colour. Brown-eyed people are taken into the meeting room and given a briefing on the next exercise, a quiz on Black history in Nova Scotia. People with lighter eye colours stay in the hallway. They are told to line up against the walls, standing, and refrain from talking to each other. Conversation draws an immediate rebuke from the supervisor of the hallway.

When the blue-eyed people are allowed into the meeting room, they sit around the edges of the room, behind the brown-eyed people. The Black history quiz begins. The brown-eyed people, already briefed, have the answers and are praised for giving them. A blue-eyed student is occasionally recognized.

If the answer is correct, they are told: "That's pretty good for someone with blue eyes." If their answer is not correct, the hapless person is belittled and told: "What can you expect from blue-eyes?" The effect is very rapid. When I went through the exercise it took me about ten minutes to completely lose my self-confidence and begin making wrong answers even when I knew the correct ones.

When the issue is poverty, an excellent reversal simulation is the board game and workshop The Poverty Game (Monkman et al. 1983). A group of low-income single mothers in Dawson Creek, B.C. developed the game from their own experience. A group of Halifax, N.S. low-income single mothers used it as the basis of a one-day poverty workshop they presented to church groups, social services staff and the boards of public housing communities. They played the role of social workers, challenging participants on some bit of money they may have been given or won, insisting they pay it back, pulling them out of the game to inspect their homes for signs of a live-in boyfriend and making them miss turns while waiting to see their worker. Participants were furious. Many insisted, "You're making this up," and were shocked when the leadership team told them the stories from their own lives on which they had based their actions. One wealthy man, sitting on a public housing board as his contribution to charity, became so frustrated with his situation in the game that he spent the debriefing session repeating: "There was no way out. I couldn't find a way out."

Another way to bring about a reversal is through a well done guided fantasy. An example is Imaginary Journey. Participants are instructed to shut their eyes and are led though a series of short relaxation exercises followed by an imaginary journey through a typical workday in a world where same-sex relationships are the norm. Heterosexuals must hide and lie to preserve their jobs, apartments, loved ones and personal safety. Fantasies can put people deeply into an imaginary experience. They should be led only by a facilitator experienced with the method.

Any kind of reversal simulation requires plenty of time for reflection afterwards. Debriefing follows the spiral — a mini-spiral within the larger spiral of the overall design. Participants are guided through reflection (What happened? How did you feel about it? etc.), analysis (Why did it happen this way? Who benefitted? Who had power? Who had to live with the results?) and strategy (What can we do about it? Who would be our allies? etc.)

Analysis Questions

History: One of the basic tools of popular education.

Use: In the Analysis component of a workshop, participants are asked to do the hard work of figuring out who benefits, who pays the price, who has power, where are they vulnerable and all the other questions that will round out their understanding of the experience they are reflecting upon.

Description: Analysis questions are usually worked out in advance by the facilitator or facilitation team and presented on a flipchart or handout. Participants can develop their own questions or add to those already provided by the leaders. Usually the participants are divided into small groups to discuss the questions, reporting back verbally if the reports will not be long. Few exercises can put a group to sleep more quickly than long report-backs. Alternative methods of reporting can involve posting flipchart sheets on the wall or publishing a photocopied "newsletter" while the group is on break or at lunch.

The following is a general set of analysis questions on the power dynamics of oppression and privilege:

- What do people in a dominant group gain from oppression? (or white people from racism, men from sexism, straight people from heterosexism, depending on the topic of the workshop)
- What do people in a dominant group lose from oppression?
- What responsibility do people in a dominant group have to end the oppression? What power do people in the dominant group have to end the oppression?
- What do those who suffer from a particular form of oppression need from members of the dominant group?
- What do people in the dominant group need from those who suffer from the oppression in order to help end it?

Iceberg

History: I developed this particular version of Iceberg to teach the concept of structural oppression. I have seen others use various forms of it to demonstrate unconscious biases, individual personality and group culture, and other concepts where the larger part of the dynamic is difficult to see.

Use: The purpose of this version of Iceberg is to communicate the structural nature of oppression.

Description: Iceberg includes a handout, reproduced in this book, but I don't always use it, or I sometimes give it out after the talk or during the next break. This leaves me free to build the talk around the language and illustrations that have emerged during the group's discussion up to that point.

Iceberg is a talk, but it must build on questions and discussion designed to bring out participants' understanding of oppression and privilege. I find it helpful to divide the class into groups to discuss questions chosen to solicit a different response from someone with a liberal worldview than from someone with a structural worldview. If the session has a focus on one form of oppression, for example, racism, the questions, of course, will relate to that form of oppression. If the workshop or course is more general in its approach to anti-oppression, I find it more effective to have each group discuss a different form of oppression. One table might discuss ableism while another discusses heterosexism. Here are my favourite questions:

- What kind of things make you think "That person is racist (sexist/heterosexist/etc.)?
- Are you racist (sexist/heterosexist/etc.)?
- What is "reverse discrimination"?
- Can racialized people be racist towards white people (women be sexist towards men/etc.)?

In response to the first question, participants with a liberal worldview will list aspects of attitude and personal treatment. They will be reluctant to call themselves racist, sexist or any other form of dominant-group discrimination,

The Iceberg
Personal and Structural Levels of Oppression

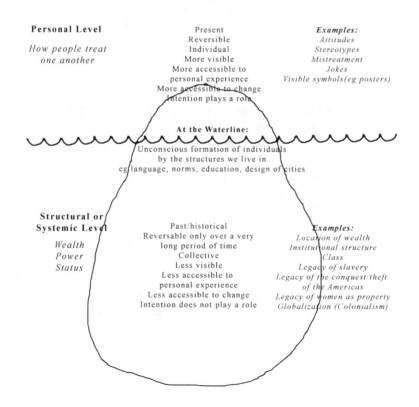

Personal Level

How people treat one another

Present
Reversible
Individual
More visible
More accessible to personal experience
More accessible to change
Intention plays a role

Examples:
Attitudes
Stereotypes
Mistreatment
Jokes
Visible symbols(eg posters)

At the Waterline:
Unconscious formation of individuals by the structures we live in eg language, norms, education, design of cities

Structural or Systemic Level

Wealth
Power
Status

Past/historical
Reversable only over a very long period of time
Collective
Less visible
Less accessible to personal experience
Less accessible to change
Intention does not play a role

Examples:
Location of wealth
Institutional structure
Class
Legacy of slavery
Legacy of the conquest/theft of the Americas
Legacy of women as property
Globalization (Colonialism)

except perhaps admitting to unintentional offence. They will believe that "reverse discrimination" exists and that the oppressed group can be racist, sexist, etc. toward members of the dominant group. Participants with a structural worldview are more likely to name the impact of policy, tradition, language, history, wealth and power in response to the first question, will understand that, as a member of a dominant group, they participate in the oppression whether they intend to or not and will grasp that an historical/structural relationship of dominance cannot be reversed in any timeframe short of many decades or centuries. In my experience, the discussion groups report back almost universally from a liberal point of view.

This discussion provides the basis for drawing the iceberg shape and waterline on a flipchart. I label the section above the water as the "Personal Level," defined by how people treat one another, and the section below the waterline as the "Structural Level," defined by wealth, power and status. Then I begin filling in other details as opposites:

- the personal level is easier to see, the structural level harder;
- the personal level is accessible to personal experience; the structural level must be figured out through analysis;
- the personal level assumes that the "majority rules"; on the structural level, more often the "minority rules," because a minority holds the institutional wealth, power and status;
- the personal level is individual; the structural level is collective;
- the personal level takes place in the present, but history made the structural level. Even when the individuals who took the actions and made the decisions that shaped it are long gone, the patterns of wealth, power and status they created continue to impact people's lives, taking from some and giving to others. I sometimes use the image of a perpetual motion machine. The maker dies, but the mechanism continues operating, doing whatever it was designed to do, with no one's hand on the controls;
- intention can play a role at the individual level; it is irrelevant at the structural level;
- the individual level is easier to change than the structural level, because many will change their attitudes, but few will willingly give up wealth, power and status;
- the personal level is reversible, because anyone can treat anyone else badly, no matter who or what they are; the structural level does not reverse except over centuries because, like the perpetual motion machine, it was created to benefit one group at the expense of another and continues operating, even after its original makers pass on.

To illustrate the last point, I often talk about my experience working with

Canadian volunteers returning from Africa, Asia and Latin America. The white volunteers would claim that they had experienced racism, because they now knew what it felt like to be the only white person on the bus, or have everyone notice them and remember their mistakes. However, during the two years they were overseas, the 80 percent of the world's resources consumed by the Northern countries did not suddenly flow back to the South, and if there had been a catastrophe, like an earthquake, the Canadian government would have used its resources, far greater than the resources of the host country, to find them first and get them to safety, or if a political disruption threatened the lives of local people, the Canadian government would get them out as soon as possible. Certain privileges travel with North Americans and Europeans no matter where we go, because we have citizenship in countries that have inherited the "white" side of colonialism.

Other examples come from the discussion that has already taken place in the workshop. For example, one group, answering the question about reverse discrimination, gave an example of a straight couple insulted in a gay bar. That is bad treatment and would be hurtful to anyone; however, there are probably a hundred other bars they can go to in the city. If the same thing happened to a LGBT couple, they might not have other options for an evening out. Also, the straight couple would not immediately think of the long history of others like themselves beaten to death for what they are and feel frightened, as any LGBT couple would.

Another example is a brilliant, concise illustration of the difference between individual and structural equality, which I have borrowed from Robert Upshaw of the Black Educators Association of Nova Scotia <www.theblackeducators.ca>. He compares Black people achieving legal equality with gaining the right to join a Monopoly game. When his people arrived on the board, every property was already bought up, with houses and hotels built on them.

When discussing the question, "Are you racist/sexist/ etc.?" my favourite illustration uses the fact that I am a white settler in relation to Aboriginal people. At the personal level, I try my best to be respectful to and supportive of Aboriginal people, although there is another factor, which I illustrate just at the waterline of the iceberg, and that is my unconscious and ignorant responses.

At the structural level, however, I have received benefits all my life, not only from the assumptions people automatically make about me because of my white skin, but because of the access to resources, income, education and opportunities that my ancestors received from the citizenship and land they were granted when they came to Canada. I have inherited all those advantages and continue to benefit from them, but whose land was that? What recompense has ever been made for the impoverishment of Aboriginal people when that land was taken from them and given to us? At this point I talk about how the phrase "I am racist" may not be totally accurate to describe this permanent, irreversible structural advantage I have, and introduce the phrase "white privilege."

Returning at some point to the waterline, I talk about how being constantly surrounded by messages about white superiority reinforces my unconscious biases, messages I don't even notice because they are invisibly encoded into the English language, our legal system, images in the media, the schooling I received and simply because privilege is invisible. I encourage people to visit the Project Implicit website at Harvard University <implicit.harvard.edu> where they can take tests designed to make their unconscious biases visible. I confess what a humbling experience it was, and continues to be, for me to check my unconscious attitudes out from time to time by taking these tests.

By this point in the talk, most people have grasped the concept of structural oppression and privilege and are depressed. It is time to talk about change. I draw a child's sun in the upper corner, make a joke about the fact that I am not praising global warming, and begin to talk about "melting the iceberg." The sun has access to the part of the iceberg that is above the water. Attitudes, stereotypes, language and biases are much easier to change than wealth, power and status. However, as the top layers melt away, the iceberg rises. Elements of the structural inequity that were hidden because they were so "normal" become more visible. For example, when an educational institution adopts an affirmative action admission policy to encourage groups that have not traditionally been able to enter their courses of study, at first the newer groups are simply happy to be there. It is later, when some of the immediate, personal barriers have been overcome, that deeper questions emerge, such as: "Why are we not reflected in the curriculum?" "Why are we assigned stereotyped projects?" and "Why, when we have any trouble at the school, is it assumed we are poor students until proven otherwise?" At this point, the institution/iceberg must make a decision. Will it continue to change, reaching ever deeper to transform its structures of wealth (resources), power (governance) and status, or will it halt, choosing not to progress beyond token change, or even reverse direction, choosing a scapegoat to blame and expel, claiming to be changed while protecting the oppression/privilege relations at the structural heart of the organization? I wrote about this process in detail in the sequel to this book, *Beyond Token Change* (2005).

I often draw a little stick person standing on top of the iceberg and talk about the discouragement I sometimes see among people who have been leading institutional change for many years. "Why are we not making any progress?" they ask. "When we started out, I thought we'd be finished in ten years, but it just gets harder." When I hear questions like these, I ask what the battles were when they started out and what they are now. Usually, the early battles were at the personal level, over respectful treatment and sometimes involving open protest when groups not traditionally included in the organization first arrived. Current battles tend to be more structural, over governance, use of resources, changes in policy or deeply entrenched privilege within the organization. Using the iceberg metaphor, it is easy to see that the little person on top cannot see the organization's progress, because as they work at melting the top layers, the iceberg is rising, bringing ever deeper structural levels to light. They perceive no change, because the distance from their perch to the waterline remains the same.

Discussion about personal and structural change is also an appropriate time to talk about the difference between guilt and responsibility. Guilt is shame over some action that was a choice, something intentional or in our control. Responsibility refers to holding ourselves accountable for a wrong that we inherited from the generations who went before us. A common and relevant quote is: "If not me, then who? If not now, then when?"[2]

Another point to be made is the difference between liberal and structural notions of accountability for change. If one takes a liberal approach, to do nothing means no responsibility for harm. It is like floating on an air mattress in the middle of a lake. If you don't paddle, you stand still. You are neutral, not involved. According to a structural approach, the harm is happening regardless, moving forward as a result of historical injustice. It is more like riding an air mattress down a flowing river. If you are not paddling against the current, you are going with it. There is no standing still. You are either part of the problem or part of the solution.

The river image is also useful for explaining why there is often conflict between those who take a liberal approach to change and those who take a structural approach. A liberal approach tries to relieve individuals' suffering. A structural approach looks for root causes. An old story tells of two people walking along a river when they see a young child trying to swim against the current, but being carried relentlessly downstream. They immediately wade in and save the child. Then they spot another child and save him, then another, and another, and another. Finally, one of the people says to the other: "I have to go upstream and see where these children are coming from."

The other objects: "But if you leave, I won't be able to save all the children Despite feeling badly about walking away as her friend flounders in and out of the water trying desperately to save every child, the first person leaves and walks upstream. There she finds a wharf reaching out into the current and an adult throwing children into the water. She runs back to convince her friend that they must work together to stop the person on the wharf.

When my task was to teach employees about employment equity policy, I found I could use Iceberg to help people understand that employment equity, a form of affirmative action, is not "reverse discrimination." I would explain that other laws and policies such as human rights legislation and anti-harassment policies are about individual's treatment of one another. They address the part of the iceberg above the waterline and apply to everyone. The purpose of employment equity and affirmative action on the other hand, is to overcome historical discrimination and achieve structural change in institutions and their distribution of wealth, power and status. When women, racialized people, people with disabilities and other oppressed groups have the same access to wealth, power, status, employment, resources, choices and benefits as members of the historically dominant group, the policy becomes obsolete.

An example is the *Pandora* case, which came before a Nova Scotia Human Rights Tribunal in 1992. *Pandora* was a publication by, for and about women. In 1990, the volunteer collective responsible for the magazine refused to publish a letter by a male author. He took the case to the Nova Scotia Human Rights Commission, where it was accepted as a case of discrimination. *Pandora* based its case on the Canadian Charter of Rights and Freedom's provision that allows a disadvantaged group to band together to "remedy or alleviate their disadvantage," a classic definition of affirmative action. A series of expert witnesses testified to women's lack of access to the media, the publishing industry and the field of journalism relative to men. The Tribunal ruled that *Pandora's* policy of publishing only the work of women was permissible. By definition, if and when the same kind of challenge might be brought in a time and place where this basic inequity did not exist, the ruling would go the other way. The point of affirmative action, as well as its specific expression in employment equity policies, is not to advantage women over men, but to correct women's structural disadvantage until a "level playing field" is achieved (Christensen-Ruffman 1995: 378).

After using it for many years, I know this Iceberg talk is effective. Many participants in workshops and courses, even those who already knew the language of structural oppression, speak during the closing reflection about what a revelation the iceberg metaphor was to them and what a difference it will make in their understanding of equity.

Skills

Another important aspect of educating allies is building participants' skills for identifying and responding to oppression. Possible activities include examining our everyday language, identifying the keys to recognizing oppression, developing role-plays of typical situations in different settings, and working with clippings or photographs to develop awareness of oppression. These exercises can be used in the Reflection, Analysis or Strategy parts of the workshop and are best with willing participants. Participants with denial or backlash tendencies will disrupt the exercise by arguing with the basic premise. This can be turned into learning, but takes a great deal of time from more open participants that could better be spent doing other things.

In the racism workshop I developed with Valerie Carvery (Bishop and Carvery 1994) we used an exercise from Judith Katz (1978: 115–16) to reflect on racism in language. Small groups list all the words or phrases they can think of with "light," "fair" or "white" in them; then all they can think of with "dark" or "black" in them. Next they mark which of these have a negative and which a positive connotation. They share their lists and reflect on them. This exercise invariably makes people take a new look at language they have always taken for granted. It can also lead to a discussion of liberal/individual discrimination versus structural oppression. Participants with a liberal worldview will focus on the intent of those using words with an oppressive history, their innocence because they were not aware of the buried meaning. In a structural worldview, the development of language and its subsequent impact on those who use it is structural and unconscious. It is another "perpetual motion machine," not dependant on any individual's intension for its effect.

For identifying oppression at work in various settings, we include an exercise from the Doris Marshall Institute called When I See, Hear, Feel (Arnold et al. 1991: 89–90; cuso 1988). In small groups, participants complete the sentences: "When I see … when I hear … when I feel … I know that racism is at work."

Working with photographs and clippings can be fun and revealing. It is depressingly easy to collect a portfolio of examples of any form of oppression. You can then make several copies for participants to analyze in small groups and report back. The challenge is to see how many examples they can find in the documents they have been given.

Strategy and Action

This is my favourite handout for working with a group to develop a strategy for action. It outlines a detailed and time consuming process. If there is less time, the Spiral, illustrated earlier in this toolkit, works well.

Closing

Closing exercises need to be short, fun and summarize the experience in some way. For example, ask people to sum up their feelings about the workshop in one sentence or even one word, and then have each say their sentence or word in rap-rhythm, to the accompaniment of everyone clapping their hands and snapping their fingers.

Another method uses a ball of yarn. One person sums up their feelings about the workshop and throws the ball to someone else, holding on to the yarn. The next person says how they feel and throws the ball, again hanging on to the yarn. At the end you have a web of yarn woven back and forth, connecting everyone in the group. Comment on the connections among you, and lay the web carefully on the floor.

Building a Social Change Strategy

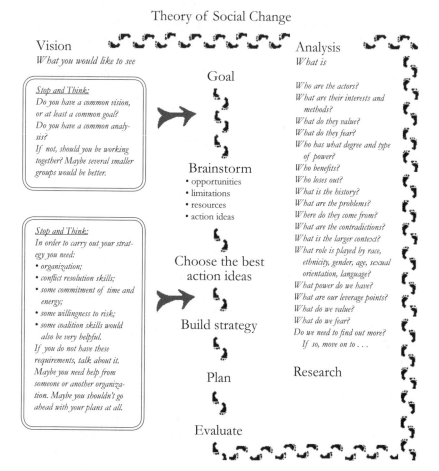

Theory of Social Change

Vision
What you would like to see

Stop and Think:
Do you have a common vision,
or at least a common goal?
Do you have a common analy-
sis?
If not, should you be working
together? Maybe several smaller
groups would be better.

Stop and Think:
In order to carry out your strat-
egy you need:
• organization;
• conflict resolution skills;
• some commitment of time and
energy;
• some willingness to risk;
• some coalition skills would
also be very helpful.
If you do not have these
requirements, talk about it.
Maybe you need help from
someone or another organiza-
tion. Maybe you shouldn't go
ahead with your plans at all.

Goal

Brainstorm
• opportunities
• limitations
• resources
• action ideas

Choose the best
action ideas

Build strategy

Plan

Evaluate

Analysis
What is

Who are the actors?
What are their interests and
methods?
What do they value?
What do they fear?
Who has what degree and type
of power?
Who benefits?
Who loses out?
What is the history?
What are the problems?
Where do they come from?
What are the contradictions?
What is the larger context?
What role is played by race,
ethnicity, gender, age, sexual
orientation, language?
What power do we have?
What are our leverage points?
What do we value?
What do we fear?
Do we need to find out more?
If so, move on to . . .

Research

Other Sources

There are many, many learning exercises appropriate for use in ally education. I have contributed exercises to the following collections:

CUSO Education Department. 1985/88. *Basics and Tools: A Collection of Popular Education Resources and Activities.* Ottawa: CUSO.

Bishop, Anne, and Valery Carvery. 1994. *Unlearning Racism: A Workshop Guide to Unlearning Racism.* Halifax, NS: OXFAM/Deveric.

Bishop, Anne, with Jeanne Fay. 2004. *Grassroots Leaders Building Skills: A Course in Community Leadership.* Black Point, NS: Fernwood.

A few more of my favourite sources are:

Arnold, Rick, Bev Burke, Carl James, D'Arcy Martin, and Barb Thomas. 1991. *Educating for a Change*. Toronto: The Doris Marshall Institute for Education and Action and Between the Lines Press.

Central Vancouver Multicultural Society Diversity Team. *Diversity Resources*. <www.diversityteam.org/resources>.

Curry-Stevens, Ann. 2003. *An Educator's Guide for Changing the World: Methods, Models and Materials for Anti-oppression and Social Justice Workshops*. Toronto: Centre for Social Justice <www.socialjustice.org/uploads/pubs/EducatorsGuideforChangingtheWorld.pdf>.

Lopes, Tina and Barb Thomas. 2006. *Dancing on Live Embers: Challenging Racism in Organizations*. Toronto: Between the Lines.

National Campus and Community Radio Association, 2013. *Anti-oppression Toolkit: Workshop and Exercise Outlines for Anti-oppression Training at Community Radio Stations* <www.ncra.ca/equity>.

Organizing for Power, Organizing for Change. *Anti-oppression Resources and Exercises* <organizingforpower.org/anti-oppression-resources-exercises>.

Thiagarajan, Sivasailam. 1990. *Barnga*. Yarmouth, ME: Intercultural Press.

____. 2003. *Design Your Own Games and Activities*. San Francisco: John Wiley and Sons.

____. 2006. *Tiagi's 100 Favourite Games*. San Francisco: John Wiley and Sons.

I encourage you to check out other resources in book form and on the Internet, participate yourself in ally education and learn from experienced practitioners what works for them.

notes

1. A film, entitled *The Eye of the Storm*, recording the original Blue Eyes, Brown Eyes experiment, was made in 1971 (Elliot 1971). In 1985 PBS Frontline interviewed the students fifteen years later and produced a documentary called *A Class Divided* (Elliot 1985). More recently, the video *Blue Eyed* (Elliot 1995) includes footage of a group of adults participating in the exercise and an interview with Jane Elliot. There is also a book on the exercise, including interviews with the original grade three students twenty years later (Peters 1987). Another powerful video of a classroom experiment in learning about race and class, useful in the education of allies, is *War Between the Classes* (1985), from Marlin Motion Pictures, 211 Watline Ave., Mississauga, ON, L4Z 1P3.

2. This quote appears in many places, usually accredited as "paraphrased" or "derived from" first-century Jewish scholar Hillel the Elder, who said: "If I am not for myself, who will be for me? If I am only for myself, what am I and if not now, when?"

References

Abella, Irving. 1974. *On Strike: Six Key Labour Struggles in Canada, 1919–1949*. Toronto: James Lewis and Samuel.

Ackbar, Mark, Jennifer Abbot and Joel Bakan. 2003. *The Corporation*. (Movie) <www.thecorporation.com> or watch the whole movie on YouTube.

Agger-Gupta, Neils. 1997. *Terminologies of Diversity*. Edmonton: Alberta Community Development, Government of Alberta.

Allen, Paula Gunn. 1986. *The Sacred Hoop: Recovering the Feminine in American Indian Traditions*. Boston: Beacon Press.

Allen, Richard. 1973. *The Social Passion: Religion and Social Reform in Canada, 1914–1928*. Toronto: University of Toronto Press.

Allen, Robert C. 1992. *Enclosure and the Yeoman*. Oxford: Clarendon.

Altman, Denis. 1989. "Fear and Loathing." *New Internationalist* 201 (November).

Anderson, Sarah (ed.). 2000. *Views from the South*. Chicago: Food First Books and International Forum on Globalization.

Anonymous. 2011. "Can We Stop Using the Term Ally?" *The Queer Proletariat*. <http://thequeerproletariat.tumblr.com/post/3985274011/can-we-stop-using-the-term-ally>.

Arnold, Rick, Deborah Barndt and Bev Burke. 1985. *A New Weave: Popular Education in Canada and Central America*. Toronto: Ontario Institute for Studies in Education.

Arnold, Rick, and Bev Burke. 1983. *A Popular Education Handbook: An Educational Experience Taken from Central America and Adapted to the Canadian Context*. Toronto: Ontario Institute for Studies in Education.

Arnold, Rick, Bev Burke, Carl James, D'Arcy Martin and Barb Thomas. 1991. *Educating for a Change*. Toronto: Between the Lines.

Asher, Shirley Joseph. 1988. "The Effects of Childhood Sexual Abuse: A Review of the Issues and Evidence." In Lenore E. Walker (ed.), *Handbook on Sexual Abuse of Children: Assessment and Treatment Issues*. New York: Springer.

Badgley, R.F. 1988. *Child Sexual Abuse in Canada: Further Analysis of the 1983 National Survey*. Ottawa: Heath and Welfare Canada.

Bakan, Joel. 2004. *The Corporation: The Pathological Pursuit of Profit and Power*. New York: Free Press.

____. 2011. *Childhood Under Siege: How Big Business Targets Children*. Toronto: Penguin.

Barlow, Maude, and Tony Clarke. 1998. MAI *Round 2: New Global and Internal Threats to Canadian Sovereignty*. Toronto: Stoddart.

Barnet, Richard, and Ronald Muller. 1974. *Global Reach*. New York: Simon and Schuster.

Barnett, Walter. 1979. *Homosexuality and the Bible*. Wallingford, PA: Pendle Hill Publications.

Barry, Kathleen. 1979. *Female Sexual Slavery*. New York: Avon Books.

____. 1985. "Social Etiology of Crimes Against Women." *Victimology: An International Journal* 10.

Bartlett, John. 1980. *Familiar Quotations: A Collection of Passages, Phrases and Proverbs Traced to Their Sources in Ancient and Modern Literature*. Boston: Little Brown and Company.

Bell, Myrtle P., Mary Connerley, and Faye K. Cocchaiara. 2008. "The Case for Mandatory Diversity Education." Briarcliff Manor, NY: Academy of Management Learning and Education/Pace University. <dopey.cs.vt.edu/courses/grad5984-F11/readings/Academia/2008-Bell-A%20Case%20for%20Mandatory%20Diversity%20Education.pdf>.

Bishop, Anne. 2005. *Beyond Token Change: Breaking the Cycle of Oppression in Institutions*. Black Point, NS: Fernwood.

Bishop, Anne, and Valery Carvery. 1994. *Unlearning Racism: A Workshop Guide to Unlearning Racism*. Halifax, NS: OXFAM/Deveric.

Bishop, Anne, with Jeanne Fay. 2004. *Grassroots Leaders Building Skills: A Course in Community Leadership*. Black Point, NS: Fernwood.

Blackbridge, Persimmon, and Sheila Gilhooly. 1985. *Still Sane*. Vancouver: Press Gang.

Blackstock, Cindy. 2003. "First Nations Child and Family Services: Restoring Peace and Harmony in First Nations Communities." In Kathleen Kufeldt and Brad McKenzie (eds.), *Child Welfare: Connecting Research Policy and Practice*. Waterloo: Wilfrid Laurier University Press.

Blackstock, Cindy, and Nick Trocmé. 2005. "Community Based Child Welfare for Aboriginal Children: Supporting Resilience Through Structural Change." *Social Policy Journal of New Zealand* 24 (March).

Blumenfeld, Warren J. (ed.). 1992. *Homophobia: How We All Pay the Price*. Boston: Beacon Press.

Bowles, Paul, and Henry Veltmeyer (eds.). 2014. *The Answer Is Still No: Voices of Pipeline Resistance*. Black Point, NS: Fernwood.

Boyd, Jocelyn, and the Metro Committee for a Non-Racist Society. 2004. *Racism: Whose Problem? Strategies for Understanding and Confronting Racism in Our Communities*. Second edition. Halifax: Metro Committee for a Non-Racist Society.

Bregman, Peter. 2012. "Diversity Training Doesn't Work." *Harvard Business Review* March 12. <blogs.hbr.org/2012/03/diversity-training-doesnt-work>.

Brickman, Julie. 1984. "Feminist, Non-Sexist and Traditional Models of Therapy: Implications for Working with Incest." *Women and Therapy* 3.

____. 1992. "Female Lives, Feminist Deaths: The Relationship of the Montréal Massacre to Dissociation, Incest and Violence Against Women." *Canadian Psychology* 3, 2 (April).

Brignall, Tom III. 2002. "The New Panopticon: The Internet Viewed as a Structure of Social Control." *Theory and Science* 3. <theoryandscience.icaap.org/content/vol003.001/brignall.html>.

Brock-Utne, Birgit. 1973. *Sexual Suicide*. New York: Quadrangle Press.

____. 1981. "The Soldier and the Mother." Paper prepared for UNESCO experts meeting, New Delhi, July 11–12.

Brooks, Imelda. 1991. "What I Remember: Residential School Memories Never Forgotten." *Micmac Maliseet Nations News* 2, 5 (May).

Brown, Nancy. 1982. "Conditions Under Which Racial Learning Occurs." NTL *Reading Book for Human Relations Training*. NTL Institute.

Butler, Sandra. 1978. *Conspiracy of Silence: The Trauma of Incest.* San Francisco: Volcano Press.

Cahill, C., S.P. Llewelyn, and C. Pearson. 1991. "Long Term Effects of Sexual Abuse Which Occurred in Childhood: A Review." *British Journal of Clinical Psychology* 30.

Calhoun, Sue. 1983. *The Lockeport Lockout: An Untold Story in Nova Scotia's Labour History.* Halifax: Oxfam Canada Atlantic Region.

Campbell, Mary. 1991. "Natives Carry Scars of Residential School." *Micmac Maliseet Nations News* 2, 3 (March).

Canadian Council on the Status of Women. 1987. *Battered but Not Beaten: Preventing Wife Battering in Canada.* Ottawa: Canadian Advisory Council on the Status of Women.

Canadian Centre for Justice Statistics. 2001, 2002, 2003, 2007. *Family Violence in Canada: A Statistical Profile.* Ottawa: Statistics Canada.

Canadian Centre for Policy Alternatives. 2012. "The 99% vs the 1%." (Infographic) <www.policyalternatives.ca/publications/commentary/infographic-99-vs-1>.

Carniol, Ben. 2010. *Case Critical: Challenging Social Services in Canada.* Sixth edition. Toronto: Between the Lines.

Carty, Victoria. 2009. "SMOs, Cyberactivism and Entertainment as Politics: How MoveOn Is Expanding Public Discourse and Political Struggle." In David Fasenfest (ed.), *Engaging Social Justice: Critical Studies of Twenty-First Century Social Transformation.* Chicago: Haymarket.

CBC. 2013. "The Real Avatar." *The Nature of Things.* <www.cbc.ca/natureofthings/episodes/the-real-avatar>.

Chossudovsky, Michel. 2013. "The Anti-Globalization Movement and the World Social Forum: Is Another World Possible?" <www.globalresearch.ca/the-anti-globalization-movement-and-the-world-social-forum-another-world-is-possible/5335181>.

Christiansen-Ruffman, Linda. 1995. "Women's Conceptions of the Political: Three Canadian Women's Organizations." In Myra Marx Ferree and Patricial Yancy Martin (eds.), *Feminist Organizations: Harvest of the New Women's Movement.* Philadelphia: Temple University Press.

Clark, Campbell. 2013. "Canada Falls Out of Top 10 in U.N.'s Human Development Index." *Globe and Mail* March 14. <www.theglobeandmail.com/news/national/canada-falls-out-of-top-10-in-uns-human-development-index/article9758218/>.

Clarke, Tony. 2002. *Blue Gold: The Battle Against the Corporate Theft of the World's Water.* Toronto: Stoddart.

Coffin Jr., William Sloan. 1983. "Homosexuality: A Sermon by Dr. William Sloan Coffin." In Committee on Gay and Lesbian Concerns, Hartford Meeting, Society of Friends, *Study Packet on Gay and Lesbian Concerns.* Hartford, MA.

Cole, Susan. 1989. *Pornography and the Sex Crisis.* Toronto: Amanita.

Coles, Robert, and Jane Hallowell Coles. 1990. *Women of Crisis II.* Reading, MA: Addison-Wesley.

Committee on Sexual Offences Against Children and Youths (The Badgley Committee Report). 1984. *Sexual Offences Against Children.* Ottawa: Supply and Services Canada.

Conlogue, May. 1991. "Different Views of the Montréal Massacre." *Globe and Mail* Dec. 4.

Connell R.W. 2005. *Masculinities.* Second edition. Berkley: University of California Press.

Counts, David R., and Dorothy A. Counts (eds.). 1991. *Coping With the Final Tragedy.* Amityville, NY: Baywood.

Courtois, Christine A. 1988. *Healing the Incest Wound: Adult Survivors in Therapy.* New

York: Norton.

Courtois, Christine A., and Judith E. Sprei. 1988. "Retrospective Incest Therapy for Women." In Lenore E. Walker (ed.), *Handbook on Sexual Abuse of Children*. New York: Springer Publishing.

Cripps, Joanne. 2001. *Deaf Culture*. Toronto: Deaf Culture Centre. <www.deafculturecentre. ca/public/Default.aspx?I=294&n=Deaf+Culture>.

Curry-Stevens, Ann. 2005. "Pedagogy for the Privileged: Transformation Processes and Ethical Dilemmas." Canadian Association for the Study of Adult Education 2005 National Conference Online Proceedings. <casae-aceea.ca/~casae/sites/casae/ archives/cnf2005/2005onlineProceedings/CAS2005Pro-Curry-Stevens.pdf>.

CUSO. 1988. *Racism: A Cooperant Preparation Workshop*. Ottawa: CUSO.

Dworkin, Andrea. 1981. *Pornography: Men Possessing Women*. New York: Perigee Books.

Easlea, Brian. 1987. "Patriarchy, Scientists and Nuclear Warriors." In Michael Kaufman (ed.), *Beyond Patriarchy: Essays by Men on Pleasure, Power, and Change*. New York: Oxford University Press.

Eisler, Riane. 1990. *The Chalice and the Blade*. San Francisco: Harper.

Elghawaby, Amira. 2012. "Musings on the State of Women's Equality in Canada: Based on a True Forum." *Rabble.ca* Nov. 13. <rabble.ca/news/2012/11/musings-state-womens-equality-Canada-based-true-forum>.

Elliot, Jane. 1971. *Eye of the Storm*. ABC News. <www.trainerstoolchest.com/show_product. php?idnum=464>.

____. 1985. "A Class Divided." PBS Frontline. <www.pbs.org/wgbh/pages/frontline/ shows/divided>.

____. 1995. "Blue Eyed." Video, 90 minutes. California Newsreel. <www.trainerstoolchest. com/show_product.php?idnum=315>.

Eltantawy, Nahed, and Julie B. Weist. 2011. "The Arab Spring/The Egyptian Revolution: Considering Resource Mobilization Theory." *International Journal of Communication* 5. <ijoc.org/index.php/ijoc/article/view/1242>.

Emcheta, Buchi. 1989. "Natural Gesturers." *New Internationalist* November 11–12.

Enloe, Cynthia. 1983. *Does Khaki Become You? The Militarization of Women's Lives*. Boston: South End Press.

Faderman, Lillian. 1981. *Surpassing the Love of Men: Romantic Friendship and Love Between Women from the Renaissance to the Present*. New York: William Morrow.

Faguy, Steve. 2013. "The New Convergence Utopia: Who Owns What in the Canadian Media." <blog.fagstein.com/2013/07/03/media-ownership-chart>.

Farber, Bernie. 2013. "Why We Can No Longer Call Canada an Advocate for Human Rights." *Huffington Post* Jan. 2. <www.huffingtonpost.ca/bernie-farber/canada-human-rights-record_b_2598003.html>.

Fasenfest, David (ed.). 2009. *Engaging Social Justice: Critical Studies of Twenty-First Century Social Transformation*. Chicago: Haymarket.

Fidler, Richard. 1978. *RCMP: The Real Subversives*. Toronto: Vanguard Publications.

Findlay, Barbara. 1991. *With All of Who We Are*. Vancouver: Lazara.

Finkelhor, David. 1979. *Sexually Victimized Children*. New York: Free Press.

____. 1994. "Current Information on the Scope and Nature of Child Sexual Abuse." *The Future of Children* Summer/Fall 1994.

Fontaine, Theodore. 2010. *Broken Circle: The Dark Legacy of Indian Residential Schools: A Memoir*. Victoria: Heritage House.

Frank, Blye. 1987. "Hegemonic Heterosexual Masculinity." *Studies in Political Economy* 24, 15.

Freeland, Chrystia. 2012. *Plutocrats: The Rise of the New Global Super-Rich and the Fall of Everyone Else.* Toronto: Doubleday.

Freire, Paulo. 1970. *Pedagogy of the Oppressed.* New York: Seabury.

____. 1972. *Cultural Action for Freedom.* Harmondsworth, UK: Penguin.

____. 1973. *Education for Critical Consciousness.* New York: Seabury.

Gehl, Lynn. Undated. "Ally Bill of Responsibilities." <www.lynngehl.com>.

Gelday, Katherine. 1990. "The Famine Within." Video. Montréal: National Film Board of Canada, Studio D.

George, Susan. 1976. *How the Other Half Dies: The Real Reasons for World Hunger.* New York: Penguin.

____. 1988. *A Fate Worse Than Debt.* San Francisco: Food First.

____. 2004. *Another World Is Possible If …* London: Verso.

____. 2010. *Whose Crisis, Whose Future.* Cambridge, UK: Polity Press.

____. 2013. *How to Win the Class War: The Lugano Report II.* Washington: Transnational Institute.

Gerbaudo, Paolo. 2012. *Tweets and the Streets: Social Media and Contemporary Activism.* London: Pluto Press. <dl.acm.org/citation.cfm?id=2462754>.

Gimbutas, Marija. 1982. *Goddesses and Gods of Old Europe.* Berkeley: University of California Press.

____. 1989. *The Language of the Goddess.* San Francisco: Harper and Row.

Gonner, E.C.K. 1966. *Common Land and Enclosure in England 1450–1850.* London: Frank Cass.

Göttner-Abendroth, Heide (ed.). 2009. *Societies of Peace: Matriarchies: Past, Present and Future.* Toronto: Inanna.

____. 2012. *Matriarchal Societies: Studies on Indigenous Cultures Around the Globe.* New York: Peter Lang.

Grahn, Judy. 1984. *Another Mother Tongue: Gay Words, Gay Worlds.* Boston: Beacon Press.

Gramsci, Antonio. 1988. *Antonio Gramsci Reader: Selected Writings, 1916–1935.* New York: Schocken Books.

Green, Margaret. 1987. "Women in the Oppressor Role: White Racism." In Sheila Ernst and Marie Maguire (eds.), *Living with the Sphinx: Papers from the Women's Therapy Centre.* London: Women's Press.

Griffith, Gwyn. 1982. "Images of Interdependence: Meaning and Movement in Learning/Teaching." EdD thesis, University of Toronto.

Gruen, Arno. 1987. *The Insanity of Normality: Realism as Sickness—Toward Understanding Human Destructiveness.* New York: Grove Weidenfeld.

Guillén, Ligia. 1979. *Los Niños de Nicaragua.* Costa Rica: Editorial Universitaria Centroamericana.

Haig-Brown, Celia. 1988. *Resistance and Renewal: Surviving the Indian Residential Schools.* Vancouver: Arsenal Pulp Press.

Haiven, Max. 2014. *Crises of Imagination, Crises of Power: Capitalism, Creativity and the Commons.* Black Point, NS: Fernwood.

Halifax *Daily News.* 1992. "A Kinder, Gentler Kind of Warfare." Feb. 16.

____. 1993. "Pumsy the Dragon: Boosting or Brainwashing?" Apr. 4.

Halifax *Mail Star.* 1992. "The Tailhook Affair: U.S. Navy Lands Its Biggest Scandal." Sept. 18.

Hamilton, T. 1995. *A Guide to Key Anti-Racism Terms and Concepts*. Second edition. Toronto: Anti-Racism Secretariat of Ontario.

Hanmer, Jalna, and Mary Maynard (eds.). 1987. *Women, Violence and Social Control*. Atlantic Highlands, NJ: Humanity Press International.

Hanson, R.F., H.S. Resnick, D.G. Kilpatrick, and C.L. Best. 1999. "Factors Related to Reporting of Childhood Rape." *Child Abuse and Neglect* 23: 559–69.

Harrison, David. 1981. *The White Tribe of Africa: South Africa in Perspective*. Berkeley: University of California Press.

Heinbecker, Paul. 2010. "Security Council Failure Was of Canada's Own Making." *Ottawa Citizen*, Oct. 13. <www2.canada.com/ottawacitizen/news/archives/story. html?id=b5257f25-7446-4644-8bb6-5e8207795308>.

Helms, Janet E. (ed.). 1990. *Black and White Racial Identity: Theory, Research, and Practice*. Westport, CT: Praeger.

Hennessey, Trish. 2014. "Hennessey's Index: Inequality." ccpa *Monitor* 20, 8.

Henry, Frances. 1973. *Forgotten Canadians: The Blacks of Nova Scotia*. Toronto: Longman.

Hill, Christopher. 1972. *The World Turned Upside Down: Radical Ideas During the English Revolution*. New York: Viking.

Hoagland, Sarah L. 1988. *Lesbian Ethics*. Palo Alto, CA: Institute of Lesbian Studies.

Hood, Bruce. 2012. *The Self Illusion: How the Social Brain Creates Identity*. Toronto: Harper Collins.

hooks, bell. 1990. *Yearning: Race, Gender and Cultural Politics*. Toronto: Between the Lines.

Howard, P.N., A. Duffy, D. Frelon, M. Hussain, W. Mari and M. Mazaid. 2011. "Opening Closed Regimes: What Was the Role of Social Media During the Arab Spring?" Seattle: Project on Information Technology and Political Islam. <pitpi.org/index. php/2011/09/11/opening-closed-regimes-what-was-the-role-of-social-media-during-the-arab-spring>.

Huysamer, C., and E.M. Lemner. 2013. "Hazing in Orientation Programs in Boys-Only Secondary Schools." *South African Journal of Education* 33, 3. <www.ajol.info/index. php/saje/article/viewFile/91936/81396>.

IshiyamaIshu. 2006. *Anti-Discrimination Response Training: Leaders' Manual*. Framingham, MA: Microtraining.

Jackins, Harvey. 1973. *The Human Situation*. Seattle: Rational Island Publishers.

James, Carl. 1989. *Seeing Ourselves: Exploring Race, Ethnicity and Culture*. Toronto: Sheridan College.

Jensen, Robert. 1998. "White People Need to Acknowledge Benefits of Unearned Privilege." *Baltimore Sun*. <lilt.ilstu.edu/gmklass/pos334/..%5Cfoi/read2/unearned_privilege

____. 1999. "More Thoughts on Why the System of White Privilege Is Wrong." *Baltimore Sun*, July 4 <uts.cc.utexas.edu/~rjensen/freelance/whitefolo.htm>.

____. 2002. "I know I am racist but…" <uts.cc.utexas.edu/~rjensen/freelance/notracist. htm>.

____. 2005. *The Heart of Whiteness: Confronting Race, Racism and White Privilege*. San Francisco: City Lights.

____. 2007. "The Problem with Solutions." Common Dreams.org <uts.cc.utexas. edu/~rjensen/freelance/lastsunday2.html>.

Johnson, Allan G. 2005a. *The Gender Knot: Unravelling Our Patriarchal Legacy*. Philadelphia: Temple University Press.

____. 2005b. *Privilege Power and Difference*. New York: McGraw-Hill.

Johnson, Beverly D. 1991. "Black Perspectives on Foster Care: A Project Exploring the Experience of Foster Care Placement on Black Children Placed in White Foster Homes." MSW thesis, Maritime School of Social Work, Dalhousie University, Halifax, NS.

Johnson, Carl E.K. 1988. "Retrospective Incest for Men." In Lenore E. Walker (ed.), *Handbook on Sexual Abuse of Children: Assessment and Treatment Issues*. New York: Springer.

Jung, C.G. 1966. *Two Essays on Analytical Psychology*. Princeton: Princeton University Press.

Kalev, Alexandra, Frank Dobbin and Erin Kelly. 2006. "Best Practices or Best Guesses? Assessing the Efficacy of Corporate Affirmative Action and Diversity Policies." *American Sociological Review* 71, 4 (August): 589–617. <scholar.harvard.edu/dobbin/files/2007_contexts_dobbin_kalev_kelly.pdf>.

Kanter, Rosabeth Moss. 1977. *Women and Men of the Corporation*. New York: Basic Books.

____. 1993. *A Tale of "O": Being Different*. Video produced by Barry M Stein. Boston: Goodmeasure Inc. <www.trainerstoolchest.com/show_product.php?idnum=356>.

Katz, Judith. 1978. *White Awareness: Handbook for Anti-Racism Training*. Norman, OK: University of Oklahoma Press.

Kaufman, Michael (ed.). 1987. *Beyond Patriarchy: Essays by Men on Pleasure, Power, and Change*. New York: Oxford University Press.

Kimmel, Michael. 2012. *Manhood in America: A Cultural History*. Third edition. New York: Oxford University Press.

____. 2014. *Angry White Men: American Masculinity at the End of an Era*. New York: Nation Books.

Kinzer, Stephen. 1991. *Blood of Brothers: Life and War in Nicaragua*. New York: Doubleday.

Kirkham,Kate. 1988/89. "Teaching About Diversity: Navigating the Emotional Undercurrents." *The Organizational Behavior Teaching Review* 13, 4.

Klein, Naomi. 2007. *The Shock Doctrine: The Rise of Disaster Capitalism*. Toronto: Alfred A. Knopf.

Kleinberg, Seymour. 1987. "The New Masculinity of Gay Men." In Michael Kaufman (ed.), *Beyond Patriarchy: Essays by Men on Pleasure, Power, and Change*. New York: Oxford University Press.

Knockwood, Isabelle, with Gillian Thomas. 2001. *Out of the Depths: The Experiences of Mi'kmaw Children at the Indian Residential School at Shubenacadie, Nova Scotia*. Third edition. Black Point, NS: Roseway Publishing.

Kohn, Alfie. 1986. *No Contest: The Case Against Competition*. Boston: Houghton Mifflin.

Kuyek, Joan Newman. 1990. *Fighting for Hope: Organizing to Realize Our Dreams*. Montréal: Black Rose.

Laidlaw, Toni Ann, Cheryl Malmo and Associates. 1990. *Healing Voices: Feminist Approaches to Therapy with Women*. San Francisco: Jossey Bass.

Lalonde, Michelle. 1991. "I Am Not a Feminist." *Montréal Gazette*, November 30.

Lambley, Peter. 1980. *The Psychology of Apartheid*. Athens, GA: University of Georgia Press.

Landry, Normand. 2014. *Threatening Democracy: SLAPPs and the Judicial Repression of Political Discourse*. Black Point, NS: Fernwood.

Lee, Enid. 1985. *Letters to Marcia: Anti-Racist Education in School*. Toronto: Cross Cultural Communication Centre.

Leemon, Thomas. 1972. *The Rites of Passage in a Student Culture*. New York and London: Teachers College Press.

Lerner, Harriet Goldhor. 1985. *The Dance of Anger: A Woman's Guide to Changing the Patterns of Intimate Relationships*. New York: Harper and Row.

Lill, Wendy. 1987. "The Occupation of Heather Rose." In Diane Bessai and Don Kerr (eds.), *NeWest Plays by Women*. Edmonton: NeWest Press.

____. 1991. *Sisters*. Vancouver: Talonbooks.

Lopes, Tina, and Barb Thomas. 2006. *Dancing on Live Embers: Challenging Racism in Organizations*. Toronto: Between the Lines.

Lorde, Audre. 1980. *Cancer Journals*. Argyle, NY: Spinsters Ink.

Lyttelton, Ned. 1983/4. "Men's Liberation: Men Against Sexism and Major Dividing Lines." *Resources for Feminist Research* 12, 4 (December/January).

MacDonald, Ann-Marie. 2014. "Love, Anger and Pride." *Globe and Mail*, June 21.

Macdonald, David. 2014. *Outrageous Fortune: Documenting Canada's Wealth Gap*. Ottawa: Canadian Centre for Policy Alternatives. <www.policyalternatives.ca/outrageous-fortune>.

MacKinnon, Catherine. 1987. *Feminism Unmodified: Discourses on Life and Law*. Cambridge, MA: Harvard University Press.

Malinowski, Bronislaw. 2001 [1927]. *Sex and Repression in Savage Society*. Milton Park, UK: Routledge Classics.

Mander, Jerry. 1991. *In the Absence of the Sacred: The Failure of Technology and the Survival of the Indian Nations*. San Francisco: Sierra Club.

____. 2012. *The Capitalism Papers: Fatal Flaws of an Obsolete System*. Berkeley: Counterpoint.

Mann, Edward, John Allen Lee, and Norman Penner. 1979. *RCMP vs. the People: Inside Canada's Security Service*. Toronto: General Publishing.

Marcus, Bruce, and Michael Taber (eds.). 1983. *Maurice Bishop Speaks: The Grenada Revolution, 1979–83*. New York: Pathfinder Press.

Martin, A. Damien. 1984. "The Perennial Canaanites: The Sin of Homosexuality." *Et Cetera* 41, 4.

McCaskell, Tim. 1988. "Racism as a White Problem." In *Facilitator's Handbook for Students' Multicultural/Multiracial Camp*. Toronto: Toronto Board of Education.

McDougall, Sheila. 1991. "Thank God for the Shubie School." *Micmac Maliseet Nations News* 2, 8 (August).

McGillivray, Don. 1990. "Men Must Face Massacre Reality." *Vancouver Sun*, November 19.

McIntosh, Peggy. 1990. "White Privilege: Unpacking the Invisible Knapsack." *Independent School* 49, 2 (Winter), available in many locations on the Internet including, for example, <amptoons.com/blog/files/mcintosh.html>.

McLeod Group (Alan Martin, Betty Plewes, Carolyn McAskie, Edward Jackson, Elizabeth J. McAllister, Hunter McGill, Ian Smillie, John Sinclair, Laura Macdonald, Mark Stiles, Rieky Stuart, Stephen Brown). 2013 "Making Choices: A Policy Agenda for International Cooperation in 2015 and Beyond." <www.mcleodgroup.ca>.

McMurtry, John. 2013. *The Cancer Stage of Capitalism: From Crisis to Cure*. Black Point, NS: Fernwood.

McQuaig, Linda. 1987. *Behind Closed Doors: How the Rich Won Control of Canada's Tax System and Ended Up Richer*. Markham: Viking.

____. 2001. *All You Can Eat: Greed, Lust and the New Capitalism*. Toronto: Viking.

____. 2010. *Holding the Bully's Coat: Canada and the United States Empire*. Toronto: Doubleday.

McQuaig, Linda, and Neil Brooks. 2012. *Billionaires Ball: Gluttony and Hubris in an Age of*

Epic Inequality. Boston: Beacon Press.

Mellor, John. 1983. *The Company Store: James Bryson McLachlan and the Cape Breton Coal Miners, 1900–1925*. Toronto: Doubleday.

Merchant, Carolyn. 1980. *The Death of Nature: Women, Ecology, and the Scientific Revolution*. San Francisco: Harper and Row.

Merriam-Webster Dictionary. <www.merriam-webster.com/dictionary/ally>.

Michener, James. 1980. *The Covenant*. New York: Random House.

Mies, Maria, and Vandana Shiva. 1993. *Ecofeminism*. Black Point, NS: Fernwood Publishing.

Miller, Alice. 1981. *Prisoners of Childhood: The Drama of the Gifted Child and the Search for the True Self*. New York: Basic Books.

____. 1983. *For Your Own Good: Hidden Cruelty in Child-Rearing and the Roots of Violence*. New York: Farrar, Straus and Giroux.

____. 1986. *Thou Shalt Not Be Aware: Society's Betrayal of the Child*. New York: New American Library.

Milloy, John S. 1999. *A National Crime: The Canadian Government and the Residential School System 1879 to 1986*. Winnipeg: University of Manitoba.

Mills, Lisa Nicole. 2002. *Science and Social Context: The Regulation of Recombinant Bovine Growth Hormone in North America*. Montreal: McGill-Queens University Press.

Mingay, G.E. 1990. *A Social History of the English Countryside*. London: Routledge.

____. 1997. *Parliamentary Enclosure in England: An Introduction to Its Causes, Incidence, and Impact, 1750–1850*. New York: Longman.

Monkman, Penny, Garth Tyler-Neher, and Joyce Tyler-Neher. 1983. "The Poverty Game." The Poverty Game, 2-956 Cornwall Crescent, Dawson Creek, B.C. V1G 1N9.

Morgan, Dan. 1979. *Merchants of Grain*. New York: Penguin.

Mortimer, Robert A. 1980. *The Third World Coalition in International Politics*. New York: Praeger.

Muszynski, Alicja. 1991. "What Is Patriarchy?" In Jesse Vorst et al. (eds.), *Race, Class, Gender: Bonds and Barriers*. Second edition (revised). Winnipeg: Society for Socialist Studies.

Nelson, Joyce. 2013. "The Harper Government's War on Science." *CCPA Monitor* 20, 2 (June).

Neufeld, Gordon, and Gabor Maté. 2005. *Hold On to Your Kids*. Toronto: Random House.

New Internationalist. 1989. "Pride and Prejudice: Homosexuality." 201 (November).

Niezen, Ronald. 2013. *Truth and Indignation: Canada's Truth and Reconciliation Commission on Indian Residential Schools*. Toronto: University of Toronto Press.

Nutt, Samantha. 2011. *Damned Nations: Greed, Guns, Armies and Aid*. Toronto: McClelland and Stewart.

O'Brien, Michelle. 2003. "Whose Ally? Thinking Critically About Anti-Oppression Ally Organizing." Colors of Resistance. <www.coloursofresistance.org/370/whose-ally-thinking-critically-about-anti-oppression-ally-organizing-part-1/> and <www.coloursofresistance.org/374/374>.

Obear, Kathy. 1990. *Opening Doors to Understanding and Acceptance: A Facilitator's Guide to Presenting Workshops on Lesbian and Gay Issues*. Cambridge, MA: Campaign to End Homophobia.

Obedkoff, Vicki. 1989. *Exploring Racism: Workshop Materials for Congregational Groups*. Toronto: United Church of Canada.

Okun, Tema. 2010. *The Emperor Has No Clothes: Teaching about Race and Racism to People Who Don't Want to Know*. Charlotte, NC: Information Age Publishing.

olsson, jona. 1997. *Detour Spotting for White Anti-Racists: A Tool for Change*. Questa, NM:

Cultural Bridges. <http://www.racialequitytools.org/resourcefiles/olson.pdf>.

Orbach, Susie. 1978. *Fat Is a Feminist Issue: A Self-Help Guide for Compulsive Eaters.* New York: Berkeley Books.

Pachai, Bridglal. 1987. *Beneath the Clouds of the Promised Land: The Survival of Nova Scotia's Blacks. Vol. 1, 1600–1800.* Halifax, NS: Black Educators Association.

Paton, Alan. 1982. *Ah, But Your Land Is Beautiful.* New York: Scribner.

Payne, Anthony, Paul Sutton and Tony Thorndike. 1984. *Grenada: Revolution and Invasion.* London: Croom Helm.

PBS (Public Broadcasting System). 1990. *Out in America.*

Personal Counsellors Inc. 1962. *Fundamentals of Co-counselling Manual: Elementary Counsellors Manual.* Seattle: Rational Island Publishers.

Peters, William. 1987. *A Class Divided, Then and Now.* Expanded edition. New Haven, CT, and London: Yale University.

Pharr, Suzanne. 1988. *Heterosexism: A Weapon of Sexism.* Oakland: Chardon Press.

Piketty, Thomas. 2014. *Capital in the Twenty-First Century.* Cambridge, MA: Belknap Press. <mpra.ub.uni-muenchen.de/52384/1/MPRA_paper_52384.pdf>.

Pogrebin, Letty Cottin. 1991. "Ain't We Both Women? Blacks, Jews and Gender." In *Deborah, Golda and Me: Being Female and Jewish in America.* New York: Crown Publishers.

Polster, Claire. 2014. "War on Science: Metaphor Apt But May Limit Our Thinking." CCPA *Monitor* 20, 8 (Feb).

Porto Alegre. 2013. "World Social Forum History." <www2.portoalegre.rs.gov.br/fsm2013_ing/default.php?p_secao=4>.

Raghavan, Iyer. 1973. *The Moral and Political Thought of Mahatma Gandhi.* New York: Oxford Press.

Regan, Paulette. 2011. *Unsettling the Settler Within: Indian Residential Schools, Truth Telling and Reconciliation in Canada.* Vancouver: UBC Press.

Reynolds, Malvina. 1975. "World in Their Pocket." New York: Schroeder Music.

Rich, Adrienne. 1978. *The Dream of a Common Language: Poems 1974–77.* New York: Norton

____. 1986. *Your Native Land, Your Life: Poems.* New York: Norton.

Richardson, Boyce (ed.). 1989. *Drumbeat: Anger and Renewal in Indian Country.* Toronto: Summerhill Press.

____. 1997. "Corporations: How Do We Curb Their Obscene Power?" "MAI? No Thanks! On-Line Library." <islandnet.com/plethora/mai/cancorp1.html>.

Robinson, Marcus, Delyte Frost, Joan Buccigrossi, Charles Pfeiffer. 2003. *Gender, Power and Privilege.* Rochester, NY: WetWare Inc. <www.workforcediversitynetwork.com/docs/Gender_4.pdf>.

Roscoe, Will (ed.). 1988. *Living the Spirit: A Gay American Indian Anthology.* New York: St Martin's Press. <www.willsworld.org>.

Rose, Suzanna. 1991. "The Contribution of Alice Miller to Feminist Therapy and Theory." *Women and Therapy* 11, 2.

Royal Commission on Aboriginal Peoples. 1996. *Report of the Royal Commission on Aboriginal Peoples, Chapter 10.* Ottawa: Minister of Supply and Services Canada. <www.aadnc-aandc.gc.ca/eng/1307458586498/1307458751962>.

Salter, Anna C. 2003. *Predators: Pedophiles, Rapists and Other Sex Offenders: Who They Are, How They Operate and How We Can Protect Ourselves and Our Children.* New York: Basic Books.

Salutin, Rick. 1980. *Kent Rowley, The Organizer: A Canadian Union Life*. Toronto: Lorimer.

Sanday, Peggy Reeves, and Mita Choudhury. 2003. *Women and the Centre: Life in a Modern Matriarchy*. Ithaca, NY: Cornell University Press.

Santayana, George. 2006 [1905]. *The Life of Reason: Five Volumes in One*. Fairford, Gloucestershire: Echo Library.

Sawatsky, John. 1980. *Men in the Shadows: The RCMP Security Service*. Toronto: Doubleday.

Schacht, Stephen P. 2001. "Teaching About Being an Oppressor: Some Personal and Political Considerations." <www.nostatusquo.com/Schacht/teaching.html>.

Schacht, Stephen P., and Doris Ewing. 1998. *Feminism and Men: Reconstructing Gender Relations*. New York: New York University Press.

Scheff, Thomas J. 1979. *Catharsis in Healing, Ritual, and Drama*. Berkeley: University of California.

Schwalbe, Michael. 1996. *Unlocking the Iron Cage: The Men's Movement, Gender Politics and American Culture*. London: Oxford University Press.

Sellars, Bev. 2013. *They Called Me Number One: Secrets and Survival at an Indian Residential School*. Vancouver: Talon Books.

Sherr-Klein, Bonnie, and Linda-Lee Tracy. 1981. "Not a Love Story." Video. Montréal: National Film Board of Canada, Studio D.

Shiva, Vandana. 2005. *Earth Democracy: Justice, Sustainability and Peace*. Cambridge, MA: SouthEnd Press.

____. 2010. *Staying Alive: Women, Ecology and Development*. Boston: SouthEnd Press.

Singh, Siddharth. 1993. "Indian Farmers Protest Cargill's Designs: Opposition to GATT Emerges." <www.larouchpub.com/eiw/public/1993/envir20n05-19930129/envir20n05-19930129_007-indian-farmers-protest-cargills.pdf>.

Singham, A.W., and Shirley Hume. 1986. *Non-Alignment in an Age of Alignments*. London: Zed Books.

Smith, William. 1978. *The Meaning of Conscientization: The Goal of Paulo Freire's Pedagogy*. Boston: University of Massachusetts Press.

Snodgrass, Jon (ed.). 1977. *A Book of Readings for Men Against Sexism*. Albion, CA: Times Change Press.

Some Angry Women. 1992. "Why Did Jane Hurshman Have to Die?" *New Maritimes* 10, 6 (July/August).

Somé, Malidoma Patrice. 1995. *Of Water and the Spirit: Ritual, Magic and Initiation in the Life of an African Shaman*. London: Penguin.

____. 2002. *The Healing Wisdom of Africa*. New York: Tarcher.

Sparks, Allister. 1990. *The Mind of South Africa*. New York: Knopf.

Spronk, Susan. 2006. "Roots of Resistance to Urban Water Privatization in Bolivia: The New Working Class, the Crisis of Neo-Liberalism and Public Services." <www.cpsa-acsp.ca/papers-2006/Spronk.pdf>.

Starhawk. 1982. *Dreaming the Dark: Magic, Sex and Politics*. Boston: Beacon Press.

____. 1987. *Truth or Dare: Encounters with Power, Authority, and Mystery*. San Francisco: Harper and Row.

____. 1993. *The Fifth Sacred Thing*. New York: Bantam.

Steinem, Gloria. 1992. *The Revolution from Within: A Book about Self Esteem*. Boston: Little, Brown and Co.

Stepanova, Ekaterina. 2011. "The Role of Information Communication Technologies in the 'Arab Spring': Implications Beyond the Region." *PONARS Eurasia Policy Memo*

No. 159 (May). <www.ponarseurasia.com/sites/default/files/policy-memos-pdf/pepm_159.pdf>.

Stoltenberg, Jon. 1999. *The End of Manhood: Parables on Sex and Selfhood*. London and New York: UCL Press.

____. 2000. *Refusing to Be a Man*. London and New York: UCL Press.

Swanson, Jean. 2001a. *Poor-Bashing: The Politics of Exclusion*. Toronto: Between the Lines.

____. 2001b. "Gap Between Rich and Poor Expands." *The Long Haul* VIII, 1 (April).

Swenarchuk, Michelle. 1999. *Liberalized Investment and Investor-State Suits: Threats to Government Powers*. Toronto: Canadian Environmental Law Association.

Telegraph. 2012. "G8 Summit: Protests Timeline." May 18. <www.telegraph.co.uk/news/worldnews/g8/9273813/G8-summit-protests-timeline.html>.

Thiagarajan, Sivasailam. 1990. *Barnga: A Simulation Game on Cultural Clashes*. Boston: Intercultural Press.

____. 2006. *Thiagi's One Hundred Favourite Games*. San Francisco: John Wiley.

Thomas, Barb. 1984. "Principles of Anti-racist Education." *Currents: Readings in Race Relations* 2:3 (Fall).

Thomas, Barb, and Charles Novogrodsky. 1983a. *Combatting Racism in the Workplace: A Course for Workers*. Toronto: Cross Cultural Communication Centre.

____. 1983b. *Combatting Racism in the Workplace: Readings Kit*. Toronto: Cross Cultural Communication Centre.

Thomas de Benitez, Sarah. 2011. *The State of the World's Street Children*. London: Consortium for Street Children. <www.streetchildrenresources.org/resourcesren-research/>.

Thompson, Audrey. 2003. "Tiffany, Friend to People of Colour: White Investments in Anti-Racism." *Qualitative Studies in Education* 16, 1: 7–29.

Thompson, Cooper. 1990. *A Guide to Leading Introductory Workshops on Homophobia*. Cambridge, MA: Campaign to End Homophobia.

Thwaites, R.C. (ed.). 1906. *The Jesuit Relations and Allied Documents*. 71 volumes. Cleveland, OH: Burrows Brothers.

Tolson, Andrew. 1977. *The Limits of Masculinity*. London: Tavistock.

Troiden, Richard. 1988. *Gay and Lesbian Identity: A Sociological Analysis*. Dix Hills, NY: General Hall.

Truth and Reconcilliation Commission of Canada. 2014. <www.trc.ca>.

Velasquez, Mauricio. 1998. "Why Diversity Training Must Change." Herndon, VA: The Diversity Training Group. <home.diversitydtg.com/article/basics/changes-in-diversity-training>.

Walker, James St. G. 1980. *A History of Blacks in Canada*. Ottawa: Supply and Services Canada.

Ward, Brian. 2014. "First Nations Fight Against the Frackers: The Mi'kmaq People of New Brunswick Against Texas Southwestern Energy Co." <www.globalresearch.ca/first-nations-fight-against-the-frackers-the-mikmaq-people-of-new-brunswick-against-texas-southwestern-energy-co-swn/5363944>.

Wikipedia. 2013. "Canadian Newspapers: Percentage Circulation by Ownership. <en.wikipedia.org/wiki/file:Canadian_Newspapers_circulation_by_ownership.pdf>.

____. 2014a. "Concentration of Media Ownership." <en.wikipedia.org/wiki/concentration_of_media2014b. "Occupy Movement." <en.wikipedia.org/wiki/Occupy_Movement>.

Wink, Walter. 1992. *Engaging the Powers: Discernment and Resistance in a World of*

Domination. Minneapolis: Fortress Press.

Winks, Robin. 1971. *The Blacks in Canada: A History*. New Haven, CT, and London: Yale University Press.

Winter, James. 2007. *Lies the Media Tells Us*. Montreal: Black Rose.

Wise, Tim. 2009. *Between Barack and a Hard Place: Racism and White Denial in the Age of Obama*. San Francisco: City Lights.

____. 2011. *White Like Me: Reflections on Race from a Privileged Son*. Berkely: Soft Skull Press. <www.timwise.org>.

Wright, Ronald. 1992. *Stolen Continents: The "New World" Through Indian Eyes*. Harmondsworth: Penguin.

Yelling, J.A. 1977. *Common Field and Enclosure in England 1450–1850*. London: Macmillan.

Index

ableism 1, 4, 13, 14-19, 50, 54, 62, 63, 65-66, 69, 74, 91, 116, 117, 133, 137, 138, 143, 144, 153

Aboriginal people 15, 21, 23, 29, 41, 49, 54, 56-57, 59, 60-61, 64, 69, 71, 72, 77, 88, 98-99, 107, 122, 133, 138, 139, 140, 143, 148, 159

abuse
   Canadian statistics 47
   healing from 80
   in military training 32
   of allies 1, 96
   of children 21, 48, 57, 71
   pre-colonial Aboriginal attitude toward children 22
   of children by corporations 48-49
   of women 15, 21, 54, 61, 106
   sexual 46, 47, 48, 56, 57

abuse survivors, need to control 30, 45-57, 91

action as part of educating allies 109, 116, 119, 145, 163

action as part of liberation 78, 81, 91, 94, 101, 108, 109, 110

action, non-violent 84-85

active witnessing 123

activism 8, 29, 37, 38, 44
   internal conflict among activists 1, 31
   Internet activism 1, 36-37

addiction/addiction recovery 49, 83, 94, 151

adultery 133

adultism 18, 48

affirmative action 134, 138, 140, 160, 161, 162

Africa 42, 49, 53, 56, 57, 59, 75, 111, 122, 145, 146, 159

African-Nova Scotian people 4, 64, 72, 74, 86, 87, 88, 124, 134, 135, 136, 140, 144, 145, 148

Afrikaner people 59

ageism 18, 66

ahistorical/historical worldview 9, 78, 91, 108, 110, 111, 112, 134, 138, 140, 142, 158, 161, 162, 163

Allen, Paula Gunn 20-23, 57

allies 1, 3, 8-13, 85, 86, 87-105, 130, 143, 149, 151, 154, 155, 162, 164, 165
   abuse of 1, 96
   characteristics of 91, 101-104, 109
   educating 108-126
   how not to be 101-104, 107
   literature 12-13
   working with 100-101

Ally Bill of Responsibilities (Dr. Lynn Gehl) 98-100

analysis 62, 67, 78, 81, 82, 85, 92, 94, 101, 108, 109, 116, 117, 118, 130, 134, 145, 147, 155, 156, 158

Analysis Questions (exercise for educating allies) 156

anger 8, 29, 51, 61, 76, 78, 82, 83, 85, 89, 93, 95, 96, 101, 114, 121, 131, 139, 154

Ango-Boer War 56, 59

Anti-discrimination Response Training 123

anti-globalization movement 1, 37

anti-heterosexism/heterosexism 11, 12, 13, 17, 18, 32, 63, 73, 74, 82, 125, 134, 139, 140, 141, 143, 147, 156, 157

anti-oppression education 108

anti-racism/racism ix, 10-12, 14-19, 21-

23, 50, 52-53, 56, 60-61, 63, 64, 66, 67, 69, 72, 73, 74, 75, 86, 87-88, 91, 93, 94, 95, 98, 105, 109, 110, 111, 112, 120, 121, 122, 123, 124, 134, 135, 136, 154, 156, 157, 159, 160, 163
anti-Semitism 68, 133
anti-sexism/sexism ix, 4, 6, 11, 12, 13, 14-30, 32, 41, 49, 59, 60-61, 66-67, 68, 73, 74, 75, 76, 82, 85, 86, 93, 96, 120, 121, 122, 134, 138, 139, 140, 141, 143, 144, 145, 147, 156
apartheid 42, 56
archeology 19, 20-21, 78
Armenian people 77
Asia 38, 49, 108, 111, 136, 145, 146, 159
assimilation 15-19, 21-23, 40
authority 22, 30, 31, 48, 58, 83

backlash 41, 78, 87, 113, 114, 115, 126, 134, 145, 162
backlashers (response to equity education) 87, 88, 109, 111, 112, 115, 117, 119, 122, 152
ball of yarn closing (exercise for educating allies) 163
Barnga (exercise for educating allies) 118, 152
becoming an ally
    guidelines 94-100, 101-104
    key blocks 109-112
    steps 12
Beyond Token Change 3, 147, 160
bigotry 2, 87
bisexual 50, 135, 139, 141, 145, 146, 147, 148
Black people 11, 34, 41, 53, 62, 64, 69, 71, 72, 86, 133, 134, 135, 140, 144, 145, 148, 154, 159
blaming the victim 39
Blue Eyes, Brown Eyes (exercise for educating allies) 155
boarding schools 56, 59, 65, 70
bodies as a source of power 82
breaking silence 76, 78
Building a Social Change Strategy (exercise for educating allies) 164

Butler, Sandra 58, 81

Canada 2, 6, 33, 35, 36, 37, 38, 40, 41, 42, 43, 46, 47, 56, 58, 59, 64, 71, 75, 108, 109, 110, 118, 133, 134, 136, 138, 140, 142, 159, 162
cancer 76
capitalism as cancer 29-30, 35-42, 111, 112, 136
Caribbean 49, 108, 145, 146
changing organizational culture 113-115
childbirth 82
children 16, 17, 18, 21-22, 30, 46-57, 58, 63, 65, 67, 68-71, 72, 76, 77-78, 84, 99, 134, 140, 143, 144, 146
class 1, 9, 11, 16, 19, 23, 30, 35-42, 56-57, 64-67, 69, 91, 94, 108, 116, 128, 136, 137, 138, 141, 143, 145, 165
class culture 65
closing (exercises for educating allies) 163
collective action 77, 80
colonialism 23, 42, 56, 111, 112, 122, 146, 159
commons 23-30, 35-42
community 4, 13, 25-27, 30, 35, 93
competition 1, 9-10, 14-19, 38, 40, 62, 69, 72, 85, 137, 141, 146, 147
computerized equity education 115
confession 83
conflict in social justice groups 1, 31, 131
conflict over ally approach to privilege 101-104
connection 14, 31, 78, 82, 83, 91, 97, 137, 146
conquest 14-23, 30-31, 56, 73, 78, 82, 133, 134, 140, 146
conquest of North America 21-23
conquest of Old Europe 19-21
conscience 44, 130
consciousness 55, 77-80, 83, 85, 92
consensus decision making 45, 137
conspiracy theory 36
control, need by abuse survivors 30, 45-57, 91
control, of resources, labour 14-19, 30-31, 36-42, 64-67, 136, 137, 138, 143, 145

control, of women's sexuality 14-19, 70-71, 73, 81-82, 133, 140, 145

control, role of emotional repression 51, 82

cooperation 8-10, 14-19, 23, 26, 30, 31, 45-46, 55, 77-79, 83-85, 128, 131, 136, 137, 142

Corkum, Jane Hurshman 76, 78

corporate child abuse 48-49

corporations 36, 37, 39, 40, 42, 49, 50, 62, 71, 143

cultural change in organizations 113-115

cultural competence 108

culture, class 65

culture, female positive 19-23, 32, 82

culture, organizational 45-46, 84-85, 108-109, 113-115

culture, Western 4, 10, 15-30, 30-34, 39, 40, 42, 45-57, 60-61, 63-64, 67, 72, 73, 74, 77, 81-85, 92, 93, 98, 103-104, 111-112, 113-115, 129, 131, 133, 134, 136, 137, 138, 139, 145, 147, 148, 156

cycle of oppression 2, 10-12, 14-19

Deaf people 63, 72, 74, 137, 144

December 6 (Montreal massacre) 43, 105-106

defensiveness 10-11, 87, 92, 95, 102,107, 111, 117, 118, 120-122

demons 80

deniers (response to equity education) 11, 88, 89, 92, 97, 109, 110, 111, 112, 117, 118, 119, 122, 126, 162

diagonal oppressions 65-67

differences among oppressions
  Aboriginal and non-Aboriginal 64
  class and other forms of oppression 67
  specific histories 64, 86
  visible and invisible 63

Differences (exercise for educating allies) 152

Diggers 23-29

disability 1, 14-19, 50, 54, 62, 63, 65-66, 69, 74, 116, 117, 137, 138, 144, 153
  intellectual 63, 74, 137, 140

discrimination 50, 63, 66, 74, 123, 134, 139, 144, 145, 157, 162, 163
  reverse 134, 157-159, 161

dissociation 55

diversity 55, 108, 113, 114

divide and conquer 6, 9, 17, 38, 79

dream 8, 78, 131

dry lake image (Malidoma Patrice Somé) (in educating allies) 123

dualism 40, 88, 95, 109, 110, 111, 112, 147, 154

economic power 35-40, 143

educating allies 108-126
  mandatory education 2, 87, 109, 111, 113-115, 117

Eisler, Riane 19, 20

emotional repression, role in social, political control 51, 82

emotional scars 2, 45-47, 76-80, 91-92

emotions 93,115, 120-122,130
  expression 15, 82
  in educating allies 93, 120-122
  suppression 53

employment equity 6, 87, 109, 113, 138, 145, 161, 162

empowerment 84

enclosure movement 23-30

equality/equity 8, 20, 23, 29-31, 38-39, 42, 52, 55, 65-66, 69, 83, 86,, 108, 134, 138, 139, 141, 142, 145, 159, 161, 162
  difference between 139

equity education 1-2, 108, 113-114
  computerized 115
  risks 114-115

ethnocentrism 134

exercises for educating allies
  Analysis Questions 156
  Barnga 152
  Blue Eyes, Brown Eyes 154
  Building a Social Justice Strategy 164
  Closing 163
  Differences 152
  Flower of Power 148-152
  Iceberg 156-162
  Imaginary Journey 155
  Language Reflection 163

Oppression/Privilege Reflection 153
Other sources of exercises 164-165
Photographs, clippings 163
Poverty Game, The 155
Powerline 148-152
Simulated Reversals 154-155
Skill building 162
Spiral Model of Learning 116
Step Forward, Step Back 148-152
Web Chart 16
When I see, hear, feel 163
exploitation 8, 9, 14-19, 23-30, 35, 50, 67,
    111, 128, 133, 134, 138, 140, 142,
    143, 144, 146

fear 11, 29, 40, 41, 50, 51, 52, 54, 55, 63,
    73, 76, 77, 81, 82, 83, 84, 93, 94, 106,
    117, 126, 139, 146
female-positive cultures 19-23, 32, 82
feminism 4, 6, 11, 15, 41, 59, 73, 96, 106,
    138
fish in dry lake image (Malidoma Patrice
    Somé) (in educating allies) 123
Flower of Power (exercise for educating
    allies) 148-152
Freire, Paulo 13, 79, 109, 126

Gandhi 83
gay 6, 18, 32, 50, 54, 62, 63, 64, 65, 70, 72,
    73, 74, 86, 88, 101, 135, 139, 141,
    145, 147, 148, 159
Gehl, Lynn 98-100, 105
gender 1, 12, 13, 14, 23, 29, 42, 50, 56, 60,
    82, 86, 93, 94, 96, 120, 121, 136, 137,
    139, 147, 148, 150, 152
gender-equal societies 19-23, 32, 82
George, Susan x, 36, 37, 42
Gimbutas, Marija 19, 20, 21, 32
globalization 35-42
Goddess, Mother 19-21
Green, Margaret 2, 49, 52-54, 56, 57, 91-
    92, 98, 122, 124
Grenada 128, 132
grieving 51, 78, 82, 83, 85
Gruen, Arno 55
guilt 53, 89, 90, 91, 93, 95, 98, 100, 103,
    110, 120,121, 126, 154, 161

guilty (response to equity education) 87,
    89, 90, 109, 110-112, 117, 118, 119,
    120, 122, 154
Gypsy (Roma) people 70, 75, 77, 136,
    146

handouts for educating allies
    Building a Social Change Strategy 164
    Flower of Power 150
    Iceberg 157
    Spiral Model of Learning 116
harassment 32, 41, 69, 114, 120, 137
hazing 56, 59
healing (part of becoming an ally) 4, 9, 12,
    51, 52-58, 76-80, 81, 83, 85, 94, 112,
    117, 119. 128, 131, 139
    through emotional expression 51-58,
    76-80
heterosexism/anti-heterosexism 11, 12,
    13, 17, 18, 32, 63, 73, 74, 82, 125,
    134, 139, 140, 141, 143, 147, 156,
    157
hierarchy 9, 14-20, 23, 30, 38, 40, 51, 56,
    57, 62, 65, 66, 67, 74, 82, 84, 113,
    139, 142, 146
historical/ahistorical worldview 9, 78, 91,
    108, 110, 111, 112, 134, 138, 140,
    142, 158, 161, 162, 163
history 19, 21, 30, 41, 61, 63, 64, 69, 70,
    71, 72, 74, 78, 83, 85, 86, 93, 95, 97,
    98, 135, 142, 143, 158, 159
homogeneous or mixed groups in ally
    education 125
homogeneous or mixed leadership teams
    in ally education 126
homophobia 139, 140, 141, 143
hooks, bell 11-12, 13
hope 1, 8, 9, 10, 12, 86, 94, 107, 126, 129,
    130, 131, 132, 136, 152
hostile participants in ally education 88,
    110, 122
human rights 37, 42, 64, 140, 161, 162
humour 2, 68, 79, 110, 111, 117, 130, 148

Iceberg (presentation for educating allies)
    156-162
idealism 129, 132

ideological power 25, 26, 38, 39, 42, 67, 71, 72, 78, 91, 133, 134, 137, 140, 143, 146, 147
ideology 56, 65, 67, 110, 116, 138, 140, 141, 142, 143
Imaginary Journey (exercise for educating allies) 155
immigrant 134, 135, 136, 140, 144, 145, 148
income 38, 136, 138, 140, 143, 148, 159
Indian residential schools 21-23, 56-57, 71, 75
individualism 91, 93, 109, 110, 111, 112
Innu people 21-23
intellectual disability 63, 137, 140
intention 110, 112, 158, 160, 161, 163
internal conflict in social justice groups 1, 31, 131
internalized oppression 35, 57, 71, 96, 108, 141
Internet xii, 13, 37, 165
Internet activism 1, 36-37
Internet-based equity education 115
Ishiyama, Ishu 123

Jewish people 10, 49, 63, 66, 68, 70, 75, 77, 91, 101, 165

Kirkham, Kate 93, 120-122

labour, resources, control of 14-19, 30-31, 36-42, 64-67, 136, 137, 138, 143, 145
Language Reflection (exercise for educating allies) 163
Latin America 49, 53, 108, 136, 145, 146, 159
LeJeune, Fr. Paul 21-23, 57
lesbian ix, 4, 18, 41, 50, 54, 63, 64, 65, 72, 73, 74, 86, 123, 139, 146, 147, 148
leverage point 119, 141
LGBT 37, 64, 72, 88, 117, 123, 139, 141, 145, 149, 159
liberalism 9, 13, 69, 102-103, 108, 110, 116, 119, 138, 141-142,
liberation 1, 2, 11, 12, 62, 63, 72, 77, 81-84, 85, 91, 92, 94, 95, 96, 101, 107,
108, 109, 130, 132, 135, 141, 142, 147
Lorde, Audrey 13, 75

Malidoma Patrice Somé 57, 122
managers 2, 41, 113, 114
mandatory education 2, 87, 109, 111, 113-115, 117
marginalized people ix, 40, 68, 70, 74, 89, 108, 143, 145
McMurtry, John 29, 35, 42, 111
media 8, 16, 30, 38, 40, 49, 70, 71, 106, 153, 160, 162
memory 47, 52, 53, 61, 77, 78
middle class 4, 65, 143
midwifery 26, 82, 148
Miller, Alice 44, 48, 51, 54, 105, 130
minorities, visible 73, 134, 135, 138, 140, 144, 145, 148
misogyny 143, 146
money 49, 111, 136, 138, 142, 143, 145
monogamy 18, 22, 139, 143
Montreal massacre 43, 105-106
morality 28, 44, 130
Mother Goddess 19-21
Multilateral Agreement on Investment 37

naming (component of popular education) 116-117, 149, 152
nature 8, 9, 14, 16, 19-27, 35, 48, 60, 70, 78, 82, 88, 98, 130, 131, 148
neoliberalism 1, 29, 37, 49142
Neolithic 19-21, 26
non-violent action 84-85
North American 21-13, 36, 38, 39, 48, 50, 51, 56-57, 64, 68, 71, 75, 78, 89, 91, 146, 159
North America, conquest 21-13
North/South 42, 62, 143, 146, 159

obedience 17, 18, 48, 56, 58
O'Brien, Michelle 101
Occupy movement 37
Okun, Tema 2, 13, 111, 112
Old Europe, conquest 19-21
Oliver, Pearline 34
olsson, jona 109

oppression, internalized 35, 57, 71, 96, 108, 141

oppression, cycle of 2, 10-12, 14-19

Oppression/Privilege Reflection (exercise for educating allies) 153

organizational culture 45-46, 84-85, 108-109, 113-115

organizational cultural change 113-115

overpersonalization 93, 95

Pacific Islands 49, 108, 145, 146

pagan 27, 81, 148

Palestinian people 77

Pandora case 162

patrilineal 18, 20, 133

peace 9, 14, 20, 39, 42, 130

people of colour 135-136

people with disabilities 50, 54, 62, 66, 69, 74, 99, 107, 117, 133, 137, 138, 140, 143, 144, 153, 162

photographs and clippings (exercise for educating allies) 163

political correctness 113, 144, 145, 147

political power 35-40

political use of psychiatry 41, 49

poor-bashing 28, 33, 42

popular education 108-126, 145, 149, 165

pornography 74, 75, 82

poverty/anti-poverty 1, 14-30, 34, 39, 42, 50, 62-67, 70, 88, 111, 114, 122, 143, 155, 160

Poverty Game, The (exercise for educating allies) 155

power 9, 14, 19, 21, 30, 31, 35, 36, 38, 39, 41, 44, 45, 46, 47, 48, 50, 51, 52, 53, 54, 55, 56, 57, 58, 59, 62, 64, 66, 67, 68, 69, 73, 74, 76, 80, 81, 82, 83, 84, 85, 89, 90, 91, 94, 98, 99, 100, 101, 108, 109, 110, 111, 112, 113, 116, 117, 119, 129, 134, 136, 137, 138, 139, 141, 142, 143, 144, 147, 150, 155, 156, 158, 160, 162
  economic 35-40, 143
  ideological 25, 26, 38, 39, 42, 67, 71, 72, 78, 91, 133, 134, 137, 140, 143, 146, 147
  political 35-40

power-over 30, 31, 38, 46, 52, 55, 57, 67, 70, 79, 83, 84, 91, 118

power-with 30, 31, 46, 83, 84, 91

power-within 30, 31, 84

Powerline (exercise for educating allies) 148-152

private property 15, 16, 17, 18, 23, 24, 25, 26, 27, 29, 30, 35, 40, 140, 145, 159

privatization 1, 29, 36, 37, 142

privilege 2, 9, 12, 13, 65, 66, 72, 89, 90, 95, 97, 98, 107, 109, 110, 111, 112, 117, 118, 134, 138, 145, 146, 150, 153, 154, 156, 159, 160, 16
  responses to learning about 93, 109-112, 120-122

profit 27, 36, 50, 76, 111

Project Implicit (Harvard University) 160

psychiatry, political use of 41, 49

queer 147

racialized people 4, 6, 52, 63, 66, 77, 96, 98, 117, 134, 135, 136, 140, 144, 145, 146, 148, 149, 157, 162

racism/anti-racism ix, 10-12, 14-19, 21-23, 50, 52-53, 56, 60-61, 63, 64, 66, 67, 69, 72, 73, 74, 75, 86, 87-88, 91, 93, 94, 95, 98, 105, 109, 110, 111, 112, 120, 121, 122, 123, 124, 134, 135, 136, 154, 156, 157, 159, 160, 163

racism in language (exercise for educating allies) 163

rape 16, 17, 32, 41, 69

realism 129

rebellion 30

re-evaluation counselling x, 53, 58, 63, 74

reflection as a component of popular education 66, 81, 109, 116, 117-118, 119-120, 145, 149, 151, 152-153, 154, 155, 156, 162

reflection as part of healing and becoming an ally 52, 78, 91, 92, 101, 109

reflection, evaluation and closure in educating allies 119

religion 16, 20, 50, 64, 68, 145

repression 39, 41, 69, 82

emotional, role in social, political control 51, 82

reproductive capacity 17-18, 81-82, 138,145

residential schools 15, 18, 21-23, 56-57, 59, 71, 75

resistance 19, 25, 29, 31, 32, 37, 42, 67, 73, 110, 130

resources, control of 14-19, 30-31,36-42, 64-67, 136, 137, 138, 143, 145

resources for educating allies 165

responses to oppressive comments 123

responsibility 11, 89, 91, 93, 95, 100, 107, 109, 110, 111, 125, 128, 154, 156, 161

reverse discrimination 134, 157-159, 161

rich 8-9, 24, 29, 38, 65-66, 101, 111, 129, 143

Rich, Adrienne 45, 128

river image (for teaching liberal vs. structural worldview) 161

Roma (Gypsy) people 70, 75, 77, 136, 146

scapegoat 66, 70, 114, 135, 160

scars, emotional 2, 45-57, 76-80, 91-92

self-esteem 48-51, 53-54, 58, 59, 72, 78, 91, 95, 148

separation 9, 13, 14, 16, 18, 23, 40, 62, 68, 71, 72, 76, 146

sexism/anti-sexism ix, 4, 6, 11, 12, 13, 14-30, 32, 41, 49, 59, 60-61, 66-67, 68, 73, 74, 75, 76, 82, 85, 86, 93, 96, 120, 121, 122, 134, 138, 139, 140, 141, 143, 144, 145, 147, 156

sexuality 15, 17, 18, 32, 51, 69, 70, 73, 75, 78, 82, 83, 86, 88, 133, 139, 146

sexuality, control of 14-19, 70-71, 73, 81-82, 133, 140, 145

sexual abuse of children 46-48, 56, 57

sexual orientation 1, 6, 12, 50, 63, 73, 76, 94, 116, 137, 141, 146, 148, 151

similarities among oppressions
  assumptions and slurs about sexuality 70
  desire to separate and distinguish 72
  power and hierarchy 67

specific similarities 72

stereotyping 69

violence 69

simulated reversal (exercises for educating allies) 118, 154-155

skills for becoming an ally 30, 31, 108, 119, 123, 137, 162

skills for educating allies 115, 116, 122

slavery 17, 21, 70, 72, 77, 140

social justice groups, internal conflict 1, 31, 131

Somé, Malidoma Patrice 57, 122

sources for exercises for educating allies 164-165

sources of power
  anger 82
  bodies 82
  childbirth and menstruation 82
  sexuality 82
  sharing common concerns 83
  sharing grief 82

Spiral Model of Learning 81, 109, 116, 145, 155

splitting and projection 54

Starhawk 19, 26, 27, 29, 30, 32, 58, 75, 77, 80, 81, 85

Step Forward, Step Back (exercise for educating allies) 118, 152

stereotypes 39, 53, 68, 69, 75, 88, 90, 109, 118, 122, 123, 160

straight people 38, 39, 70, 73, 88, 100, 117, 125, 149, 156, 159

strategy 18, 81, 101, 109, 116, 119, 130, 141, 155, 163

Strategy, Building for Social Change (exercise for educating allies) 163-164

street children 62, 74, 146

structural 49, 50, 66, 67, 88, 89, 91, 94, 101-104, 105, 108, 109, 110, 111, 112, 113, 114, 117, 118, 119, 121, 134, 135, 138, 140, 142, 145, 152, 154, 156-162, 163

struggle 10, 12, 29, 30, 45, 64, 66, 67, 68, 72, 83, 84, 86, 90, 91, 94, 95, 97, 100, 110, 118, 124, 126, 130, 131, 134, 141, 142

surprise, use of in educating allies 2, 110,

111, 115, 117, 118, 119, 151, 152

Third World 56, 146
tokenism 40, 67, 69, 113, 126, 134, 147,
    160
transgendered 50, 139, 145, 147
transsexual 145, 147
twelve-step addiction recovery 94
two-spirited 139, 140

unconscious 45, 52, 77, 103, 111, 138,
    156, 159, 160, 163
unlearning heterosexism 13
unlearning oppression 94, 97, 109, 114
unlearning racism 4, 11, 13, 52, 87, 124,
    164

values 9, 14, 16, 17, 18, 19, 23, 30, 31, 32,
    48, 49, 58, 65, 70, 83, 84, 85, 114,
    131, 138, 139, 140, 141, 144, 146
violence 15, 17, 18, 21, 32, 39, 40, 41, 42,
    43, 49, 50, 54, 57, 60, 61, 69, 70, 76,
    82, 83, 88, 99, 106, 121, 128, 139,
    148
visible minorities 73, 134, 135, 138, 140,
    144, 145, 148
vision 8, 24, 130, 131

war 14, 17, 19, 20, 21, 25, 32, 38, 67, 69,
    85, 131, 146
wealth 20, 28, 37, 38, 64, 66, 67, 110, 111,
    112, 134, 138, 139, 140, 143, 147,
    148, 158, 160, 162
wealth gap 1, 38-39
web chart (exercise for educating allies)
    15
Western culture 4, 10, 15-30, 30-34, 39,
    40, 42, 45-57, 60-61, 63-64, 67, 72,
    73, 74, 77, 81-85, 92, 93, 98, 103-
    104, 111-112, 113-115, 129, 131,
    133, 134, 136, 137, 138, 139, 145,
    147, 148, 156
When I See, Hear, Feel (exercise for edu-
    cating allies) 163
witches 26, 29, 69, 70, 148
women 4, 6, 15-18, 19-23, 26-29, 32-33,
    39, 41, 46-47, 52-54, 60-61, 62,

66-70, 71, 73-74, 76-78, 81-82, 85,
    86, 106-107, 120-122, 128, 133, 138,
    140, 141, 143, 145, 146, 148, 150,
    157, 162
women's sexuality, control of 14-19, 70-
    71, 73, 81-82, 133, 140, 145
World Economic Forum 37
World Social Forum 37
worldview, historical/ahistorical 9, 78, 91,
    108, 110, 111, 112, 134, 138, 140,
    142, 158, 161, 162, 163
worldview, individualistic 91, 93, 109,
    110, 111, 112
worldview, liberal 9, 13, 69, 102-103,
    108, 110, 116, 119, 138, 141-142,
worldview, structural 49, 50, 66, 67, 88,
    89, 91, 94, 101-104, 105, 108, 109,
    110, 111, 112, 113, 114, 117, 118,
    119, 121, 134, 135, 138, 140, 142,
    145, 152, 154, 156-162, 163